# Digital Data Communications

*Jack Quinn*

Prentice Hall
*Career & Technology*

**Library of Congress Cataloging-in-Publication Data**

Quinn, Jack.
      Digital data communications / Jack Quinn.
          p.  cm.
      Includes index.
      ISBN 0-02-397240-8
      1. Digital communications. I. Title.
   TK5103.7.Q85   1995
   004.6—dc20                               93-47974
                                                        CIP

Editor: David Garza
Production Editor: Mary Ann Hopper
Text Designer: Patricia Cohan
Cover Designer: Jane Lopez
Production Manager: Patricia A. Tonneman
Electronic Text Management: Marilyn Wilson Phelps, Matthew Williams, Jane Lopez,
   Karen L. Bretz

This book was set in Times by Prentice Hall Career & Technology and was printed and bound by R.R. Donnelley & Sons Company. The cover was printed by Phoenix Color Corp.

**© 1995 by Prentice Hall Career & Technology**
**Prentice-Hall, Inc.**
**A Paramount Communications Company**
**Englewood Cliffs, New Jersey 07632**

Printed in the United States of America
10  9  8  7  6  5  4  3  2  1

ISBN  0-02-397240-8

Prentice-Hall International (UK) Limited, *London*
Prentice-Hall of Australia Pty. Limited, *Sydney*
Prentice-Hall Canada Inc., *Toronto*
Prentice-Hall Hispanoamericana, S.A., *Mexico*
Prentice-Hall of India Private Limited, *New Delhi*
Prentice-Hall of Japan, Inc., *Tokyo*
Simon & Schuster Asia Pte. Ltd., *Singapore*
Editora Prentice-Hall do Brasil, Ltda., *Rio de Janeiro*

## Dedication

*To my sister, Jean Quinn*

# ■ Preface

This book is designed to be used in a one-semester course in digital data communications or as a supplemental text in a general electronics communications course. It was written for the electronics or computer science student who has some knowledge of digital electronics and general communications theory.

In writing the book, I have made an effort to include the technology of the 1990s, but I have also discussed the history of data communications technology, especially in the early chapters. I believe that the student who is aware of how modern data communications technology has evolved will be better prepared for the even more rapid evolution in that technology that will take place in the coming years.

Many concepts are mentioned in several chapters. In my own classroom teaching experience, I found that students retained more if topics were presented in stages. The basic point-to-point communications system, for example, is introduced in Chapter 1, but it is also referred to in several later chapters. Each time the topic is referred to, more detail is added. By the time students study serial interfaces in Chapter 6, UARTs in Chapter 8, or modems in Chapters 9 and 10, they already know from prior chapters what these devices are, where they fit into a communications system, and what functions they perform.

Throughout the book, reference is made to communications standards and the committees that develop them. Whenever possible, the book discusses published and de facto standards that are accepted throughout the industry, rather than proprietary standards that are used by a small number of equipment manufacturers.

## TOPICS COVERED

Chapter 1 is an introduction to data communications. It includes a brief history, defines some important data communications terms, and introduces the basic model of a point-to-point data communications system.

Chapter 2 covers pulse modulation, but more importantly, it attempts to take the mystery out of the sampling theorem, quantizing error, and aliasing.

Chapter 3 overviews the telephone system, today's most used medium for data communications. It presents the telephone network as it exists today—a digital system with an analog local loop between the subscriber and the central office. This chapter includes sections on fiber optics and the emerging ISDN service.

Chapter 4 covers network topologies—both point-to-point and multipoint. It also expands upon the basic point-to-point communications system that was presented in Chapter 1 and explains in more detail the data terminal equipment, the data communications equipment, and the serial interface that joins them.

Chapter 5 covers common codes used in data communications, error detection and correction, and the difference between synchronous and asynchronous communications.

Chapter 6 covers standard serial interfaces in detail. The RS-232 interface standard and the RS-449 family of interface standards are explained conductor by conductor.

Chapter 7 covers parallel interfaces and includes a detailed explanation of both the Centronics and the IEEE 488 standards.

Chapter 8 covers data terminal equipment. It uses the ACIA as an example of such a device and covers it in detail. There was no special reason for picking this chip over others. My belief is that once students learn *any* of the standard UART-type chips well, they will be able to apply what they have learned to the other chips that they encounter in the field. A specification sheet for the ACIA is included in Appendix B.

Chapter 9 is an introduction to modems and covers the importance of modem standards, the modulation types that modems use, data compression, and the difference between synchronous and asynchronous modems.

Chapter 10 discusses specific modem standards, including the AT command set, with emphasis on modern standards such as V.32, V.32 bis, and V.34. A comprehensive list of AT commands can be found in Appendix A.

Chapter 11 discusses character-oriented and bit-oriented network protocols. The chapter covers the BISYNC and HDLC protocols in detail.

Chapter 12 covers local area networks, the Open Systems Interconnect Model, and internetworking devices such as repeaters, bridges, and routers. The chapter discusses the Ethernet, Token Ring, and FDDI local area network standards in detail.

## ACKNOWLEDGMENTS

This book could not have been written without the assistance of many people and organizations. I want to thank Motorola Corporation for permission to reproduce the ACIA specification sheet and to extend special thanks to Mike Andrews of

National Semiconductor for the voluminous material he supplied on local area networks. I am grateful to David Garza, Mary Ann Hopper, Patricia Cohan, and Jane Lopez of Prentice Hall for their efforts in making this book a reality. My special thanks go to the following instructors who reviewed the manuscript and offered many suggestions for its improvement: Nathan Ballard, Electronics Institute, Kansas City; Susan Garrod, Purdue University; Carl Jensen, DeVry Institute of Technology, Woodbridge, NJ; Alex Kisha, DeVry Institute of Technology, Columbus, OH; Eric James Kline, Electronic Computer Programming Institute, Virginia Beach; John Meese, DeVry Institute of Technology, Columbus, OH; Ladimer S. Nagurney, University of Hartford; Vohra Promod, Northern Illinois University; Randy Ratliff, National Education Center, Cross Lanes, WV; Ray Roswick, DeVry Institute of Technology, Phoenix; Todd Whittington, National Education Center, Cross Lanes, WV; Lorenzo Wilson, St. Philips College.

# Contents

■ C H A P T E R  7

**PARALLEL INTERFACES    125**

■ C H A P T E R  8

**DATA TERMINAL EQUIPMENT    141**

■ C H A P T E R   9

**INTRODUCTION TO MODEMS   167**

■ C H A P T E R   10

**MODEM STANDARDS   187**

# Chapter 1

# INTRODUCTION TO DATA COMMUNICATIONS

## OBJECTIVES

After you have completed this chapter, you should be able to:

- Describe the differences and similarities between digital communications and data communications.
- Name two codes that are used in data communications.
- Describe serial and parallel communications and the advantages of each.
- Define simplex, half-duplex, and full-duplex communications.
- Name the three parts of a data communications system and describe the function of each part.

## INTRODUCTION

The field of data communications is expanding at an exponential rate. Today it is difficult to work in electronics, computers, or even business without using data communications and understanding something about how it works. This book discusses

**1**

both digital and data communications, two closely related branches of electronic communications that are rapidly merging into one. Chapter 1 overviews these two topics, presents some important vocabulary, and introduces some of the concepts that are discussed in more detail in the remainder of the book.

**Communication** is the transfer of information from one location to another. As Figure 1-1 shows, the sender of the information is called a **transmitter,** and the destination of the information is called a **receiver.** Information travels from the transmitter to the receiver through a **medium.** (The plural of *medium* is *media.*) Speech, for example, is a form of communication that uses variations in air pressure as a medium to carry information from the speaker (transmitter) to the listener (receiver). Hand signals are a form of communication that transfers information from one person to another through the medium of light waves.

**Electronic communications** is the transfer of information from one location to another with the use of electronic circuits. Radio, television, telephone, facsimile, telegraph, and recorded music are all forms of electronic communications. Electronic communications often uses radio or light waves as a medium to carry information over long distances. Radio and television are examples of electronic communications that use radio waves as a medium. Many long-distance telephone circuits use light waves as a medium to carry information through optical fibers from city to city. Data communications is one of the many types of electronic communications.

## 1-1   DATA COMMUNICATIONS DEFINED

The terms *data communications* and *digital communications* are closely related and are often used interchangeably, although they do not have quite the same meaning. Both digital communications and data communications transfer information electronically, and both use digital technology for at least part of the communications process.

As its name implies, data communications is the electronic communication of data from one location to another, but this definition will be of little use to us until we define the word *data.* In everyday usage, the word *data* means information. In the field of data communications, the word *data* is used to denote a certain type of information.

### 1-1-1   Data Versus Information

In the field of data communications the word **data** means information that is stored in digital form. An example of data is the contents of a computer's memory. The word *data* is plural. A single unit of data is called a **datum.** Although in casual speech we often hear, "The data *is* transmitted," in formal "correct" English, people say, "The data *are* transmitted."

**FIGURE 1-1**
In all forms of communication, a transmitter sends information through a medium to one or more receivers.

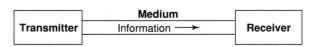

Now that we have defined the term *data,* we can be more precise in our definition of data communications. **Data communications** is the transfer of information that is in digital form before it enters the communications system. The transfer of information between two computers is an example of data communications.

## 1-1-2   Data Communications and Digital Communications Compared

In digital communications, information is transferred through the medium in digital form. The original information can be either analog or digital. Analog information is converted to digital form when it enters the communications system, is sent through the medium in digital form, and is then converted back to analog at the receiver.

As Figure 1-2 illustrates, long-distance telephone circuits use digital communications. An analog telephone circuit connects each local telephone subscriber to a telephone company office. In the telephone company office, the analog voice signal from the local telephone circuit is converted to digital form for transmission through a fiber-optic cable or other digital medium. At the other end of the long-distance telephone circuit, equipment located within another telephone company office converts the digital signal back to analog to be sent over the local telephone circuit.

Even though a long-distance telephone conversation uses digital communications, it is not an example of data communications, because the information that enters and leaves the communications system, the human voice, is analog.

Data communications is not necessarily digital communications. Computer data are often modulated onto an analog carrier so that they can be sent over an analog medium such as a local telephone line. At the receiver the data are demodulated and converted back to digital form. This is data communications. The information sent is data, because it is stored in digital form and enters the communications system in digital form. It is not digital communications, however, because the information is sent through the medium in analog form.

**FIGURE 1-2**
The long-distance telephone network is a digital communications system.

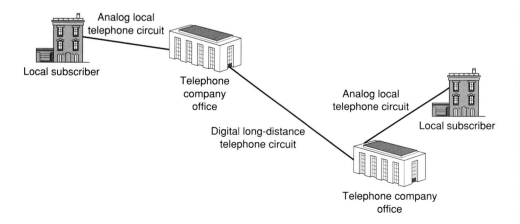

Figure 1-3 may clarify the difference between digital communications and data communications. Figure 1-3(a) shows two methods of sending data from one computer to another. The data can be modulated onto an analog carrier and transmitted in analog form over an analog transmission medium, or they can be left in digital form and transmitted over a digital communications medium. Both cases are examples of data communications. The second case is also an example of digital communications, because the data are sent through the medium in digital format.

Figure 1-3(b) shows two ways of transmitting analog information. If the information is converted to digital form and sent over a digital communications medium, it is digital communications. If it is left in analog format and transmitted over an analog medium, it is analog communications. In neither case is it data communications, because the original information is not digital.

To sum up the difference, data communications is the transfer of information that is in digital form *before* it enters the communications system. Digital communications is the transfer of information through the medium in digital form.

## 1-2     A BRIEF HISTORY OF COMMUNICATIONS

Almost all life forms carry on some form of communications. Even some plants communicate with other members of their species by means of chemical signals. The higher animals communicate by means of cries, barks, and body movements. The most common forms of short-range human communications are speech and gestures. Yells, messengers, drums, signaling towers, and smoke signals are methods of long-distance communications that were not much improved upon from man's earliest days until the early 1800s.

### 1-2-1   The Telegraph and Telephone

The era of using electric signals to communicate began in 1837 when Samuel Morse transmitted telegraph signals over wires. Human communications became more personal in 1876 when Alexander Graham Bell was granted a patent for the telephone. One year later he was producing telephones that were capable of reliably transmitting the human voice.

### 1-2-2   The Teletype

Data communications began in the twentieth century with the invention of the teletype. The teletype is an electromechanical device with a typewriter-like keyboard and carriage that can send and receive information using electrical pulses that represent 1s and 0s. Teletype soon became the standard form of rapid long-distance communications for many business applications, because unlike the telephone, the teletype leaves a printed record of the information communicated.

The first teletype code to be widely used was **Baudot** (pronounced baw-DOUGH), a code that uses 5 bits to represent each character. Baudot is still used today in some applications, although it has been largely supplanted by a 7-bit tele-

**FIGURE 1-3**

(a) In data communications, the original data are digital in nature, but they can be transmitted in either digital or analog format. (b) Likewise, analog data can be transmitted in either analog or digital format.

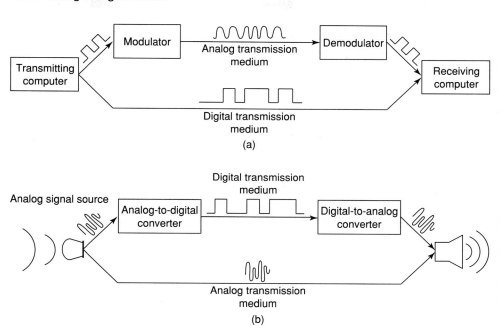

(a)

(b)

type code called the **American Standard Code for Information Interchange (ASCII)** in low-speed data communications systems and by a variety of other codes in high-speed systems.

## 1-2-3  Computers in Communications

As computers came into widespread use in the 1960s and 1970s, they began to replace teletype machines for data communications. Not only can computers send and receive data, but they can also store and manipulate data. Today, almost all data communications involves a computer at one or both ends of the communications system, and often computers are used to manage data at intermediate points in the communications system as well.

## 1-3  SERIAL COMMUNICATIONS VERSUS PARALLEL COMMUNICATIONS

As illustrated in Figure 1-4, there are two ways of transferring digital data, in parallel and in serial. When data are transferred in parallel, a number of bits are transferred from the transmitter to the receiver at the same time. Each bit requires its own conductor, and there must be at least one additional conductor to complete the circuit. Figure 1-4(a) shows that to transfer 8 bits of data in parallel therefore requires a minimum of 9 conductors, one conductor for each bit and a common return, often called a ground.

In serial communications, only one bit is sent at a time. Bits are sent one after another over the same conductor. To transfer 8 bits in serial, the first bit is sent followed by the second bit, the third bit, and so on, until all 8 bits have been sent. Figure 1-4(b) illustrates that serial data require only 2 conductors: a data line and a ground return.

Parallel communications is much faster than serial, but because of the large number of conductors required, it is almost always limited to short-distance communications, most often between two pieces of equipment located in the same room. A common use of parallel communications is to transfer data from a computer to a

**FIGURE 1-4**
(a) Parallel digital communications is fast, but it requires a conductor for each bit that is sent in parallel plus at least one common return path to complete the electrical circuit. (b) Serial communication is slow, but it requires only two conductors.

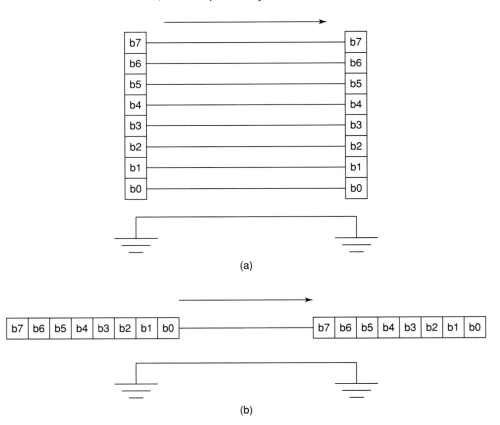

nearby printer or disk drive. Long-distance communications is almost always done in serial. Serial communications can also be used for short-distance communications, if speed is not important.

### 1-3-1 Disadvantages of Serial Communications

The main disadvantage of serial communication is its slow speed. Another disadvantage is that serial data communication is more complicated. Data are stored in parallel format within a computer. Data that are transferred in serial form between two computers must be converted from parallel to serial format at the transmitter and from serial back to parallel format at the receiver.

### 1-3-2 Advantage of Serial Communications

The main advantage of serial communication is that it requires fewer electrical conductors than parallel communication does. As we have seen, an 8-bit parallel communications system requires at least 9 conductors. Some high-speed parallel communications systems use a separate return conductor for each data bit and therefore require 16 conductors to carry 8 bits of parallel data. Additional conductors carry control signals to coordinate the transfer of data between the transmitter and receiver. Serial communication, as we have seen, requires only 2 conductors, although additional conductors may be used to carry control signals when the transmitter and receiver are located close to each other.

Parallel communications works well for short distances because of its simplicity and higher speed, but for long-distance communications, the expense of running the multiconductor cables required is prohibitive. The existing telephone network provides a communications system that can carry low-speed serial data throughout the world at low cost.

## 1-4 COMMUNICATIONS CHANNELING

A serial **communications channel** is either a 2-conductor circuit connected between the transmitter and the receiver or something that behaves as if it were a 2-conductor circuit. A telephone circuit is an example of a 2-wire communications channel. If you dial someone in a distant city, a telephone circuit is established between your telephone and the telephone of the person called. The circuit contains amplifiers, signaling equipment, switching equipment, and other sophisticated electronic devices, but for voice signals, the telephone circuit behaves as if it were constructed from a 2-conductor cable. A voice signal leaves your house over a pair of wires, and it arrives at the other end over a pair of wires. All of the equipment between is **transparent,** a term that means that during normal operation, the telephone user is unaware of the equipment's operation.

There are three types of communications that can take place between two devices. They are called simplex, half-duplex, and full-duplex and are described in the subsections that follow.

## 1-4-1 Simplex

**Simplex communications** is also called "one-way only" communication. Simplex communications can take place in only one direction, and it requires one communications channel. A common example of simplex communications is commercial radio broadcasting. The transmitted information flows in one direction only, from the announcer to the listener. The listener cannot use the radio receiver to respond to the announcer. An example of simplex data communications is a serial interface between a computer and its printer. Data are sent from the computer to the printer only. The printer does not send data back to the computer.

The process of simplex communications is illustrated in Figure 1-5(a), which shows a transmitter and a receiver connected by a single communications channel. Data can be communicated in only one direction, from terminal A, the transmitter, to terminal B, the receiver.

**FIGURE 1-5**
(a) Simplex (one-way only) communication. (b) Half-duplex (one-way alternate) communication. (c) Full-duplex (two-way simultaneous) communication.

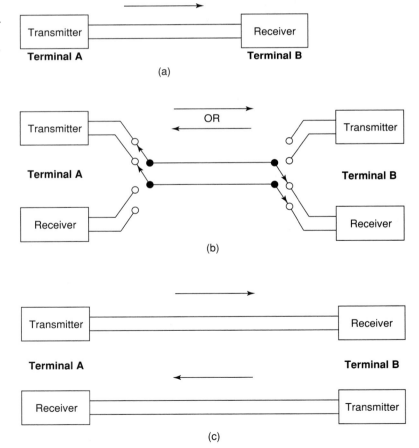

### 1-4-2 Half-Duplex (HDX)

**Half-duplex communications** can take place in either direction, but in only one direction at a time. It can be thought of as "two-way alternate" communications. Half-duplex communications requires one channel that can be switched at both ends to change its direction. An example of half-duplex communications is a two-way radio system such as citizens band. While one person transmits, the person on the other end receives. To change the direction of communications, the person who was transmitting must switch to the receive mode, and the person who was receiving must switch to the transmit mode.

Figure 1-5(b) illustrates half-duplex communications. When terminal A transmits, terminal B must be in the receive mode for communications to take place. The communications channel is then switched at both ends to enable terminal B to reply to terminal A.

### 1-4-3 Full-Duplex (FDX)

**Full-duplex communications** takes place in both directions at the same time. Also called "two-way simultaneous" communications, full-duplex requires two communications channels, one to carry information in each direction. It is difficult to find an example of full-duplex communications in everyday life, because polite conversation between two people is half-duplex; that is, only one person speaks at a time. However, full-duplex communications is common between computers. Figure 1-5(c) illustrates the principle. The two communications channels allow each terminal to both transmit and receive at the same time.

## 1-5 A DATA COMMUNICATIONS SYSTEM

Figure 1-6 is the block diagram of a common point-to-point data communications system. It is called a **point-to-point system** because it links only two terminals. Each end of the communications system consists of data terminal equipment (DTE) and data communications equipment (DCE). Data are carried between the two ends of the communications system by the medium. The various blocks that make up the system are studied in detail in later chapters of this book, and they are referred to throughout the book. Memorizing the blocks and their functions now will help you orient yourself in those later chapters.

**FIGURE 1-6**
Block diagram of a point-to-point data communications system.

### 1-5-1 The Data Terminal Equipment

The **data terminal equipment (DTE)** is where the data originate. Early DTEs were teletype machines, but today they are more likely to be computers with additional circuits that convert between the parallel data format used inside the computer and the serial format required by the medium. Functions of the DTE include sending and receiving data at the correct speed and performing error checking on received data to ensure that they were communicated correctly. If necessary, the DTE also converts data from parallel to serial form while transmitting and from serial to parallel form while receiving.

### 1-5-2 The Data Communications Equipment

The **data communications equipment (DCE)** is the interface between the DTE and the medium. It accepts serial data transmitted from the DTE and converts them to a format acceptable to the medium. If the medium is a standard telephone line, the DCE modulates the serial digital data onto a sine wave carrier that can be sent over the analog telephone system. The DCE also accepts data received from the medium and converts them to the format acceptable to the DTE. For example, the DCE demodulates the analog signal received from a telephone line, recovers the digital intelligence signal, and passes it on to the DTE.

Figure 1-7 is a block diagram of the transmitting portion of one type of DCE. The serial digital input signal from the DTE is frequency modulated onto a sine wave carrier. The frequency-modulated output of the modulator is an analog, voice-frequency signal that can be sent over a normal telephone line or a radio transmitter. Although the example in Figure 1-7 uses frequency modulation, a DCE can also use amplitude modulation, phase modulation, or a combination of amplitude and phase modulation.

**FIGURE 1-7**
The transmitting section of a DCE.

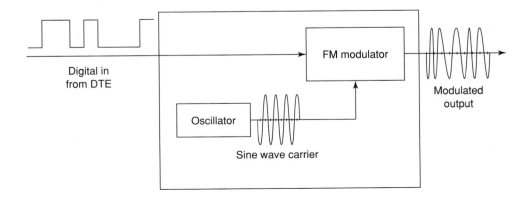

Digital in
from DTE

FM modulator

Modulated
output

Oscillator

Sine wave carrier

### 1-5-3 The Medium

The medium transports the information from the transmitter to the receiver. The medium could be a fiber-optic cable, a microwave radio link, or a pair of wires. The most common medium used in long-distance data communications is a standard analog telephone circuit. Telephone companies can also supply high-speed digital circuits as media. Digital circuits are used mainly by businesses that need to communicate large amounts of data.

■ **SUMMARY**

This chapter has been an introduction to digital and data communication. It defined data communications as the electronic transfer of information that is in digital form before it enters the communications system. The data may be transferred in their original digital form, or they may be modulated onto an analog carrier at the transmitter, transferred through an analog medium, and converted back to digital form at the receiver.

This chapter contrasted data communications with digital communications. To summarize the difference between the two, in data communications the information is in digital form before it enters the communications system. In digital communications the data pass through the communications medium in digital form, regardless of whether the information was originally in analog or digital form.

This chapter also contrasted serial communications with parallel communications. Serial communications is the transfer of information one bit at a time and requires two conductors. Parallel communications is the transfer of several bits at a time and requires a minimum of one conductor for each bit plus a common or ground conductor. Parallel communications is faster and is often used for short distances. Serial data communications requires fewer conductors and is common for long distances.

Three types of communications channeling were discussed: simplex or one-way communications, half-duplex or either-way communications, and full-duplex or both-way communications. Finally, the chapter presented the block diagram of a point-to-point data communications system. The main parts of the point-to-point data communications system are the data terminal equipment (DTE), where the data originate and which performs parallel/serial conversion; the data communications equipment (DCE), which modulates the digital data onto a sine wave carrier for transmission over an analog medium such as a telephone line; and the medium itself, which transports the data from the transmitter to the receiver.

■ **QUESTIONS**

1. Define the term *communications.*
2. a. What are *data?*
   b. What makes data different from other types of information?

3. a.   What is the difference between *data communications* and *digital communications?*

   b.   Can data communications also be digital communications?

4. a.   Give an example of digital communications that is *not* data communications.

   b.   Give an example of data communications that is *not* digital communications.

   c.   Give an example that is *both* data communications *and* digital communications.

5. a.   Who invented the telegraph?

   b.   Who invented the telephone?

6. What machine became the standard form of rapid, long-distance business communications at the beginning of the data communications era?

7. a.   How many bits does the Baudot code use?

   b.   How many bits does the ASCII code use?

   c.   What does the acronym ASCII stand for?

8. What do we mean when we say that much of the equipment that makes telephone communications possible is *transparent* to the user?

9. a.   What is the minimum number of conductors required to send serial data?

   b.   What is the minimum number of conductors required to send 8-bit parallel data?

10. Explain why parallel communications is faster than serial communications.

11. Why is serial communications preferred to parallel communications for long distances?

12. a.   What are two disadvantages of serial communications?

    b.   What is a disadvantage of parallel communications?

13. a.   What do the abbreviations HDX and FDX stand for?

    b.   Explain the differences between simplex, HDX, and FDX communications.

14. What are the main parts of a data communications system?

15. What is the purpose of the DTE in a data communications system?

16. What is the purpose of the DCE in a data communications system?

17. What is the purpose of the medium in a data communications system?

# Chapter 2

# PULSE MODULATION

**OBJECTIVES**

After you have completed this chapter, you should be able to:

- List four advantages of converting analog signals to digital format before sending them through a communications system.

- State the sampling theorem.

- Given the upper and lower frequency components of an intelligence frequency, calculate the Nyquist rate for sampling it.

- Name five types of pulse modulation and describe the main characteristics of each.

- Explain what is meant by *aliasing*.

- Explain the meaning of the terms *quantizing level* and *quantizing error*.

- Explain what a *codec* is.

- Explain the meaning of the terms *multiplexer* and *demultiplexer*.

13

## INTRODUCTION

As noted in Chapter 1, not all digital communications involve data. Almost all of the newer long-distance telephone lines carry voice signals in digital format. There are several advantages to converting analog signals to a digital format and communicating them through a digital medium. Digital signals are more immune to noise. Digital signals can be manipulated by computers to enhance their quality and to filter out noise. Several digital signals can be sent over a single channel in a process called multiplexing. Finally, converting analog signals to digital allows data and non-data signals to be transmitted over the same digital communications network.

The process of converting an analog signal to digital is called **pulse code modulation (PCM)**. PCM is one of several types of pulse modulation used in electronic communication. This chapter discusses several types of pulse modulation, including PCM.

## 2-1    SAMPLING AND THE SAMPLING THEOREM

Pulse modulation is possible because all analog waveforms contain redundant information. **Redundant information** is information that is repeated and is therefore unnecessary. For example, imagine a 1-kHz sine wave with an amplitude of 5 V peak-to-peak that repeats itself 3000 times. If you see one cycle of the sine wave displayed on an oscilloscope, you know exactly what the other 2999 cycles look like. A sine wave can be completely described by stating its frequency, its amplitude, its phase, and the number of times it repeats.

It is necessary to transmit only a small portion of almost any analog waveform to have enough information to completely reconstruct the original signal at the receiving end. Pulse modulation transmits periodic samples of an intelligence signal. At the receiver, the redundant information between the samples is filled in to construct a copy of the original waveform.

How many samples are necessary to reconstruct the signal? In 1924 H. Nyquist, working at Bell Telephone Labs, proved mathematically what has since become known as the sampling theorem. The **sampling theorem** *states that any analog signal can be reconstructed from its samples if sufficient samples per second are taken to equal at least twice the signal's maximum frequency.* This sampling rate is known as the **Nyquist rate** in honor of its discoverer.

To transmit all of the information in a voice signal that has a bandwidth of 300 Hz to 5 kHz, at least 10,000 samples per second are required (twice the signal's maximum frequency of 5 kHz). In a practical system, it is better to sample slightly above the Nyquist rate, a process known as **oversampling.** To return to our example waveform, a practical system might oversample a 300-Hz to 5-kHz voice signal 12,000 times per second. Mathematically stated:

Undersampling: $f_s < 2f_{i\,max}$
Nyquist rate:　　$f_s = 2f_{i\,max}$
Oversampling:　$f_s > 2f_{i\,max}$

where $f_s$ = the sampling frequency and $f_{i\,max}$ = the highest frequency component of the analog information signal.

■ **E X A M P L E   2 - 1**

A telephone voice signal has a bandwidth of 300 Hz to 3300 Hz. According to Nyquist, what is the minimum number of samples per second that must be sent to accurately reconstruct the voice signal at the receiver?

**SOLUTION**

The signal must be sampled at a rate equal to at least twice its maximum frequency. 2 × 3300 = 6600 samples per second minimum. (Again, a practical system would oversample the signal, perhaps at a rate of 7000 times per second.)

## 2-2   TYPES OF PULSE MODULATION

There are two general types of pulse modulation—digital pulse modulation and analog pulse modulation. Digital pulse modulation is also called pulse code modulation (PCM). PCM converts the samples of an analog signal into a series of 1s and 0s, which can be transmitted over a digital communication medium. PCM is the only type of pulse modulation that is used in digital communications systems. PCM is also the most complicated form of pulse modulation, and for that reason, we will save its discussion for last.

There are two general types of analog pulse modulation: **pulse amplitude modulation (PAM)** and **pulse time modulation (PTM).** We will begin with the simpler form, PAM.

## 2-3   PULSE AMPLITUDE MODULATION (PAM)

Figure 2-1 illustrates the principle of PAM. The sine wave at the upper left corner of the figure represents the intelligence signal to be sampled. The relay is controlled by

**FIGURE 2-1**
A simple pulse amplitude modulator.

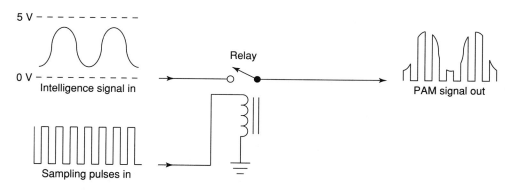

a series of sampling pulses. Each positive pulse causes the relay to close, and between pulses a spring causes the relay to open. Each time the relay closes, it allows a sample of the intelligence signal to pass through. The signal at the output of the circuit is a series of pulses that vary in amplitude. Each pulse is a sample that represents the amplitude of the intelligence signal at a specific point in time.

### 2-3-1   An Electronic Pulse Amplitude Modulator

Although the relay circuit in Figure 2-1 illustrates the principle of PAM, the technology is primitive. Semiconductor devices have replaced relays in pulse amplitude modulators. Figure 2-2 is the schematic of an electronic pulse amplitude modulator that can be built as an experiment in the electronics laboratory. The 100-Hz sine wave represents the intelligence signal and can be supplied by an audio-frequency signal generator in the laboratory. The op amp serves as a buffer to isolate the signal source from the 2N3904 transistor. The transistor is the actual modulator.

The 1-kHz square wave sampling signal turns the transistor on and off (switches it between saturation and cutoff). When the transistor is turned on, it allows a sample of the sine wave to pass through, and when the transistor is turned off, it blocks the sine wave. The intelligence signal passes through the transistor when it is turned on and is blocked by the transistor when it is turned off. The PAM output is a series of sample pulses. The amplitude of each output pulse is proportional to the amplitude of the intelligence signal at the same instant of time, just as it was in the circuit in Figure 2-1.

The PAM signals in Figures 2-1 and 2-2 have a duty cycle of 50%, but there is no reason why the pulses cannot be much narrower. The PAM signal in Figure 2-3 is

**FIGURE 2-2**
A pulse amplitude modulator that can be built in the laboratory.

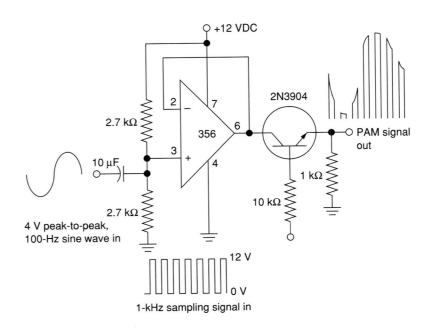

**FIGURE 2-3**
A PAM signal can consist of a
series of very narrow pulses.

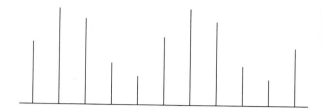

made up of a series of very narrow pulses. The advantage of such narrow pulses is that the spaces between them can be used to transmit other information, a process called *multiplexing*, which is discussed in Section 2-6 of this chapter.

### 2-3-2 Demodulating a PAM Signal

Of the various types of pulse modulation, PAM is the easiest to demodulate. The demodulator circuit can be a simple low-pass (LP) filter like the one in Figure 2-4. If the RC time constant is properly chosen, the capacitor charges with each input pulse, and it slowly discharges between the pulses. The slow discharge "smooths out" the spaces between the pulses and yields an output signal that closely resembles the original waveform. The output signal in Figure 2-4 shows what the output of a simple RC filter might look like. The quality of the demodulated signal can be greatly improved by using a more sophisticated filter design. The better the filter design, the more closely the output waveform will resemble the original waveform.

### 2-3-3 Aliasing

**Undersampling** is defined as sampling a signal at less than the Nyquist rate. We have mentioned that when an intelligence signal is sampled at less than the Nyquist rate, the intelligence signal cannot be completely recovered at the receiver. Undersampling causes a condition known as **aliasing.** Now that we have discussed one type of pulse modulation, we have laid the background to discuss why aliasing occurs.

Figure 2-5(a) illustrates the frequency spectrum required by an ordinary telephone signal, from about 300 Hz to about 3300 Hz. Figure 2-5(b) shows part of the frequency spectrum of the same signal after it has been pulse amplitude modulated onto an 8-kHz sampling pulse train.

**FIGURE 2-4**
The simplest pulse amplitude demodulator is a low-pass filter.

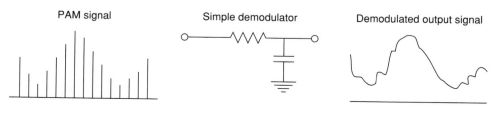

**FIGURE 2-5**
(a) The audio signal only. (b) When the sampling frequency exceeds the Nyquist rate, the audio can be recovered by an LP filter. (c) When the sampling frequency is less than the Nyquist rate, aliasing occurs.

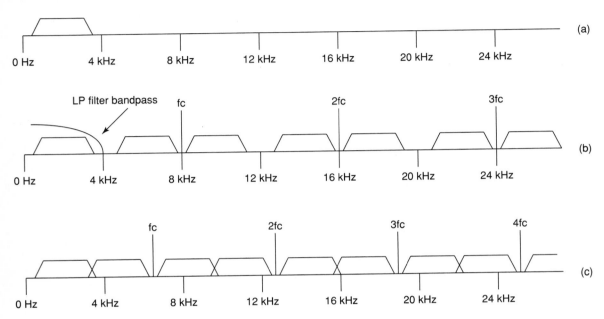

You may have learned in your studies of electronics that a perfect square wave is made up of the fundamental frequency plus an infinite number of odd harmonics. Therefore, a 1-kHz square wave has harmonics at 3 kHz, 5 kHz, 7 kHz, and so on. Of course a perfect square wave does not exist. An acceptable square wave is made up of the fundamental frequency plus all of its odd harmonics up to about the 11th.

A PAM signal approximates a square wave. It is made up of the fundamental sampling frequency and a number of both odd and even harmonics. You may have learned that when two signals of different frequency are combined in a non-linear circuit such as a modulator, four main products of modulation are produced: the two original frequencies, the sum of the two original frequencies, and the difference between the two original frequencies.

When the PAM sampling pulses are mixed with the intelligence signal in a non-linear environment (what could be more non-linear than opening and closing a switch?), each harmonic of the sampling signal mixes with the intelligence signal and produces the four products of modulation. The sum and difference frequencies appear as sidebands around the sampling frequency and around each of its harmonics. In other words, the fundamental sampling frequency mixes with the intelligence signal and produces the sum (an upper sideband of the sampling frequency) and the difference (a lower sideband). Each of the harmonics of the sampling signal also mixes with the intelligence frequency and produces upper and lower sidebands as illustrated in Figure 2-5(b).

As long as the sampling frequency exceeds the Nyquist rate, it is easy to demodulate a PAM signal from the other modulation products as shown in Figure 2-5(b). Here the sampling frequency is 8 kHz. The intelligence frequency occupies the frequency spectrum of 300 Hz to 3300 Hz. The lower sideband of the fundamental frequency of the sampling pulses extends down in frequency to 4700 Hz (the 8-kHz carrier frequency minus the 3300-Hz highest audio frequency. An LP filter can easily separate the intelligence signal from the lower sideband of the sampling pulse.

In Figure 2-5(c), which illustrates the problem that arises when the intelligence signal is undersampled, the sampling frequency is less than twice the highest frequency of the intelligence frequency. Let us assume that it is 6.5 kHz. The lower sideband of the sampling frequency extends down to 3200 Hz (6500 − 3300 Hz) and overlaps the 3300-Hz highest frequency of the intelligence signal. Because an LP filter cannot completely separate the intelligence signal from the lower sideband of the sampling pulses, aliasing occurs.

### 2-3-4 Advantages and Disadvantages of PAM

The main advantage of PAM is its simplicity. As we have seen, a simple on-off switch can serve as a modulator, and a low-pass filter can serve as a demodulator. With modern integrated circuit technology, which allows several million transistors to be placed on a single chip, simplicity is not as important an advantage as it once was.

The main disadvantage of pulse amplitude modulation (or of any other type of amplitude modulation) is that it is very susceptible to noise. Most noise is amplitude modulated, so it easily combines with electronic signals and changes their amplitude. Once a PAM signal is contaminated by noise, the noise is difficult to remove without resorting to sophisticated computer techniques.

A second disadvantage of PAM is that it requires high-bandwidth analog amplifiers if the PAM signal is to be transmitted any distance. As you are surely aware, digital circuits are preferred over analog circuits in most of today's electronic systems. Digital circuits are designed to work with signals that are either on or off. They are not designed to work with pulses of different amplitudes.

Because of its disadvantages, PAM is almost never used for long-distance communication, but it is used as an intermediate step to generate or demodulate other types of pulse modulation. The concepts of sampling, aliasing, and the frequency components of a pulse-modulated waveform that were explained in this discussion of PAM are important concepts that apply to all types of pulse modulation.

## 2-4 PULSE TIME MODULATION (PTM)

In PTM, the intelligence signal changes the timing of some characteristic of the transmitted pulses. Three timing characteristics can be varied: pulse frequency (pulse frequency modulation or PFM), pulse width (pulse width modulation or PWM), and the position of the pulse in time, making it occur slightly earlier or slightly later than expected (pulse position modulation or PPM).

**FIGURE 2-6**
In PWM, the width of the modulated pulse train is proportional to the amplitude of the intelligence signal.

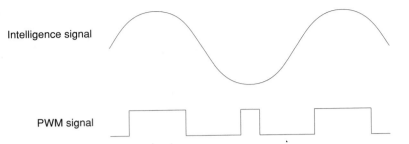

### 2-4-1   Pulse Width Modulation (PWM)

**Pulse width modulation (PWM)** is also known as **pulse duration modulation (PDM).** In PWM, all of the pulses in the modulated signal have the same amplitude. The intelligence signal varies the width of the pulses as shown in Figure 2-6. When the intelligence signal is at its maximum amplitude, it causes a wide pulse to be produced in the PWM output signal. When the intelligence signal is at its minimum level, it causes a narrow pulse to be produced as illustrated in the second pulse in the PWM signal of Figure 2-6. For simplicity, Figure 2-6 shows one output pulse for

**FIGURE 2-7**
(a) Block diagram of a pulse width modulator. (b) The waveforms of the pulse width modulator of Figure 2-6.

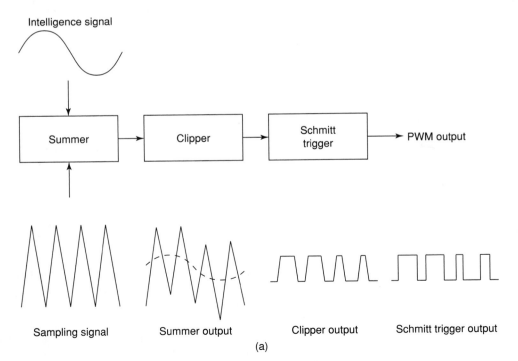

**FIGURE 2-7,** *continued*

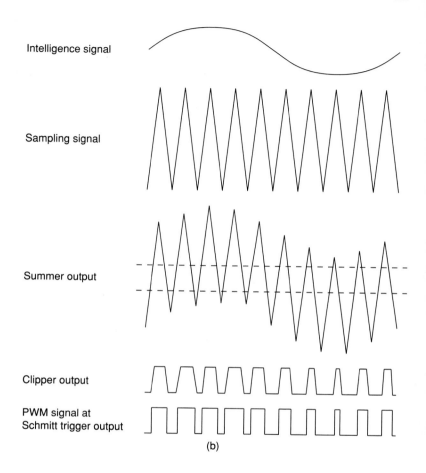

Intelligence signal

Sampling signal

Summer output

Clipper output

PWM signal at
Schmitt trigger output

(b)

each half cycle of the intelligence signal, but in actual practice more samples would be used.

A block diagram of a pulse width modulator is shown in Figure 2-7(a). The intelligence signal and a sampling signal are both fed into a summer network, which is nothing more than a resistor circuit or a linear class A amplifier. The sampling signal can be either a triangle wave, as shown in the diagram, or a sawtooth wave. In either case, the sampling signal should be at least 10 times the amplitude of the intelligence signal. Both signals appear at the summer output, where the sampling signal rides up and down, "piggy back," on the intelligence signal waveform.

The output of the summer is fed into a clipper, which removes the signal's positive and negative peaks. The result is a PWM waveform, but the leading and trailing edges of the pulse are perhaps not as steep as we would like. If necessary, the rise and fall times of the pulse edges can be made steeper by passing the signal through a Schmitt trigger.

Figure 2-7(b) shows the waveforms of Figure 2-6 in greater detail. The dashed lines drawn across the summer output waveform show the upper and lower levels at which this signal is clipped. Notice that the clipper output signal is already a PWM signal. The Schmitt trigger is optional and serves only to better define the pulses by making their leading and trailing edges sharper.

Figure 2-8 is the schematic diagram of a pulse width modulator circuit that can be built in the electronics laboratory. The op amp is operated as a voltage comparator. A voltage comparator has only two possible output voltages—a voltage very close to the op amp's positive power supply voltage on pin 7 (+12 V in our circuit) or a voltage very close to its negative power supply voltage on pin 4 (ground, in this case).

Which of the two possible output voltages is actually produced depends on which of the op amp's two inputs, pin 2 or pin 3, is more positive. Pin 3, designated by a plus sign (+), is the op amp's non-inverting input, and pin 2, designated by a minus sign (−), is its inverting input. If the non-inverting input is the more positive of the two, the output will also be positive. If the voltage on the inverting input is the more positive of the two, the output voltage of the op amp will be close to ground.

The voltage on the non-inverting op amp input of Figure 2-8 is the sum of three signals. The DC voltage acts as a reference voltage to set the duty cycle of the comparator's output signal. The triangle wave is the sampling signal that will be clipped by the comparator to form the square wave output. The sine wave signal represents the intelligence information. The three resistive inputs form a linear circuit which sums the signals at pin 3 of the op amp to form a triangle wave with a positive DC offset riding on a sine wave. The signal on pin 3 looks much like the summer output signal shown in Figure 2-7.

The summed signal drives pin 3 of the op amp alternately more and less positive than pin 2, which causes the op amp output to alternatively switch between +12 V and 0 V. The op amp clips the triangle wave to form a PWM output signal which looks like the PWM signal at the bottom of Figure 2-7(b).

There are several ways to demodulate a PWM signal. The simplest way is to use an LP filter, much like the one used to demodulate the PAM signal in Figure 2-4.

**FIGURE 2-8**
A pulse width modulator that can be built in the laboratory.

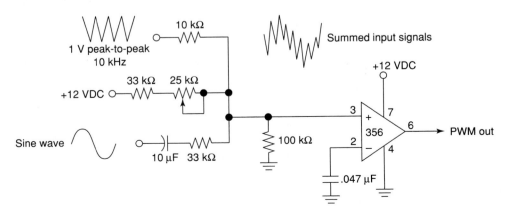

**FIGURE 2-9**
In PFM, the frequency of the
pulse train is proportional to the
amplitude of the intelligence
signal.

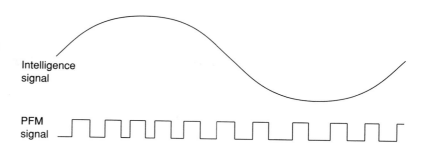

Intelligence
signal

PFM
signal

### 2-4-2  Pulse Frequency Modulation (PFM)

In **pulse frequency modulation (PFM),** the intelligence signal frequency modulates a square-wave pulse train. As Figure 2-9 illustrates, when the intelligence signal is at its maximum amplitude, the pulses in the modulated signal occur more frequently. When the intelligence signal is at its lowest amplitude, there are fewer pulses in the same period of time.

The easiest way to generate PFM is to use a square-wave voltage-controlled oscillator (VCO) integrated circuit. The frequency of a VCO is proportional to the voltage on its input pin. In Figure 2-10, the voltage divider circuit produces a DC voltage of 2.5 V at the input of the VCO. This voltage determines the center frequency of the VCO. The intelligence signal passes through the capacitor and is superimposed on the DC input. It causes the VCO input voltage to vary above and below the 2.5 VDC level. The changing input voltage in turn causes the VCO to oscillate above and below its center frequency.

Figure 2-11 shows a **phase-locked loop (PLL)** circuit connected as a PFM demodulator. A PLL consists of three principal parts: a phase detector, an LP filter, and a VCO. A properly functioning PLL circuit "locks onto" the input signal. A PLL is locked when both input signals to the phase detector are at the same frequency. In

**FIGURE 2-10**
PFM is easy to generate using a voltage-controlled oscillator IC.

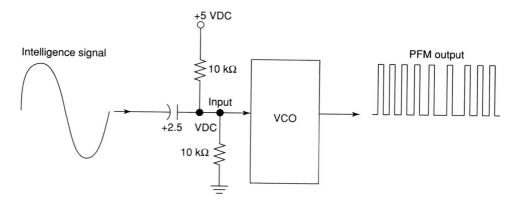

**FIGURE 2-11**
A PFM signal can be demodulated by a PLL.

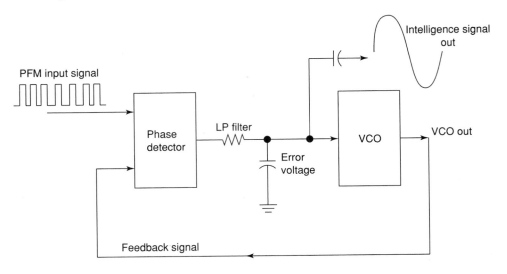

Figure 2-11, one of the inputs to the phase detector is the PFM signal that is to be demodulated, and the other is a feedback signal taken from the output of the VCO. When the PLL is locked, the phase detector outputs a signal that is filtered by the LP filter into a steady DC voltage. This voltage, called the error voltage, controls the frequency of the VCO.

When the input signal to the phase detector increases in frequency, the phase detector senses the change, and it outputs a signal that is filtered by the LP filter to increase the error voltage. The increased error voltage in turn increases the frequency of the VCO until it again matches the frequency of the input signal. Once again, the two inputs to the phase detector are at the same frequency. The phase detector and LP filter work together to hold the error voltage constant at its new, higher value.

If the input signal decreases in frequency, the phase detector senses the change and reduces the VCO frequency by outputting a lower error voltage through the LP filter. When the VCO frequency again matches the input frequency, the phase detector holds the error voltage constant at its new, lower value. The phase detector's two inputs are again at the same frequency, and the PLL is in lock.

When the input signal is a PFM signal, its frequency constantly increases and decreases in proportion to the amplitude changes of the original intelligence signal. The change in the input frequency occurs slowly enough that the PLL is able to follow it, but in order for the VCO frequency to track the input signal, the phase detector and LP filter output an error voltage that increases and decreases in step with the change in frequency of the input signal. This changing error voltage is a replica of the original intelligence signal.

### 2-4-3   Pulse Position Modulation (PPM)

Figure 2-12 illustrates another type of pulse time modulation—**pulse position modulation (PPM).** In pulse position modulation, the intelligence signal causes the individual pulses in the pulse train to occur either earlier or later than they otherwise would. In Figure 2-12, the pulses of the modulated signal occur earlier than they otherwise would have during positive swings of the intelligence signal and later than they otherwise would have during negative swings of the intelligence signal.

Figure 2-13 shows how a PPM signal can be generated from a PWM waveform. The circuit is shown in block diagram form in Figure 2-13(a), and the waveforms from various points in the circuit are shown in Figure 2-13(b). The output from a PWM generator circuit is differentiated, forming a series of short pulses that correspond to the rising and falling edges of the PWM output. The negative pulses are clipped, and the resulting positive pulses are amplified by an inverting common-emitter amplifier. The amplifier output serves as the trigger to a one-shot multivibrator.

The top series of pulses in Figure 2-13(b) is an unmodulated square wave. In our discussion, we will use this pulse train as a reference with which to compare the timing of the pulses that occur at different points in the pulse position modulator circuit. As the intelligence signal goes positive, the leading edge of the PWM signal occurs earlier in time than does the leading edge of the reference pulse; when the intelligence signal goes negative, the leading edge of the PWM signal occurs later in time than does the leading edge of the reference signal.

The differentiator output waveform in Figure 2-13(b) is the waveform that would be seen at the output of the differentiator of Figure 2-13(a) if the clipper diode and transistor were not connected to it. The leading edges of the PWM pulses would be differentiated into sharp, positive-going spikes, and the trailing edges would be differentiated into sharp, negative-going spikes. When the clipper diode is connected to the differentiator output, it conducts on negative peaks of the waveform and clips those peaks at about –0.7 V. (Incidentally, the reason the negative peaks are clipped from the waveform is to protect the emitter-base junction of the transistor from reverse breakdown.)

The transistor shown in Figure 2-13(a) has no forward DC bias on its emitter-base junction, and therefore it does not conduct between pulses. Each positive-going

**FIGURE 2-12**
In PPM, the intelligence signal causes the pulses to occur earlier or later in time than they otherwise would.

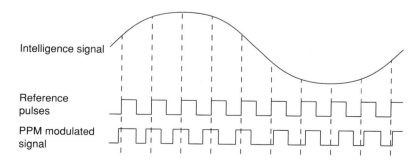

Intelligence signal

Reference
pulses

PPM modulated
signal

**FIGURE 2-13**

A PPM signal can be generated from a PWM waveform. (a) A PPM modulator circuit block diagram. (b) Waveforms from various points in the PPM modulator.

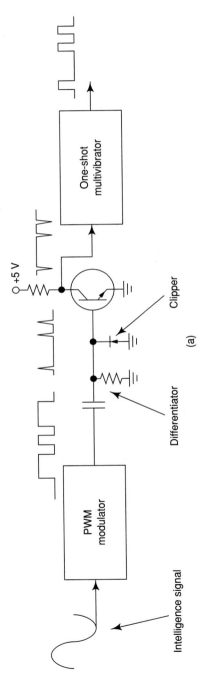

**FIGURE 2-13,** *continued*

Intelligence
signal

Reference
pulses

PWM
signal

Differentiator
output
(without clipper)

Differentiator
output
(with clipper)

Trigger
pulses

PPM signal

Reference
pulses

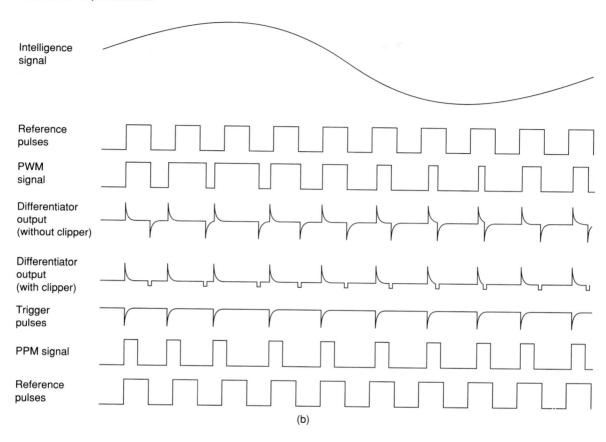

(b)

pulse on the base temporarily forward biases the emitter-base junction and causes the transistor to conduct, thus amplifying the pulse. The common-emitter amplifier also inverts each pulse. The negative-going pulses at the collector of the transistor serve as trigger signals for a one-shot multivibrator.

The output of the one-shot multivibrator is normally low. When a trigger pulse is applied to the one-shot, it produces a single pulse of a fixed length. Because the trigger pulses are derived from the leading edge of the PWM signal, which occurs earlier or later in time depending on the amplitude of the intelligence signal, the position of the PPM pulses also varies according to the amplitude of the intelligence signal.

### 2-4-4 The Advantages and Disadvantages of PTM

All of the forms of pulse time modulation are less susceptible to noise than is PAM. Noise has its greatest effect on the amplitude of the pulses, and in PTM, amplitude is unimportant. Some simple digital integrated circuits composed of gates and inverters can pass PTM, which makes expensive analog amplifiers unnecessary.

As far as disadvantages are concerned, noise corrupts the leading and trailing edges of PTM pulses, and it does have some effect on their timing. PTM may be less susceptible to noise than is PAM, but it is still not as noise immune as are digital signals. Although PTM may pass through simple combinational logic circuits, it cannot be used with more complex digital circuits that operate in time with a clock signal.

## 2-5   PULSE CODE MODULATION (PCM)

Theoretically, all of the forms of analog pulse modulation are capable of carrying an intelligence signal with 100% fidelity. A PAM pulse has an infinite number of possible amplitudes. Any slight change in the amplitude of the intelligence signal, no matter how small, causes a proportional slight change in the amplitude of the PAM pulses. In PWM, any small change in the amplitude of the intelligence signal causes a proportional small change in the width of the PWM pulses. As we shall shortly see, digital pulse code modulation cannot represent very small changes in the amplitude of the analog intelligence signal.

PCM, which is also known as **digital pulse modulation,** converts each sample of the intelligence signal into a binary number. The process of converting an analog signal into a binary code is called **quantizing,** and the levels that can be represented by the binary number are called **quantizing levels.** The number of possible amplitudes that can be represented by a binary number is $2^N$, where N is the number of bits. For example, if the intelligence signal is converted to a 2-bit binary number, as is the case in Figure 2-14, only $2^2$ or 4 levels can be represented. Those four levels are represented by the binary numbers 00, 01, 10, and 11.

### 2-5-1   Quantizing Error

If the signal is sampled between two quantizing levels as pictured in Figure 2-14, the sample cannot be accurately quantized. The sampling point indicated by the arrow in Figure 2-14 lies between quantizing levels 2 (binary 10) and 3 (binary 11). One of the two levels must be chosen to represent the signal, which means that there will be an error. The difference between the actual signal level and the quantizing level that is chosen to represent it is called a **quantizing error.**

Figure 2-15 shows how drastic the effects of quantizing error could be if samples of an analog waveform were represented by 2-bit binary numbers in PCM form. The vertical dashed lines show the times when the wave is sampled. None of the samples falls exactly on a quantizing level, so each sample is quantized to the nearest level and converted to the binary number that represents it.

**FIGURE 2-14**
A sample taken at the time indicated by the arrow must be
quantized as either binary 10 or
11.

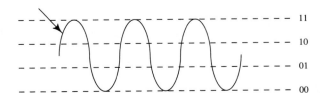

**FIGURE 2-15**
When a signal is quantized, samples whose amplitudes fall between the quantizing levels cannot be represented exactly.

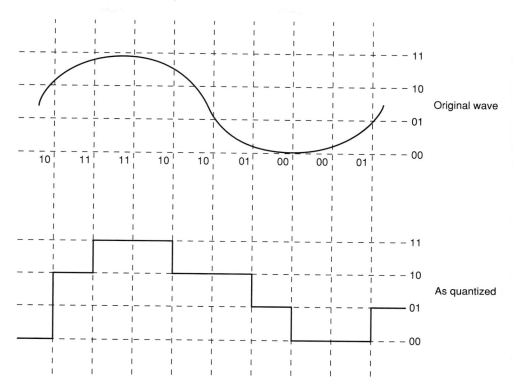

The wave at the bottom of Figure 2-15 shows what happens when the digital signal is converted back to analog. When each digital number is converted to the quantizing level that it represents, the resulting waveform changes in steps and is not an accurate representation of the original intelligence signal. Even if the waveform is filtered to smooth it out, it will still not be an accurate representation of the original signal.

Quantizing error can be reduced by increasing the number of bits. The number of possible combinations that can be represented by a digital number is $2^N$, where N represents the number of bits. Thus for 2 bits we had $2^2$ or 4 possible combinations. Adding one more bit to the system gives us $2^3$ or 8 possible quantizing levels. The more steps there are, the less room there is between steps and the more accurately the intelligence signal can be represented. But no matter how many bits are used, PCM can never perfectly represent the intelligence signal, because spaces will always occur between the quantizing levels. However, perfect fidelity is not necessary. For example, when dealing with audio, there is no point in adding more bits once the level is reached at which the human ear can no longer hear the difference. For telephone quality speech, 7 bits per sample are sufficient, which yields $2^7$ or 128 quantizing levels. High fidelity music can be well represented by 16-bit samples, which yield $2^{16}$ or 65,536 quantizing levels.

Another way to improve the quality of a digitized signal is to use **non-linear quantizing.** In non-linear quantizing, the levels are spaced closer together at the lower signal levels and farther apart at stronger signal levels, as shown in Figure 2-16. Non-linear quantizing allows low signal amplitudes to be represented more accurately. When the PCM signal is demodulated at the receiving end, a non-linear demodulator must also be used.

### 2-5-2   PCM Modulators

Figure 2-17 shows the steps required to turn a voice signal into PCM at the transmitter and to demodulate the PCM to recover the voice signal at the receiver. The voice signal enters a **sample-and-hold circuit,** which periodically takes a sample of the analog signal and holds each sample on its output line long enough for the **analog-to-digital (A/D) converter** to convert it to a binary number in parallel format. A shift register converts the parallel binary information into a serial bit stream that is sent out over the communications link.

At the receiving end, another shift register converts the incoming serial bit stream back to parallel form and outputs the parallel binary information to a **digital-to-analog (D/A) converter.** The D/A converts the parallel binary information back to analog format. Finally, an LP filter smooths the transitions between samples, and the result is a reproduction of the original analog voice signal.

A **codec** (a short form of coder/decoder) is a single integrated circuit that performs all of the functions shown in Figure 2-17. It can either convert an analog signal to PCM or convert PCM to analog.

**FIGURE 2-16**
Non-linear quantizing more accurately represents weak signal levels.

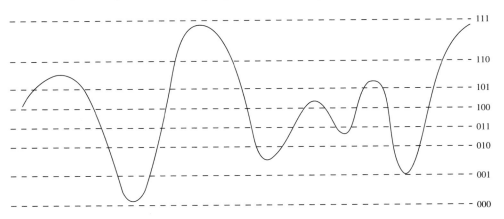

**FIGURE 2-17**
Block diagram of a PCM modulator and demodulator.

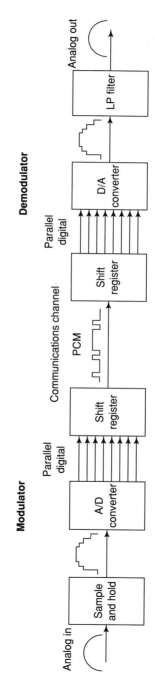

31

## 2-6    MULTIPLEXING DIGITAL SIGNALS

Several digital signals can be combined and sent over a single communications channel in a process called **multiplexing.** At the receiving end, the signals are **demultiplexed,** or separated and sent on to separate terminals. There are two types of multiplexing in use—time-division multiplexing and frequency-division multiplexing. Frequency-division multiplexing is used with analog signals and will not be discussed here. Figure 2-18 illustrates the principle of time-division multiplexing. A multiplexer acts like an electronic switch. The switch at the transmitter connects terminal A to the communication circuit for an instant of time. At the same time, an electronic switch at the receiver also connects terminal A to the circuit, and a point-to-point connection is momentarily established between the two terminals.

Then, the switches momentarily connect terminals B, then terminals C, and then the process repeats as terminals A are again connected. In practice, the process is a bit more complex than shown in the figure. For example, some sort of synchronizing signal must be sent to ensure that the transmit and receive switches do not get out of step with each other.

Figure 2-19 is a block diagram of the time-division multiplexing process. A *multiplexer,* or *MUX* unit, interleaves packets of data from terminals A, B, and C and sends them out over a common, higher speed transmission medium. In the illustration, each of the terminals is operating at 1200 bits per second (b/s). Once the data from the three terminals are combined, they are sent at 3600 b/s (3 × 1200 b/s) to the receiver. At the receiver, a *demultiplexer,* or *DEMUX,* separates the packets of data and sends each of them to the correct terminal.

**FIGURE 2-18**
Time-division multiplexing can be thought of as a switch that connects each of the terminals to the circuit for a brief period of time.

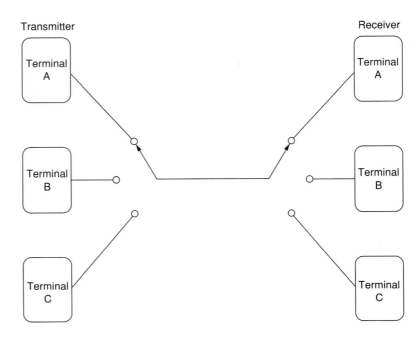

**FIGURE 2-19**
Time-division multiplexing works by interleaving packets of information from various sources.

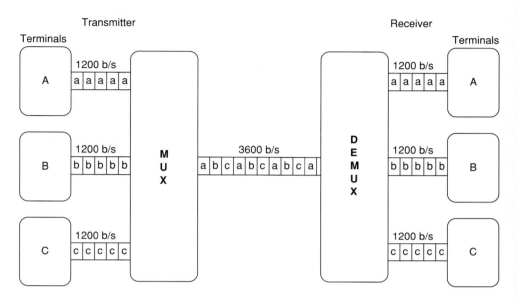

## EXAMPLE 2-2

Four terminals send information through a multiplexer and over a common communications line. One terminal operates at 300 b/s, two of them operate at 1200 b/s, and the fourth terminal operates at 2400 b/s. What is the minimum speed at which data can be sent over the common communications line?

### SOLUTION

Because the communications line must handle the bit stream from all four terminals simultaneously, it must be capable of carrying a number of bits per second equal to the sum of the bits per second produced by all of the terminals.

300 b/s + 1200 b/s + 1200 b/s + 2400 b/s = 5100 b/s

As Figure 2-20 illustrates, all digital signals can be treated alike by the communications medium, regardless of whether they are data or analog converted to digital. Data and digitized voice signals can be multiplexed together and carried over the same communications medium. A new telephone service called integrated services digital network (ISDN) carries all information in digital format. Computer data, facsimile images, and voice can be multiplexed together and carried over an ISDN line. ISDN allows two persons in different parts of the world to view the same image on

**FIGURE 2-20**
Digital multiplexing allows data and voice signals to be carried over the same communications medium.

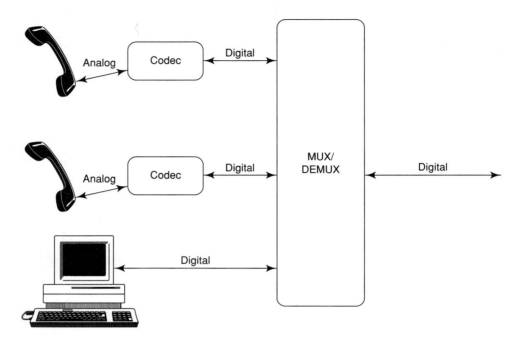

their computers and to make changes to the image while simultaneously carrying on a voice conversation, all over the same telephone connection. ISDN is discussed in greater detail in Chapter 3 of this book.

## ■ SUMMARY

This chapter has discussed pulse modulation. Pulse modulation is made possible by the fact that analog signals contain redundant information. Redundant information is information that is repeated in the original intelligence signal and therefore needs to be transmitted only once. In pulse modulation, periodic samples of the intelligence signal are taken, and each sample is converted into one or more pulses. According to the sampling theorem, the minimum number of samples needed to convey all of the information contained in the intelligence signal is equal to twice the highest frequency component of the analog intelligence signal. This rate is known as the Nyquist rate. If an intelligence signal is sampled at less than the Nyquist rate, new frequency components are generated in a process called aliasing. To avoid aliasing, practical pulse modulation systems sample the intelligence signal at slightly more than the Nyquist rate.

Pulse modulation is divided into analog pulse modulation and digital pulse modulation. In analog pulse modulation, some characteristic of the pulse can be continuously varied to accurately represent the amplitude of the intelligence signal. The two general types of analog pulse modulation are pulse amplitude modulation (PAM) and pulse time modulation (PTM). The three types of PTM discussed in the chapter are pulse width modulation (PWM), which is also referred to as pulse duration modulation (PDM); pulse frequency modulation (PFM); and pulse position modulation (PPM). Analog pulse modulation is rarely used in long-distance communications.

Digital pulse modulation is commonly referred to as pulse code modulation (PCM). During PCM, the samples of the analog intelligence signal are first quantized, or assigned a level that is then represented by a binary number. The number of possible quantizing levels is equal to $2^N$, where N is the number of bits used in the binary number. Because it uses a finite number of quantizing levels, PCM cannot represent the amplitude of the samples with 100% accuracy. The difference between the actual amplitude of a sample and the quantizing level assigned to that sample is called a quantizing error. PCM can be performed by a single integrated circuit known as a codec (coder/decoder).

The disadvantages of PCM are that it is complex and that it cannot represent the intelligence signal with 100% fidelity. These disadvantages are outweighed by PCM's advantages over other types of modulation. PCM has very high noise immunity, and PCM signals can be multiplexed with other digital signals such as digital data from computers and carried over the same communications lines.

## ■ QUESTIONS

1. List four advantages of converting analog signals to digital format before sending them over a communications system.

2. What is meant by the expression *redundant information?*

3. What is the sampling theorem?

4. It is desired to sample an analog signal that has a frequency range of 50 Hz to 15,000 Hz. According to the sampling theorem, what is the *minimum* number of samples per second that can be taken in order to have enough information to completely reconstruct the original signal from the samples?

5. What is another name for *digital pulse modulation?*

6. What are the two general types of analog pulse modulation?

7. What is the simplest method of demodulating a PAM signal?

8. If an intelligence signal is sampled at less than the Nyquist rate, new frequencies are generated in a process known as _____.

9. a. What is the main advantage of PAM?

   b. What is the main disadvantage of PAM?

10. a. What does the abbreviation *PTM* stand for?

b.  List three types of PTM.

11.  What is another name for pulse width modulation?

12.  What is the simplest method of demodulating a PWM signal?

13.  What is the easiest way to generate a PFM signal?

14.  What type of circuit can be used as a PFM demodulator?

15.  What two advantages do all of the forms of PTM have over PAM?

16.  What is another name for pulse code modulation?

17.  How many quantizing levels are possible in PCM if a 3-bit binary number is used?

18.  a.  In PCM, what is the definition of the term *quantizing error?*

b.  Which of the following two PCM systems will have the larger quantizing error, an 8-bit system or a 12-bit system?

19.  How can non-linear quantizing improve the quality of a PCM signal?

20.  What function is performed by a codec chip?

21.  a.  What are the two types of multiplexing?

b.  Which of these two types of multiplexing is used with digital signals?

22.  Briefly describe the principle of time-division multiplexing.

23.  What is ISDN?

# Chapter 3

# THE TELEPHONE SYSTEM

**OBJECTIVES**

After you have completed this chapter, you should be able to:

- Define the terms *subscriber, station equipment, switching equipment, transmission equipment, local loop, trunk circuit, central office, toll office, local office switch,* and *tandem switch.*

- Name the major components of the DDD network.

- Briefly describe how DTMF signaling works.

- List some disadvantages of using today's telephone network for data communications.

- List some advantages of using leased lines instead of dial-up lines for data communications.

- Describe the differences between basic ISDN and primary rate interface ISDN.

- Explain why optical fibers are the preferred medium for long-distance telecommunications.

## INTRODUCTION

The telephone network was designed for voice communications, not to carry data. As a data communications medium it has some severe technical limitations. It is an analog medium, and data are digital. The narrow bandwidth of a telephone circuit restricts the rate at which it can carry data to several tens of thousands of bits per second (b/s), which is very slow by today's standards.

Despite the telephone network's technical limitations, its convenience makes it the world's most used data communications medium. It extends to almost all parts of the world to which one would wish to send data. For instance, an anthropologist working in a small village in South America can use the telephone network to communicate with a university computer in North America or Europe.

Anyone who works in the data communications field should have a basic idea of how the telephone system works, what its limitations are, and what changes in the system can be expected in the future.

This chapter provides a brief survey of the telephone system as it exists today and of the changes that are taking place. The telephone system of the near future will be digital from end to end, and it will carry a mixture of audio, data, and video signals as easily as the present system carries voice communications.

## 3-1    THE ORGANIZATION OF THE DDD NETWORK

The telephone network is made up of almost all of the world's telephone companies (called **telcos** for short). Customers of the telcos are called **subscribers.** Telcos provide their subscribers with two basic types of service—access to the worldwide **direct distance dial (DDD) network,** which is the type of telephone service that almost all of us have in our homes and businesses, and the private line service, which provides dedicated, semi-permanent telephone connections between fixed points.

The three major components of the DDD network are *station equipment, switching equipment,* and *transmission equipment.* **Station equipment** includes all parts of the telephone network that are located on the subscriber's premises such as the telephone set itself, switchboards (which are called **private branch exchanges** or **PBXs** in telephone jargon), and the wiring within the subscriber's home or business. **Switching equipment** is located in telco offices and makes the connections between the station equipment of two or more subscribers. **Transmission equipment** consists of the telephone circuits that carry information from one location to another.

There are two general types of telephone circuits—local loops and trunks. **Local loops** connect the subscribers' station equipment to the switching equipment in the telco local office. **Trunks** carry communications from one item of switching equipment to another or from one telco office to another. Circuits that connect a large subscriber's PBX to the local office can also be called trunks (the PBX is an item of switching equipment, even though it is on the subscriber's premises), but they will be referred to as local loops in this chapter.

### 3-1-1    Station Equipment

Station equipment, as mentioned earlier, includes all telephone equipment and wiring located on the subscriber's premises. In a private residence, subscriber equipment usually consists of one or more telephones (a **telset** in telco jargon), the telephone wiring on the subscriber's premises, and perhaps a telephone answering machine. A business may have a PBX that allows a large number of telsets to be serviced by a much smaller number of local loops. Other common items of station equipment used by business subscribers are facsimile (fax) machines and computer modems.

Figure 3-1 is a simplified schematic diagram of a traditional telset, the type with the rotary dial that was widely used into the 1960s. Most newer telsets are built around an integrated circuit and do not contain the separate components shown in Figure 3-1. The integrated circuit performs the same functions as the components shown in the figure, so it may be helpful to refer to the figure as you read the following paragraphs.

The main components of a telset are the **ringer,** which sounds to alert the subscriber when there is an incoming call; the **hook switch,** which is open when the telephone handset is "on the hook" and which closes when the handset is lifted; an ear piece (called a **receiver** or **Rx**); and a microphone (called a **transmitter** or **Tx**).

**FIGURE 3-1**
Simplified schematic of a telset.

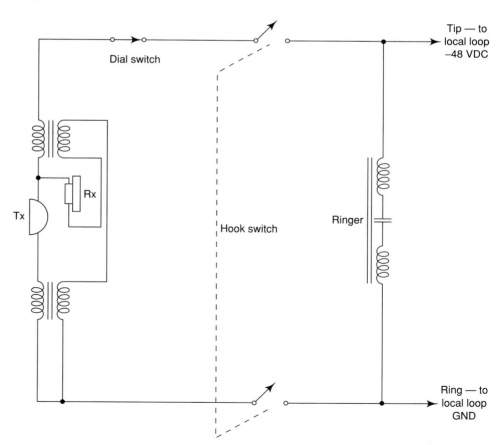

**FIGURE 3-2**
The tip and ring connections of a common audio plug gave their names to the conductors of a telephone circuit.

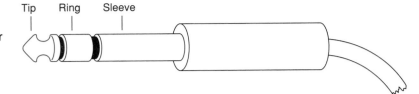

The two conductors that connect the telset to the local telephone loop (and the conductors of the local loop itself) are called the **tip** and the **ring.** As shown in Figure 3-2, these conductors take their names from a common audio plug used by the telcos. When the telset is on-hook, and the hook switch is open, the tip is at a potential of –48 VDC, and the ring is at ground potential. The telco central office supplies these voltages over the local loop. When the telset goes off-hook, current flow through the local loop causes these voltages to change.

The ringer is connected across the local loop at all times. A capacitor in series with the ringer coils blocks DC to prevent the ringer from shorting the –48 V to ground. Equipment located in the telco local office sends an AC voltage over the local loop to ring the telephone.

### 3-1-2  The Local Loop

Figure 3-3 shows how the subscriber's telset has traditionally been connected through the local loop to the telco central office. The schematic of the telset has been further simplified from that shown in Figure 3-1 to keep from cluttering the diagram with unnecessary detail.

The local loop consists of a pair of copper wires. The –48 V and ground potential are applied to the loop through the *line relay* located at the local office. A capacitor bypasses voice frequencies around the line relay. A transformer passes the voice

**FIGURE 3-3**
When the subscriber's telephone goes off-hook, a DC connection is made which closes the line relay in the telco central office.

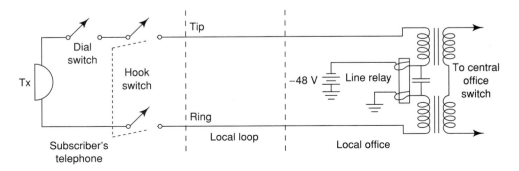

frequencies on the central office switching equipment and isolates the switching equipment from the DC voltages on the loop.

When the subscriber takes the telset off-hook, the hook switch in the telset closes. Current flows in the local loop and through the telset between the −48 V supply and ground. The current causes the line relay to close. This is called a **line start operation** or a **loop start operation.** The line relay activates a **linefinder switch** (not shown in the figure) in the central office, which connects the loop to the central office switch and returns a **dial tone** to the telset. The dial tone notifies the subscriber that the switch is ready to receive dialing pulses.

To dial each digit of the telephone number on a traditional telset, the subscriber rotates the dial to the right and releases it, and a spring returns the dial to its resting position. As the dial returns, it opens and closes the dial switch causing pulses of current to flow through the local loop. If the subscriber dials the digit 6, the dial switch opens and closes six times. If a 9 is dialed, the dial switch opens and closes 9 times, and so on. The pulses of current also cause the line relay in the central office to open and close. Contacts on the line relay forward the dial pulses to the central office switch.

### 3-1-3 Touch-Tone Dialing

Most of the telsets used in North America today do not use pulse dialing, although pulse dialing is still common in other parts of the world. In modern telsets, pulse dialing has been replaced by **dual-tone multifrequency signaling (DTMF),** more commonly known as **Touch Tone.** As illustrated in Figure 3-4, DTMF uses seven audio oscillators, one for each of the four rows and one for each of the three columns of buttons on the telset. Each time a number is dialed, two oscillators are activated simultaneously, one for the row in which the button is located and one for the column in which it is located. For example, when an 8 is dialed, both the 852-Hz and the 1336-Hz oscillators sound, and the two frequencies that they generate are sent over the telephone line.

DTMF tones are superior to dial pulses for two reasons. DTMF tones can be sent much more rapidly than dial pulses. Unlike DC dialing pulses, DTMF tones can pass through the audio amplifiers that are part of the telephone system.

Using two tones instead of one for dialing reduces the possibility that random frequencies that occur on the line will be interpreted as a dialed digit. It is unlikely that two random frequencies will occur at a high enough amplitude to be confused with a DTMF signal.

The circuit pictured in Figure 3-5 can be used to decode DTMF signals. The rectangular boxes represent tuned amplifiers. Each of the amplifiers normally outputs a logic low. When an amplifier detects the frequency to which it is tuned, its output switches to a logic high. The tone that corresponds to the row on the telset keypad activates one of the top four amplifiers, and the tone that corresponds to the column on the keypad activates one of the bottom three. For example, a received DTMF signal that consists of a 770-Hz tone and a 1336-Hz tone causes the outputs of both the 770-Hz and the 1336-Hz tuned amplifiers to go high. These outputs are

**FIGURE 3-4**
DTMF signaling transmits a two-tone signal each time a digit is dialed.

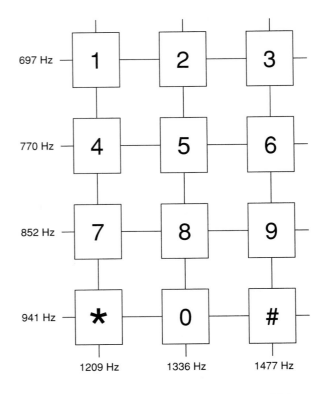

ANDed together by (and *only* by) AND gate number 5 whose output goes high to signify that the DTMF tones for the digit 5 have been detected.

When there is an incoming call, the local office sends an AC voltage over the local loop to the telset. The AC voltage activates the ringer to inform the subscriber of the call. When the subscriber lifts the telephone receiver, the hook switch closes, allowing current to flow between the tip and ring through the closed dial switch and the telset transmitter and receiver in parallel. This current flow through the local loop is sensed at the local office and causes the ringing voltage to be removed from the loop, and the telset of the subscriber receiving the call is connected to the telset of the calling party.

### 3-1-4  Switching Equipment

Switching equipment establishes a telephone circuit between one subscriber and another. When a subscriber's telset is taken off hook, or when it receives an incoming telephone call, it is connected to the **local office switch.** The local office switch serves all of the subscribers of a local telephone exchange and establishes the connection when one subscriber telephones another subscriber on the same exchange. A local exchange in the United States or Canada serves all subscribers whose telephone numbers begin with the same three digits, which are known as a **prefix.** For example, the 275 telephone exchange in a given city serves all subscribers in that city

**FIGURE 3-5**
A DTMF decoder circuit.

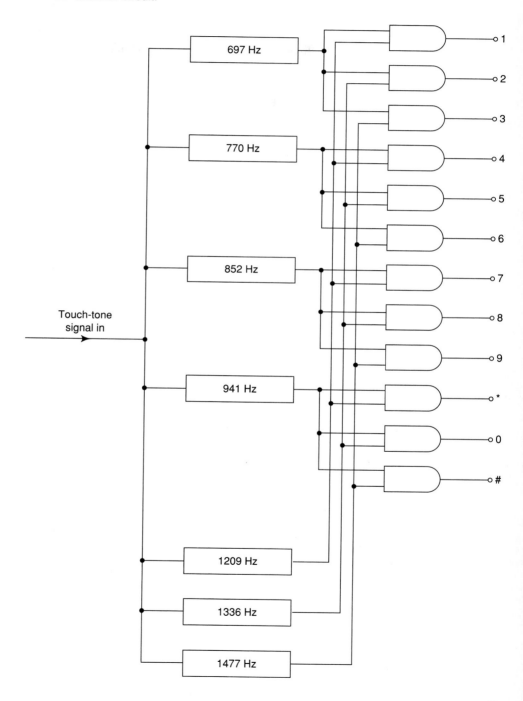

whose telephone numbers have the prefix 275, which is to say, all numbers in the range of 275-0000 to 275-9999.

Most urban areas are served by a number of local office switches. When a subscriber from one exchange telephones a subscriber on a different exchange, the call must pass through two or more switches. As shown in Figure 3-6, local office switches are interconnected by trunk circuits called **interoffice trunks.** When a subscriber dials a telephone number, the subscriber's local office switch determines from the number's prefix whether the call is for another subscriber served by the same switch or if the call needs to be routed through another switch.

If the call does need to be routed to another switch, the subscriber's local office switch searches for an interoffice trunk to make the connection. If it does not find one, it sends a busy signal back to the subscriber, and the call is not completed. If the switch does find an interoffice trunk, it connects the subscriber's local office loop to that trunk and forwards the dialed telephone number to the second switch. The second switch connects the trunk to the called subscriber's local loop and sends a ringing voltage over the loop to the called subscriber's telset.

In a large urban area with many local office switches, it is impractical to interconnect all switches with sufficient trunks to handle the volume of interexchange

**FIGURE 3-6**
A tandem switch is used to establish connections between local office switches.

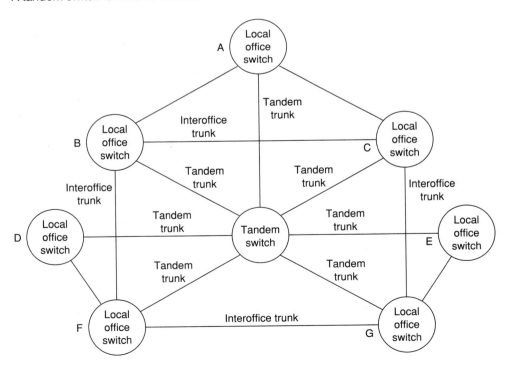

calls that occur during peak calling hours. To reduce the number of interoffice trunks required, a **tandem switch** establishes many of the interoffice connections. A **tandem switch,** shown in Figure 3-6, is a switch that connects other switches. **Tandem trunks** connect the tandem switch to the local office switches.

In Figure 3-6, if a subscriber in the exchange served by local office switch F calls a subscriber in the exchange served by local office switch E, the call must be routed through the tandem switch. There is no interoffice trunk connecting the two local office switches. If a subscriber in the exchange served by local office switch F calls a subscriber in the exchange served by local office switch G, the call is routed over an interoffice trunk, if one is free. If all of the interoffice trunks that connect the two exchanges are busy, the call is routed through the tandem switch, if trunks are available between the tandem switch and both local office switches. If there are no free interoffice or tandem trunks that can be used to complete the call, the calling subscriber receives a busy signal.

## 3-1-5  The DDD Long-Distance Network

When a call is placed outside the local area, it goes through the long-distance network. The long-distance network was developed by AT&T, which used to supply all of the long-distance telephone service in the United States. However, with AT&T's monopoly now ended, a number of companies currently compete with each other to provide long-distance telephone service in the United States. All of those companies are required to maintain equipment that is compatible with the system established by AT&T. The United States and Canada are divided into geographic areas, and each area has a three-digit area code.

## 3-1-6  The Long-Distance Switching System

Figure 3-7 shows the different levels of switching offices in the long-distance network. The offices are arranged in a **hierarchical network** that can be thought of as a pyramid-shaped organization with a few regional switching centers at the top and many toll centers at the bottom. The various levels of the hierarchy, from bottom to top, are toll centers, primary centers, sectional centers, and regional centers. The local switch routes all long-distance calls over trunk lines to a **toll center,** from which it is routed through the long-distance network to the toll center that handles the called subscriber. From there it is routed to the called subscriber's local office switch.

As Figure 3-8 illustrates, there are many possibilities for routing a long-distance call from one toll center to another. It may be routed directly from the toll center serving the exchange where the call originated to the destination toll center over a single trunk. If no free trunks directly connect the two toll centers, the call is routed through one or more primary centers. The call may also be routed higher up the hierarchy to a sectional or regional center. A number of trunk circuits, as many as seven, may be connected in tandem (end to end) to complete the telephone circuit.

**FIGURE 3-7**
The telephone system is organized as a hierarchical network.

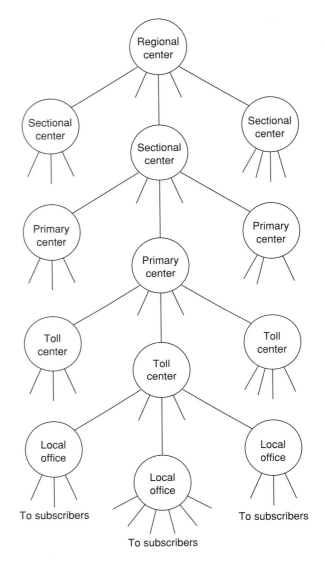

The selection of trunk circuits to make the connection is more or less random, and it is unlikely that the same combination of trunk circuits will be used each time a call is placed. As more trunks are added to the circuit, certain limitations of the trunks, such as their noise level, become cumulative. Older switches add impulse noise to the telephone circuit. The more switches that are used to form the circuit, the higher the levels of impulse noise are likely to accumulate. Impulse noise is of short duration and has minimal effect on voice communications, but it can have a detrimental effect on data communications by covering up individual bits. Thankfully, most telephone switches in use today use digital technology, and they do not

**FIGURE 3-8**
There are many possible paths to route a toll call between two subscribers.

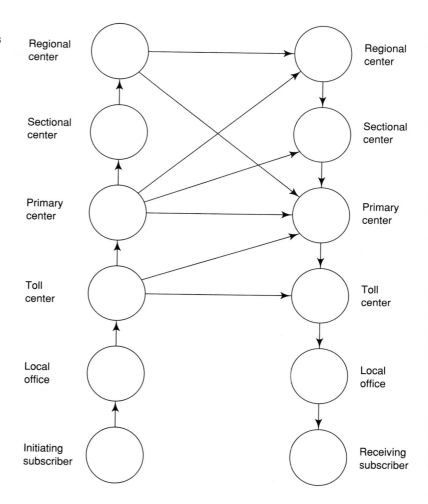

add noise to the telephone circuit. Almost all of the long-distance trunk circuits in North America are also digital, and they do not add noise to the connection.

The quality of the telephone circuit between two subscribers can vary greatly each time a call is placed between them, especially if the call is routed through the older, analog equipment that is still used in many parts of the world. Worse yet, from the standpoint of data communications, the quality cannot be predicted and compensated for, because the combination of switching equipment and trunk circuits that will be used is random and cannot be known before the connection is established.

## 3-2 THE PRIVATE LINE SERVICE

In the private line service, facilities are leased from the telephone company. Generally these facilities consist of leased telephone lines that connect two or more points.

The connection is semi-permanent. The telephone company maintains the connection for as long as the subscriber leases the line, and the line is available to the subscriber 24 hours a day.

### 3-2-1  Leased Lines

A **leased line** is made up of normal telephone facilities. A local loop is used from the subscriber's premises to the local telco office, and trunk circuits are used for the remainder of the link. However, the switching equipment is bypassed, and the trunks are hardwired together to form the circuit.

There are several advantages to using leased lines instead of the DDD network for data communications. If the line is used many hours a day, the leased line is cheaper than a DDD connection. A leased line is continuously available whenever it is needed. The quality of a leased line is guaranteed from end to end. Because the connection exists for as long as the line is leased, the quality of the circuit is consistent, which allows the subscriber to add equalizers at both ends of the circuit. **Equalizers** compensate to a certain extent for the frequency response of the line or for certain other types of distortion. Bypassing the switching equipment minimizes impulse noise if part of the circuit passes through an older electromechanical central office switch.

For an extra fee, the telco will *condition* the line. A **conditioned line** has its frequency response and delay characteristics optimized for the transmission of data. In the 1980s, the maximum rate at which data could be reliably sent over the DDD network was 2400 b/s. Conditioned leased lines could carry data at 9600 b/s. Today, improved data communications equipment and higher quality telephone connections through the DDD network have made communications speeds of 14,400 b/s commonplace, and the most advanced data communications equipment operates at even higher speeds.

### 3-2-2  Digital Leased Facilities

Many of the trunk circuits that connect telco switches operate over **T1 digital carrier systems.** T1 systems in North America and Japan carry information in digital format using PCM and operate at 1.544 Mb/s, often over fiber-optic cables. T1 systems carry up to 24 digitized voice channels using time-division multiplexing. In Europe, a similar carrier system called an E1 line operates at 2.048 Mb/s and can carry 32 digitized voice channels.

T1 and E1 systems can also carry digital data. For high-speed data communications, one or more of these channels or even an entire T1 or E1 system can be leased. Three channels, for example, could provide $3 \times 64$ kb/s or a 192-kb/s data channel. If only one part of the T1 system is leased, it is referred to as **fractional T1.**

In North America, four T1 carrier systems can be multiplexed along with some extra bits to perform control functions to form a **T2 carrier system,** which operates at 6.312 Mb/s. Seven T2 systems can be multiplexed along with some extra control bits to form a **T3 carrier system,** which operates at 47.736 Mb/s.

The advantages of leasing digital communications lines instead of analog circuits are much higher data speeds, fewer transmission errors, and the fact that no modem is needed. The most serious disadvantage is that the subscriber must pay the cost of having a digital circuit installed from the nearest telco central office to the subscriber's premises. If high-speed data communications is not required, it is much cheaper to put up with the disadvantages of the analog system and use a normal analog loop.

## 3-3  DIGITAL TELEPHONE SERVICES

The telephone network has largely been converted from an analog to a digital system. More than 90% of the long-distance trunks in North America are digital. Most of them operate over fiber-optic cables, and most of the old analog switches in the DDD network have been replaced by digital switching machines. Digital switches are computers that can be programmed to perform such functions as call waiting, call forwarding, speed dialing, and answering machine services. Analog information that arrives from the local loop to the central office is converted to digital PCM as it enters the switch, and it remains in digital format until it reaches the local loop at the other end of the telephone connection. At that point, it is converted back to analog form.

The advantages of multiplexing, computer control, and low-cost VLSI digital circuitry have made high-volume communications cheaper to handle in digital format than in analog, and digital technology has the additional advantages of lower noise and higher sound quality. The only part of the DDD network that remains to be digitized is the local loop. Each local loop still carries one analog communications channel to the subscriber. For years, observers of the telephone industry have been expecting the telcos to also convert the local loop to a digital circuit.

Analog local loops are a bottleneck to data communications in the present telephone system. They require the subscriber who wants to send data over a standard telephone line to use a **modem** to interface the digital computer or terminal to the analog local loop by modulating the data onto a voice-frequency analog carrier. High-speed modems may operate at 14.4 kb/s, which is much slower than the 64-k/bs capacity of a digital telephone trunk.

At the telephone company office, the analog carrier and the digital information that it carries are converted to a 56-kb/s or a 64-kb/s digital bit stream and sent through the digital central office switch and over digital trunk circuits. The 64-kb/s digital signal is converted back to analog at the receiving local office to be sent over the analog local loop. At the premises of the receiving subscriber, a modem demodulates the analog carrier to recover the original digital data.

How much simpler and more efficient it would be to leave the data in digital form throughout the telephone system. And how much faster data could be sent if the subscriber had direct access to the 64-kb/s digital telephone system instead of having to pass data through the bottleneck created by the combination of the modem and the analog local loop.

### 3-3-1  Integrated Services Digital Network (ISDN)

ISDN, or **Integrated Services Digital Network,** is a digital system that is very slowly being installed in North American, Japan, and Europe. In the few places where it is available, it brings the digital telephone network right to the subscriber's station equipment.

There are two types of ISDN service. **Basic ISDN** is designed for residential subscribers and operates over existing local loop wiring. **Primary ISDN** is intended for business subscribers and requires a wide-band communication medium such as a fiber-optic cable to connect the subscriber's PBX to the local office switch.

#### Basic ISDN

Proponents of ISDN believe that Basic ISDN will someday be provided to all residential subscribers. Basic ISDN is also referred to as **Basic Rate Interface (BRI)** and as **2B+D** because of its channel configuration. BISN uses a 144-kb/s digital signal transmitted over the local loop to connect the subscriber to the central office.

The 144-kb/s bit stream is time-division multiplexed into three channels. Two of the channels, called **bearer** or **B channels,** each operate at 64 kb/s. The B channels carry such information as digitized voice, facsimile, and computer data. The third channel, called the **data** or **D channel,** operates at 16 kb/s and carries control information and low-speed data. The D channel is low-speed only by comparison with the B channels. The 16-kb/s D channel alone can carry as much data as an analog telephone circuit. Each B channel can carry several times as much data as can be sent over an analog dial-up telephone circuit.

It is not easy to send data at 144 kb/s over an existing local loop. A local loop consists of a single pair of wires and may be several miles long. To send digital data over this long length of wire, BRI ISDN uses a coding scheme that is called *2 binary, 1 quaternary,* or *2B1Q* for short. A **quaternary coding** scheme uses four different voltage levels to represent information. As Figure 3-9 illustrates, each voltage level represents a group of two bits. The first bit is called a *sign bit.* The sign bit determines whether the voltage is positive or negative. A sign bit of 1 causes a positive voltage to be placed on the local loop, and a sign bit of 0 causes a negative voltage to be placed on the loop.

The second bit is called a *magnitude bit.* The magnitude bit determines whether the voltage is 1 V or 3 V. A magnitude bit of 1 causes the voltage to be 1 V, and a

**FIGURE 3-9**
Truth table for 2B1Q modulation.

| First bit (sign) | Second bit (magnitude) | Quaternary symbol |
|:---:|:---:|:---:|
| 1 | 0 | +3 V |
| 1 | 1 | +1 V |
| 0 | 1 | −1 V |
| 0 | 0 | −3 V |

**FIGURE 3-10**
An example of 2B1Q coding.

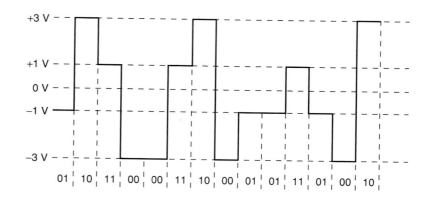

magnitude bit of 0 causes a voltage of 3 V. Figure 3-10 shows how a 2B1Q signal would look on an oscilloscope.

ISDN is a direct-dial service. If ISDN becomes universally available to residential subscribers, it will allow a person working at a personal computer at home to dial the office to confer with an associate. If desired, both B channels can be used for communication, one for high-speed data transfer between the computers and the other for pulse code modulated voice. With the proper software, the person at each end of the telephone connection will see the same image on a computer screen. When one of them makes a change to the image, that change will be communicated over the ISDN telephone link and also appear on the other computer screen. The two employees can communicate by voice over the second B channel to discuss the changes they make to the screen as they work together.

However, it is not necessary that the two B channels be used for communication to the same location. They are multiplexed over the local loop to the central office switch, but there they can be demultiplexed and routed separately. They give the subscriber two independent telephone lines, both of which use the same existing local loop wiring. Any household with a teenager will appreciate the ability to add a second telephone line without the expense of installing additional wiring.

Figure 3-11 shows how analog telephone local loops can coexist with basic ISDN during the transition phase from an analog to a digital telephone system. Today, digital central office switches are interfaced to analog local loops by a plug-in circuit board called a *line card*. An analog line card contains a codec to convert between analog voice and PCM.

When a subscriber converts to ISDN, an ISDN interface will be installed at the subscriber's premises to multiplex the two 64-kb/s B channels and the 16-kb/s D control channel from the station equipment into a 144-kb/s bit steam. This ISDN interface is called a **network terminator** or an **NT.** At the central office, the analog line card will be removed from the switch, and an ISDN line card will be installed. This ISDN line card is called a **line termination** or an **LT.** The LT will demultiplex the ISDN 144-kb/s bit stream into the two B channels and the D channel and feed them to the switching circuitry.

**FIGURE 3-11**
During the transition period from analog to ISDN, both analog and digital telephones will be serviced by the same central office switch.

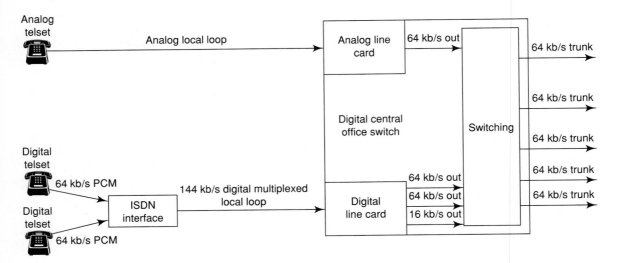

### Primary ISDN

Primary ISDN, also known as primary rate interface **(PRI),** operates at 1.544 Mb/s in North America and Japan and at 2.048 Mb/s in Europe to match the speed of a T1 or E1 line. Primary ISDN provides an interface between the PABX of a business subscriber and a telco central office switch.

The subscriber's PABX demultiplexes the 1.544-Mb/s data stream into 23 B channels and one D channel (31 B channels and one D channel in Europe). This effectively gives the large business subscriber 24 local loops to the central office switch, 23 of which can be used for either digitized voice or high-speed data. As with basic ISDN, the channels can be demultiplexed again at the central office switch and routed over the DDD telephone network. B channels can be combined into a single higher speed channel. For example, four B channels can be combined to form a single 256-k/bs channel. Small businesses that do not require the equivalent of 24 present-day local loops can use one or more basic ISDN circuits.

### 3-3-2 Fiber Optics

The tremendous increase in electronic communications in recent decades and the switch from analog to digital trunk circuits have created a demand for communications media capable of carrying more information. Analog trunk circuits require a bandwidth of 4 kHz to carry telephone-quality voice signals. Copper wire pairs worked fine when all telephone circuits had such a narrow bandwidth, but a modern T3 system has a bandwidth of several MHz and requires a wide bandwidth medium.

Fiber-optic cables are very thin strands of glass or plastic that have the ability to carry rays of light over long distances, much as metallic waveguides carry microwave

Fiber-optic cables. Courtesy of Sieman's Corporation.

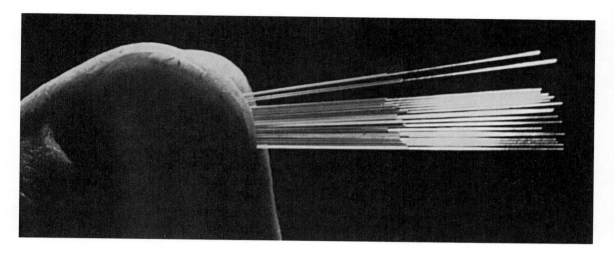

radio signals. The light beam can be modulated by turning it on and off in time to a digital signal. A high-quality glass fiber has a bandwidth of several GHz.

Plastic fiber is cheaper and easier to work with than glass, but it is usually used only for short-distance communications within a room or a building, because it has a higher attenuation. Glass fiber is more suitable for the longer distances involved in telephone communications. Glass fibers are so thin that hundreds of them can be made into a single cable.

Figure 3-12 shows how an optical fiber guides light. The fiber is constructed of two layers of glass. The central layer is called the **core,** and it is surrounded by another layer called the **cladding.** The boundary between the core and the cladding is not visible to the eye, because both the core and cladding are made of transparent glass. However, the cladding has a slightly lower **index of refraction,** which means that light travels through the cladding faster than it does through the core. When light reaches the boundary between the core and the cladding, the change in velocity causes it to **refract** or bend back toward the core, just as light rays bend when they pass from air into water. The core and cladding acting together thus act as an *optical waveguide,* guiding the light beam from its source to its destination.

**FIGURE 3-12**
Optical fibers guide light waves, much as a radio waveguide guides microwave signals.

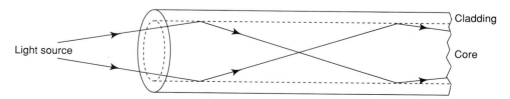

For fiber-optic communications, either a light-emitting diode (LED) or a laser diode is used as the light source. LEDs are cheaper, but laser diodes emit a purer form of light that is better suited to long-distance propagation through a fiber. The light source is switched on and off by the digital pulse train. At the receiving end, a light detector senses the pulses of light from the optical fiber and converts them back into electrical signals.

Light waves are capable of carrying very high data rates. To date, only a fraction of fiber optic's data-carrying ability has been exploited. To mention a few of the fiber-optic systems that are in use in the United States and Canada, a T1 carrier system operates at 1.544 Mb/s. A T3 system carries 672 64-kb/s voice channels over a single optical fiber. The Spanish national telephone company, Telefónica de España, is operating a 150-mile long 2.5-Gb/s fiber-optic link from Valencia to Cuenca, Spain. The system can carry 30,720 voice channels over a single fiber. Future systems are expected to operate at much higher speeds.

## ■ SUMMARY

This chapter has discussed the telephone network, present and future. The telephone network is the most frequently used medium for communicating data over long distances, so a basic understanding of how it works is important to the data communications student. The advantage of the telephone network as a data communications network is that it reaches to almost all parts of the world to which one would want to send data. Its disadvantage is that it is still an analog system. The subscriber who wants to send data over the telephone network must use a modem to modulate the digital data onto a carrier when transmitting and demodulate it from the carrier when receiving.

However, most of the telephone network is digital. The part of the network that is still analog is the local loop, the pair of wires that connects the subscriber to the network. A digital system called the integrated services digital network or ISDN may replace the analog local loop. ISDN has already been installed at some locations in North America, Europe, and Japan. ISDN will make the telephone system digital from end to end resulting in higher digital transmission speed with greater quality.

## ■ QUESTIONS

1. What is another name for a telco customer?
2. a. What are the three major components of the DDD network?
   b. What function does each of these components perform?
3. a. What are the two types of telephone circuits?
   b. What is the difference between these two types of circuits?
4. Give at least four examples of station equipment that can be found on a subscriber's premises.
5. What are the main components of a telset?

6. a. What is the name of each of the two conductors that form the local loop?
   b. What voltage potential is found on each of these conductors?
7. Describe briefly what happens when a subscriber takes the telset off-hook.
8. a. What does the acronym DTMF stand for?
   b. What is another name for DTMF?
9. What is the name of the switch to which the subscriber's telset is connected by means of the local loop?
10. What is the name of the telephone circuits that interconnect local offices?
11. What type of switch is used to connect two local office switches when there are no free trunk circuits directly connecting them?
12. a. How many digits are there in an area code in the United States and Canada?
    b. What is special about the second digit of an area code?
13. What are the names of the different types of telephone offices in the long-distance DDD network? List them in the order in which they are arranged in the switching hierarchy from top to bottom.
14. Is impulse noise caused by older analog switches more of a problem for analog communications or for data communications? State the reason for your answer.
15. a. What are the advantages of a leased analog line over a dial-up line for data communications?
    b. What disadvantage is there?
16. a. At how many bits per second does a T1 carrier system operate?
    b. How many PCM voice channels can a T1 system carry?
17. What is the last portion of the DDD telephone network to remain largely analog?
18. a. What does the acronym ISDN stand for?
    b. For what type of subscriber is basic ISDN designed?
    c. For what type of subscriber is primary ISDN designed?
19. a. What are the three channels of basic ISDN called?
    b. At how many bits per second does each basic ISDN channel operate?
    c. For what purpose can each channel of basic ISDN be used?
20. a. What is the name of the coding system that is used to transmit basic ISDN over the local loop?
    b. Briefly describe, in your own words, how the coding system works.
21. Name at least three advantages that basic ISDN will provide over the present analog telephone system.
22. a. At how many bits per second does primary ISDN operate?
    b. Into how many channels is primary ISDN divided?
23. What big advantage do fiber-optic cables have over wire cables for long-distance telephone communications?

# Chapter 4

# NETWORK CONFIGURATIONS

## OBJECTIVES

After you have completed this chapter, you should be able to:

- Define the following terms: *point-to-point network, multipoint network, contention, address, terminal select code, polling,* and *selecting.*

- Describe the main characteristics, the advantages and the disadvantages of each of the following multipoint networks: star, bus, ring, mesh, and hierarchical.

- Discuss the function that data terminal equipment and data communications equipment perform in interfacing a data terminal to an analog communications medium.

- Describe where in the communications system the RS-232 interface resides and the voltage levels it uses to represent both a mark and a space.

## INTRODUCTION

This chapter discusses several methods of connecting terminals to form a communications network. It also introduces the block diagram of a simple point-to-point communications system and discusses the function of each of its sections. This overview of communications networks is designed to prepare you for the more detailed discussions in the remaining chapters of the book.

Communications systems may be divided into two basic types, *point-to-point systems* and *multipoint systems.* A point-to-point system permits communication between two terminals. Multipoint systems permit three or more terminals to communicate over a single network without interfering with each other. Many types of multipoint communications systems exist, and some of the most important of them are discussed in this chapter.

All communications systems must follow a *protocol.* A **protocol** is the system of rules that controls the operation of a communication system. The protocol's rules govern such factors as the communications speed, which terminal has permission to send data, and what to do when communications errors occur. The more complicated the communications system is, the more complicated its protocol must be to make sure that the system operates efficiently. This chapter mentions several of the tasks that a protocol must perform. Several specific protocols are discussed in detail in Chapter 11.

## 4-1 POINT-TO-POINT NETWORKS

A **point-to-point link,** illustrated in Figure 4-1, is the simplest type of communications network. It consists of two terminals and the medium that connects them. A point-to-point network can be used for communication between two devices in the same room, for example, a computer sending data to a printer, or it can be used for communication between devices in two different parts of the world, such as the communications link between a computer in the headquarters of a multinational corporation and a computer in a branch office on another continent. A point-to-point link can be simplex, half-duplex, or full-duplex. (These terms were defined in Chapter 1. To review the definitions of these terms, consult the glossary at the back of the book.)

### 4-1-1 Simplex Point-to-Point Networks

In a simplex point-to-point network, one of the terminals is the transmitter, and the other is the receiver. Data travel through the network in one direction only, from the transmitter to the receiver. Because one terminal always has permission to transmit and the other is always prepared to receive data, a simplex point-to-point network usually needs only a simple protocol to managing the flow of data.

**FIGURE 4-1**
A point-to-point network.

Terminal A ———— Communications link ———— Terminal B

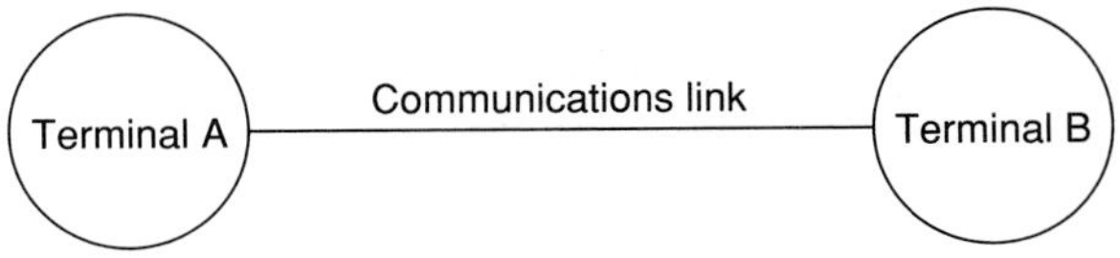

### 4-1-2 Half-Duplex Point-to-Point Networks

Half-duplex transmission requires a more complex protocol, because transmission can occur in either direction, even though only one terminal can transmit at any given time. The network protocol of a half-duplex communications system must ensure that when one terminal is in the transmit mode, the other is in the receive mode, or data will be lost. If both terminals attempt to transmit at the same time, the result is a **contention** situation. The terminals *contend* with each other for the use of the communications channel.

One method to avoid contention on a half-duplex point-to-point communication system is to use a protocol in which one of the terminals supervises the operation of the other. The controlling terminal is called the **master** or **primary,** and the other terminal is called the **slave** or **secondary.** The system is called a **master-slave system.**

The primary in a master-slave communication system normally operates in the transmit mode. The secondary normally operates in the receive mode. The secondary may switch to the transmit mode only when the primary commands it to do so. The primary may transmit at any time as long as it has not relinquished this privilege to the secondary.

As part of the protocol of some master-slave systems the primary periodically *polls* the secondary by sending it a brief message commanding the secondary to transmit. The primary then switches itself to the receive mode and awaits the secondary's reply. The secondary responds to the poll by transmitting any data it has to send. If it has no data, it sends a brief message to acknowledge that it has received the poll and that it has nothing further to transmit. After sending its message, the secondary switches itself back to the receive mode, and it does not transmit again until it receives another poll from the primary.

### 4-1-3 Full-Duplex Point-to-Point Networks

There are no contention problems in a full-duplex point-to-point system because both terminals are free to transmit and receive at the same time. The protocol can be relatively simple, but a protocol is still necessary to determine such factors as communications speed and to determine what to do if there are communications errors.

## 4-2 MULTIPOINT NETWORKS

A **multipoint network** connects three or more terminals to each other so that they form a single communications system. The more terminals the network contains, the more care must be taken to keep them from interfering with each other. The terminals must be connected in a systematic manner that ensures that data can be communicated rapidly, efficiently, and with a minimum of errors. The physical layout of a network is called its **topology.** The most popular multipoint network topologies are discussed in this section.

### 4-2-1   The Star Network

The **star network,** illustrated in Figure 4-2, is a multipoint topology that has a single central terminal and a number of remotes. The central terminal is called a **hub.** Each remote is connected to the hub by means of its own point-to-point link. One of the key advantages that the star network has compared with the other multipoint topologies discussed in this chapter is that each remote can be in constant communication with the hub, and all remotes can communicate with the hub at the same time.

However, the star also has several disadvantages when compared with the other multipoint networks. It can be expensive to install an individual point-to-point communications link to each remote. The star topology is worth the cost if each remote has enough traffic to keep its point-to-point link to the hub busy a high percentage of the time. If the remotes communicate infrequently, it is usually cheaper to use a topology that allows all of the remotes to share a single communications link.

**FIGURE 4-2**
A star network.

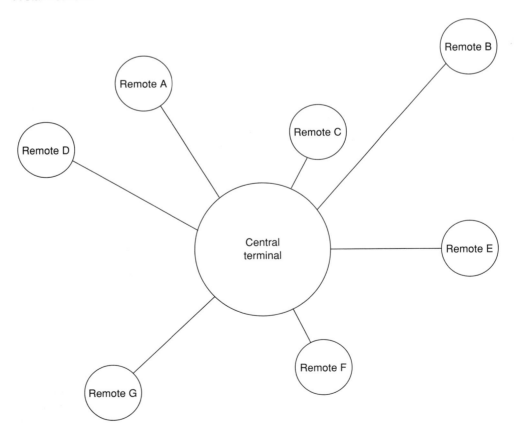

The fact that all communication passes through the hub is the star topology's main disadvantage. If the hub goes out of service, the entire network is shut down. Fortunately, modern electronics is very reliable, and hub failures are infrequent.

## 4-2-2  The Bus Network

Figure 4-3 illustrates the bus network topology. A **bus network** uses a single communications channel to connect all terminals. The bus network is sometimes called a **multidrop network,** and the short communications link that connects each remote terminal to the bus is called a **drop.**

The advantage of the bus network compared with the star topology is that the bus uses a single communications link. This simplifies the network's wiring and can reduce the cost of installing the network. A disadvantage of the bus network is that only one terminal can transmit at a time.

A bus network's protocol must include some form of network control to ensure that only one terminal transmits at any time. If the bus network has a master terminal like the one pictured in Figure 4-3, no remote may transmit unless it is first polled by the master. Some bus networks have no master terminal, and each terminal has an equal right to access the bus. In this case, before a terminal transmits, it must monitor the bus to make sure that it is free. If two terminals do begin to transmit at the same time, one of them must be programmed to relinquish the bus until the other has sent its data.

The electronics of modern communications terminals is very reliable, but the activity in a busy office building can cause a communications link failure. An electrician may accidentally cut a cable, or someone may unplug a connection to move a terminal and forget to reconnect it. If there is a disruption in a communications link in a star network, only the remote connected to that specific link is affected. The rest of the network continues to operate normally.

If there is a break in the communications link that forms the bus between terminals A and B in Figure 4-3, terminals B and C cannot communicate with the master, and they are both out of service. If the bus network does not have a master, terminals B and C can continue to communicate with each other, but they cannot communicate with terminal A. As more terminals are added to a bus network, and as the bus becomes longer, there is a greater chance of a communications link failure.

**FIGURE 4-3**
A bus network.

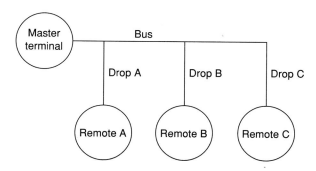

Because of the simpler wiring involved, the bus topology was once preferred over the star network, especially if each individual terminal used the network only a small percentage of the time. It was especially popular in *local area networks (LANs)* for communications among computers located in the same building. In new installations with many terminals, the star network is preferred today, because it is more reliable.

### Selecting the Remotes

As part of the protocol of a bus network, each remote terminal connected to the bus has an address. When a remote is not receiving traffic, it monitors the network, listening for its address. For example, if the master terminal in Figure 4-3 has a message to send to remote terminal B, it first transmits terminal B's address followed by the message. All of the remote terminals receive the address, but only terminal B responds to the address by receiving the message that follows it. When a terminal receives its address, we say that it is *selected.* The process of choosing a terminal on a network to receive data is called **selection.** Only terminals that have been selected can receive messages.

A terminal can transmit the same message to more than one remote at the same time if it first sends either a *group address* or a *broadcast address.* A **group address** is an address assigned to more than one remote. For example, in Figure 4-3, in addition to having their individual addresses, remotes B and C may have a common group address. If the master sends this group address before a message, both terminals B and C are selected and receive the message. Terminal A ignores the message, but it continues to monitor the network looking for its address.

A **broadcast address** is an address that is assigned to all terminals on the network. When the master transmits the broadcast address, all remotes are selected, and all copy the message that follows.

In summary, it is possible for one terminal to have all three types of addresses. It can have its individual address which is unique to it. It can have one or more group addresses that it shares with other terminals on the network, and it can have a broadcast address, which it shares with all of the other terminals on the network.

### Polling the Remotes

**Polling** is the process of asking each remote terminal, one at a time, if it has data to send. Polling is used only in networks that are under the control of a master terminal. The master polls each remote one at a time by sending a special code called a **transmitter start code (TSC)** over the network. A TSC is similar an address, but there is an important difference in the way a terminal responds to the two. *An address selects the terminal to receive a message. A TSC commands a terminal to transmit.* A terminal may have more than one address, but a terminal can have only one TSC. Each TSC is unique. That is, each TSC is associated with one and only one terminal.

When a terminal receives its TSC, it responds by transmitting. For example, assume that the master terminal in Figure 4-3 sends the TSC of remote A. If remote A has data to send, it responds by sending that data. Otherwise, it transmits a short message to say it has no data. When terminal A finishes its transmission, it switches itself back to the receive mode.

After terminal A has been polled and has responded to its TSC, the master polls terminal B by sending its TSC. After terminal B responds, the master sends the TSC of terminal C. When terminal C responds, the polling process begins by sending the TSC of terminal A. The terminals are always polled one at a time. There are no group or broadcast TSCs, because contention would result if more than one terminal recognized a TSC and began transmitting.

### 4-2-3  The Ring Network

Figure 4-4 illustrates a **ring network,** which gets its name from the fact that the terminals are connected together in a loop or ring. Data are relayed around the ring from terminal to terminal in one direction. To illustrate the procedure, assume that terminal C has data for terminals B, A, and F. Terminal C transmits all of the data to terminal B. Terminal B, in turn, removes data addressed to it, adds any data that it has to send to other terminals on the network, and transmits all of the data to terminal A. Terminal A receives the data from terminal B, extracts any data destined for it, adds data that it has to send to other terminals on the network, and transmits to terminal F. The data continue to cycle around the ring from terminal to terminal in this manner as long as the network is in operation, with each terminal removing data addressed to it and adding data it is sending to other terminals.

The main disadvantage of a simple ring network is that if a single communications link is lost, data can no longer circulate, and the whole network is out of ser-

**FIGURE 4-4**
A ring network.

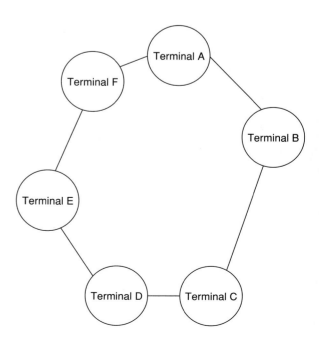

vice. More sophisticated ring networks can send data in either direction, which allows the ring to be **self-healing** if one communications link is lost. If Figure 4-4 were a self-healing network, a broken communications link between terminals B and C would not stop the network's operation. Terminal C would still be able to communicate with terminal B, or any other terminal, by sending information counterclockwise around the ring.

If two communications links are lost, a self-healing ring network may be split in two. For example, suppose the communications links between both terminals D and E and between terminals A and B are broken. Terminals E, F, and A would be able to communicate with each other, and terminals B, C, and D would be able to communicate. While this situation is not ideal, the terminals will be able to carry on at least limited communications until one or both of the links are repaired.

### 4-2-4　The Mesh Network

The **mesh network,** as shown in Figure 4-5, has numerous connections between the terminals. This topology provides alternate transmission paths in case of a communications link failure. For example, if terminal H has data to send to terminal A, there are several possible routes over which to send it. The shortest route is over the communications link that directly connects the two terminals. If for some reason the direct link is out of service, the data can be sent to terminal C, D, E, or G for relay to terminal A. If all of these links are busy, the data can be sent to terminal F, relayed to terminal G, and finally to terminal A. There are also many other possible paths available.

The main advantage of the mesh network topology is its ability to handle large volumes of data among many terminals. In addition, communications link problems seldom put the network out of service because there are many possible data routes between any two terminals. A disadvantage of the mesh topology is the high cost of installing and maintaining the large number of communications links. The task of managing such a complex network usually requires a sophisticated computer-controlled network management system.

### 4-2-5　The Hierarchical (Tree) Network

Figure 4-6 illustrates a **hierarchical network,** which is sometimes called a **tree** because it branches out from a central point. In a hierarchical network, each terminal reports to one terminal higher up the tree. If terminal L has data to send to terminal N, it must send the data up the hierarchy through terminals F and B to terminal A. Terminal A then sends the data down another branch through terminals D and J to terminal N.

The hierarchical topology is best suited to networks in which most communication occurs between the central terminal, which is typically a powerful computer, and the terminals at the ends of the branches. This topology is inefficient if most communication occurs among the remote terminals.

**FIGURE 4-5**
A mesh network.

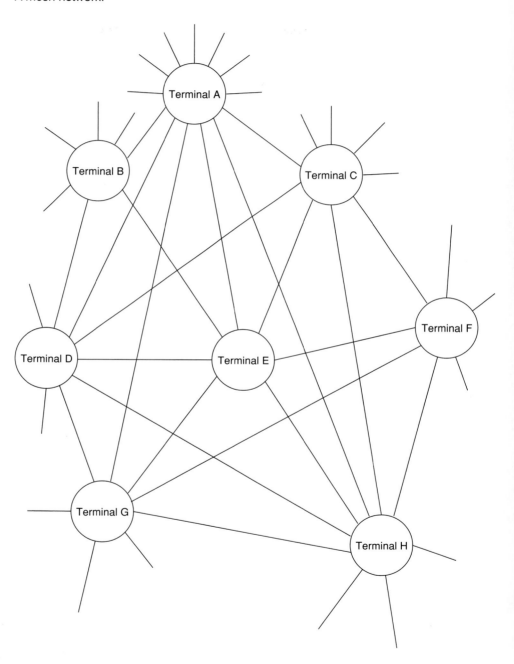

**FIGURE 4-6**
A hierarchical or tree network.

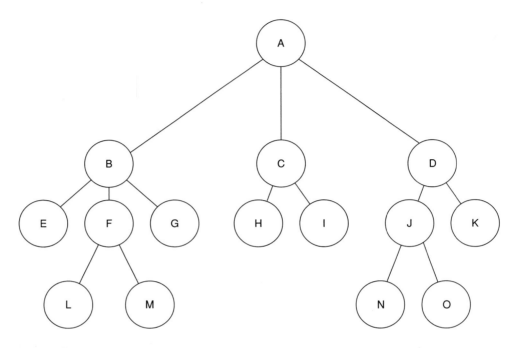

### 4-2-6    Combinations of Network Types

Many networks use a variety of the techniques presented in this chapter to route communications from one terminal to another. Figure 4-7, for example, shows a **combinational network** composed of a ring network that connects two bus networks and a star network. Such a combinational network is often the result of a decision to link existing independent networks. The first step in the evolution of the combinational network in Figure 4-7 may have been a decision by individual departments in a large company to link their personal computers. For instance, the engineering department and the marketing department may have installed separate bus networks to allow the computers within each department to communicate with each other. The accounting department may have installed a star network to meet its data communications needs. Later, the company's management may have installed a high-speed ring network to link these individual communications networks to allow employees in different departments to share data. A network that links smaller networks is called a **backbone network.** The devices that link the backbone network to each of the smaller networks are called **bridges.**

## 4-3    A POINT-TO-POINT COMMUNICATIONS SYSTEM

Figure 4-8 is the block diagram of a typical point-to-point long-distance serial communications system. Many data communications systems either fit this block dia-

**FIGURE 4-7**
A combinational network.

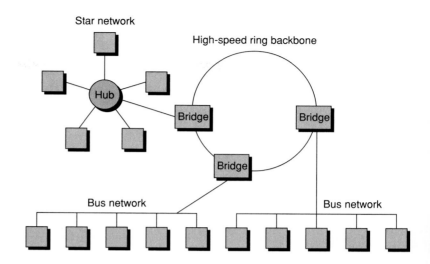

gram or are derived from it, so every data communications technician and engineer needs to be familiar with it. Learning the block diagram well now will give you some of the background you need to understand the more detailed discussions of each of the diagram's component parts in later chapters of this book.

Each end of the communications system in Figure 4-8 consists of identical equipment: a **terminal,** where the data originates, **data terminal equipment (DTE),** which converts between the parallel data format used by the terminal and the serial data format used by the communications system, and **data communications equipment (DTE),** which converts the digital data to a form that can be sent over an analog communications medium, in this case, a telephone line.

### 4-3-1 The Terminal

There are many types of terminals that fit the block diagram, such as an automatic teller machine that communicates with the central computer of a bank or a facsimile (fax) machine that transmits pictures or graphics to another fax machine at the other end of the communications link.

In our example we will assume that the terminals are personal computers and that the information to be sent already exists as parallel digital data within the computers' memory. We will also assume that the communications link is an analog telephone line, although the block diagram also holds true for other types of analog media.

To transmit, a computer outputs data in parallel format to the DTE. To receive, the computer inputs data in parallel format from the DTE. A computer may be able to input or output millions of bytes of data per second, (a byte is 8 bits of digital information), whereas a communications system that uses a telephone line as its communications medium can typically handle only a few hundred to a few thousand bytes per second. Because the computer is so much faster than the communications

**FIGURE 4-8**
Block diagram of a serial point-to-point data communications system that uses a telephone line as a communications medium.

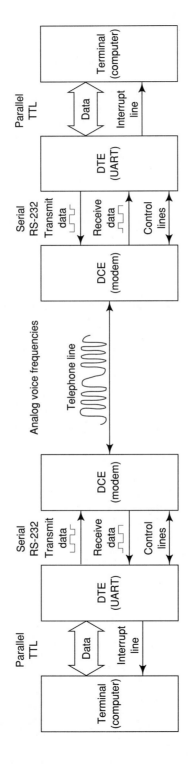

system, the computer spends only a small fraction of its time exchanging data with the DTE.

As an example, assume that the computer is sending data. It begins the transmission by outputting one or more bytes of parallel data to the DTE. Because the DTE transfers data very slowly compared to the speed of a computer, the computer has time to turn its attention to another task. In our example, let us assume that the computer is running a word processing program while the DTE is transmitting. When the DTE is ready for more data, it signals the computer by outputting a control signal called an **interrupt.** The DTE sends the interrupt to the computer over a control lead called the **interrupt line,** which is pictured in Figure 4-8.

When the computer receives the interrupt, it temporarily suspends or *interrupts* the word processor program and outputs more data to the DTE. Then the computer returns to the word processing program and ignores the DTE until it receives another interrupt. Each interrupt is taken care of so quickly (typically in much less than a millisecond) that the computer user may not notice any slowing of the word processing program. Transmission proceeds in this manner, with the DTE interrupting the computer every time it is ready for another byte of data, until the entire message has been transmitted.

The DTE interrupts the computer every time it receives data. The computer responds to each interrupt by leaving any program it may be running, inputting the data from the DTE, and storing them to memory. Then the computer returns to the program until it receives another interrupt, which informs the computer that the DTE has received another byte of data.

## 4-3-2 The Data Terminal Equipment (DTE)

The DTE is often a single integrated circuit which may be known by such names as **universal asynchronous receiver/transmitter (UART), universal synchronous receiver/transmitter (USRT),** or **asynchronous communications interface adapter (ACIA).** As mentioned earlier, the task of the DTE is to serve as the interface between the terminal and the communications network. This task can be divided into a number of functions.

While transmitting, the DTE:

1. Converts data from parallel to serial form.
2. Adds extra bits (parity bits) to the data to aid in checking for communications errors.
3. Clocks out serial data at the correct speed to the DCE.
4. Notifies the terminal each time a character has been sent, so the terminal can make more data available.

While receiving, the DTE:

1. Clocks in serial data at the correct speed from the DCE.
2. Converts received data from serial to parallel form.

3. Looks for certain types of errors in the received data and notifies the terminal if it finds any.

4. Notifies the terminal each time data has been received, so that the terminal can input them.

### 4-3-3   The Data Communication Equipment (DCE)

The main purpose of the DCE is to interface between the digital DTE and the analog communications medium, such as the local loop of a telephone circuit. In casual conversation, communications engineers and technicians sometimes say that the DCE converts the data from digital to analog or from analog to digital, but that is not quite accurate. The DCE is *not* an analog-to-digital or digital-to-analog converter, and it does *not* convert data from digital to analog. The DCE is a modulator/demodulator or **modem** for short. The modem modulates digital data onto an analog carrier during transmission, and it demodulates the analog carrier to recover the digital intelligence signal during reception.

The three main types of modulation that modems use are amplitude modulation (AM), frequency modulation (FM), and phase modulation (PM). When applied to modems, frequency modulation is called **frequency-shift keying (FSK),** and phase modulation is called **phase-shift keying (PSK).** AM is combined with PSK in a type of modulation called **quadrature amplitude modulation (QAM).** The PSK and QAM modulation schemes that modems use are complicated, so we will postpone their explanation until Chapter 9. In the following brief introduction to DCEs, we will use an FSK modem as our example.

#### The Modulator Section

Figure 4-9(a) is a functional block diagram that illustrates the modulator section of an FSK modem. Any FM modulator is a type of voltage-to-frequency converter. The modulator in the figure is a voltage-controlled oscillator (VCO). The output frequency of the VCO is directly proportional to its input voltage. If the input voltage of the VCO doubles, it causes the frequency of the sine wave at the VCO's output to double as well. The center frequency of the VCO is set by the +12 VDC power supply and the voltage divider network connected to the VCO's input. The voltage divider formed by the two 10 kΩ resistors sets the DC voltage on the VCO's input pin to half of the supply voltage or 6 VDC.

The serial digital data are applied to the VCO's input through a large-value DC-blocking capacitor. The voltage of the digital input signal is superimposed upon the 6 VDC on the VCO's input pin and causes the instantaneous voltage on the VCO's input pin to vary above and below 6 V in time with the input. The VCO output frequency varies in step with the input voltage. Figure 4-9(b) shows the relationship between the VCO's input voltage and its output frequency.

Figure 4-9 illustrates the principle of FSK modulation, but you are not likely to find a separate VCO circuit in a modern modem. Today's modems combine many functions onto each integrated circuit. The actual modulation may be performed by a

**FIGURE 4-9**
(a) A simplified block diagram of the modulator section of a modem. (b) The input and output signals of the VCO compared.

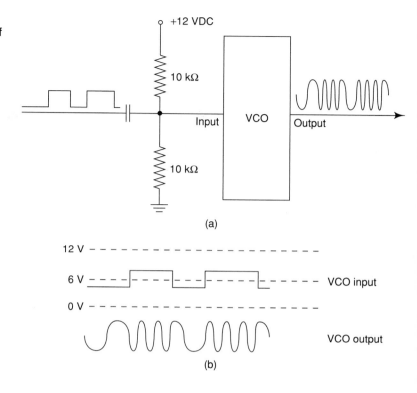

*digital signal processor (DSP)* embedded within an integrated circuit. Nevertheless, such a DSP modulator performs the same function as the circuit shown in Figure 4-9.

### The Demodulator Section

The demodulator section of an FSK modem can be a phase-locked loop (PLL) connected as shown in Figure 4-10. A PLL connected in such a manner acts as a frequency-to-voltage converter. A PLL has three major sections: a phase detector, a low-pass filter, and a VCO.

The phase detector has two inputs, one of which is called a *reference input.* A feedback signal, which comes from the output of the VCO, is fed into the phased detector's second input. A properly operating PLL attempts to maintain the same frequency on both of its inputs.

In Figure 4-10, the FSK signal to be demodulated is fed into the phase detector's reference input. The PLL has no control over this signal, but it can control the frequency of the feedback signal by controlling the VCO. The phase detector and the low-pass filter together generate an error voltage. The error voltage, in turn, controls the VCO frequency. When the phase detector's two input signals are the same frequency, the error voltage remains at a steady DC level. When the FSK signal changes frequency, it no longer matches the feedback frequency. The phase detector varies the error voltage, which in turn varies the VCO frequency.

**FIGURE 4-10**
A PLL used as an FSK demodulator.

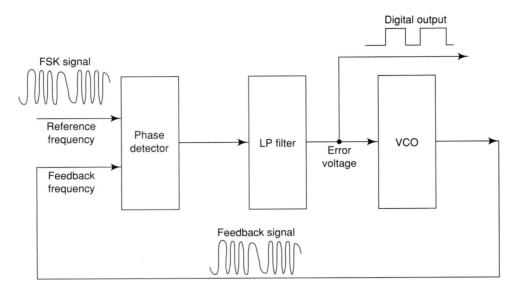

When the VCO frequency again matches the reference frequency, the phase detector holds the error voltage at its new DC value, and the PLL stabilizes at its new operating frequency. Every change in the frequency of the received FSK signal causes a proportional change in the PLL's error voltage. The error voltage is the demodulated digital intelligence signal. It is a copy of the original intelligence signal that was fed into the modulation section of the sending modem at the other end of the communications link.

In Figure 4-11 the PLL FSK demodulator circuit has been redrawn to show step by step the changes that take place when the frequency of the received FSK signal changes. The numbers that follow refer to the numbers in the figure.

1. The received signal from the telephone line increases in frequency. For an instant, the two inputs to the phase detector are of different frequencies, a condition that the PLL attempts to correct.

2. Because the feedback signal is lower in frequency than the phase detector's reference frequency input, the phase detector and low-pass filter acting together increase the error voltage.

3. The increase in the error voltage increases the frequency of the VCO. When the feedback frequency again equals the FSK input frequency, the error voltage and VCO output frequency stabilize at their new value.

If the input frequency decreases, the phase detector and the low-pass filter working together decrease the error voltage, which in turn decreases the VCO frequency

**FIGURE 4-11**
A change in the reference frequency (1) causes a change in the error voltage (2), which changes the VCO frequency (3).

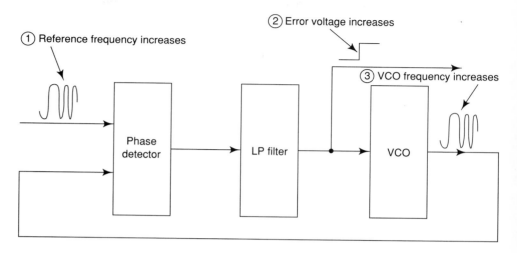

until it equals the reference frequency. The error voltage thus rises and falls in step with the shifts in the received FSK signal.

Just as was the case with the modulator, modern modems are unlikely to have a separate PLL demodulator such as the one pictured in Figures 4-10 and 4-11. Demodulation may be performed by the same DSP circuit that modulates the transmitted signal. However, whatever type of circuit is used as an FSK demodulator, that circuit performs the same function as the circuit in the figures.

## 4-3-4 The RS-232 Interface

The DTE and the DCE are often connected by an RS-232 standard serial interface. Although the RS-232 serial interface is discussed in detail in Chapter 6, the following brief introduction to the standard now will contribute to your overview of communications networks.

The Electronics Industries Association (EIA) published the specifications for the RS-232 in the 1960s. The standard describes **RS-232** as a standard interface between a DTE and a DCE, although it is also used to connect many other types of devices. The letters *RS* are an abbreviation for the words *recommended standard*. The number *232* is the number of the standard. The standard has been revised several times, and a letter following the standard indicates the revision. For example, RS-232C is the C revision. Often the revision letter is dropped, and the standard is referred to simply as RS-232.

Figure 4-8 does not show all of the conductors that make up the RS-232 interface. As you will see in Chapter 6, the complete interface has 25 conductors, most of which are control signals. In most installations, not all of the control signals are required. Most RS-232 serial ports on personal computers, for example, use only 9 of the 25 conductors described in the standard.

The RS-232 interface uses *negative logic*. It uses a negative voltage to represent a logic 1 and a positive voltage to represent a logic 0. An RS-232 device outputs a logic 1 as any voltage between –5 V and –15 V and a logic 0 as any voltage between +5 V and +15 V. The specific voltages used are determined by the equipment manufacturer, as long as they fall within the specified range. It is common to use +12 V for a logic 0 and –12 V for a logic 1, because these are common power supply voltages. Desktop computers may output +5 V as a logic 0 and –12 V as a logic 1. Most desktop personal computers use a +5 V supply to power the computer's digital logic chips, and using that power supply as one of the RS-232 voltage sources saves the expense of adding a separate +12 V supply.

To allow for equipment aging, noise, and so on, the RS-232 standard requires devices that accept information from an RS-232 line to recognize a wider range of voltages. An RS-232 device recognizes any input voltage between +3 V and +25 V as a logic 0 and any input voltage between –3 V and –25 V as a logic 1. Voltages between –3 V and +3 V are undefined. They should not exist on an RS-232 line, and if they do, it is a sign of a malfunction.

Those of us who are used to working with TTL logic have become sloppy in our habits. We refer to a logic 1 as a "high" and to a 0 as a "low." In negative logic systems, such as RS-232, a 1 is a lower voltage than is a 0. In other words, a 1 is a "low" and a 0 is a "high." Communications engineers and technicians avoid confusion by using the terms *mark* and *space* to refer to the logic level of a data signal. A **mark** is a logic 1, and a **space** is a logic 0.

Most DTEs in use today are single-chip devices that use TTL logic levels. A voltage level converter is required to connect them to an RS-232 interface. Level converters are available in integrated circuit packages. Figure 4-12 shows schematically the function that a level converter performs. The converter in the figure is supplied with both +12 V and –12 V DC supplies. In the TTL input, a space is represented by 0 V and a mark is represented by +5 V. At the output, the space has been converted to +12 V and the mark to –12 V.

**FIGURE 4-12**
Integrated circuits are available on the market to interface between TTL and RS-232 logic levels.

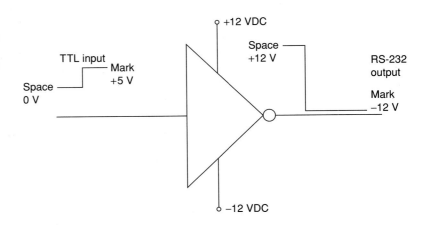

## ■ SUMMARY

This chapter has covered network topologies. The simplest topology is a point-to-point network that connects two terminals. Point-to-point networks can be simplex (communication in one direction only), half-duplex (communication in either direction, but only one direction at a time), or full-duplex (communication in both directions simultaneously).

Networks that consist of three or more terminals are called multipoint networks. Some of the more common types of multipoint networks are the star, the bus, the ring, the mesh, and the hierarchical. A star network has communications links radiating from a central terminal to its remotes so that each remote has its own dedicated point-to-point link that connects it to the master. In a bus network, which is sometimes called a multidrop network, all terminals share a common communications link. In a ring network, as its name implies, all terminals are connected in the form of a circle or ring.

The mesh network uses a large number of communications paths to connect terminals and usually offers a number of paths for communications between any two terminals. The hierarchical network, also called the tree network, is organized in the form of a pyramid with a single master terminal at the top and increasing numbers of terminals at each lower level.

Networks need a system of rules to prevent two or more terminals from trying to transmit at the same time over the same communications channel and to be sure that the proper terminal receives messages. Such a system of rules is called a protocol. When a master transmits a message over a communications link to which several remotes are connected, it selects one or more of the remotes to receive the message. It selects the terminal by broadcasting the terminal's address. A group address selects two or more terminals on the network, and a broadcast address selects all of the terminals on a network.

The master polls the remotes on a network one at a time to allow them to transmit messages. A remote is polled when the master transmits its transmitter start code (TSC). A remote responds to its TSC by transmitting any messages that it has been holding for the network or by transmitting a short message indicating that it has nothing further to send.

A typical terminal location on a network consists of the terminal itself and the data terminal equipment (DTE), which converts data between the serial format used on the network and the parallel format used by the terminal. If the communications network operates over an analog communications link, the terminal location also has data communications equipment (DCE). The DCE is a modem that modulates outgoing serial data onto an analog carrier and demodulates a received carrier to recover data. The DCE and DTE are connected by an RS-232C interface.

The topics presented in this chapter are explored in more detail in the remaining chapters of the book. The RS-232 interface is explained in detail in Chapter 6. DTEs are explained in Chapter 8, and DCEs are covered in Chapters 9 and 10. Several protocols are covered in Chapter 11. The multipoint network topologies are referred to in several chapters, but the overview in this chapter will be especially helpful when you study local area networks in Chapter 12.

## ■ QUESTIONS

1. What is a protocol?

2. Which of the following types of communications channeling presents the fewest problems with regard to managing the flow of data: simplex, half-duplex, or full-duplex?

3. a. What is the name for the situation that occurs in a half-duplex point-to-point system if both terminals attempt to transmit at the same time?

   b. How can this situation be avoided?

4. a. What does a primary station do when it polls a secondary?

   b. How does the secondary respond to the poll if it has data to transmit?

   c. How does the secondary respond to the poll if it does not have data to transmit?

5. Can contention situations occur on a full-duplex point-to-point network? Give a reason for your answer.

6. What is the minimum number of terminals that a multipoint network can contain?

7. Name the multipoint networks that are discussed in this chapter.

8. a. How is the central terminal connected to the remotes in a star network?

   b. What is the advantage of the star network over other multipoint network topologies?

   c. What are some disadvantages of the star topology?

9. How did the bus network topology get its name? What is another name for this topology?

10. a. What advantage does the bus topology have over a star network?

    b. What are some of the bus's disadvantages compared with the star?

11. a. What is the difference between *selecting* a remote and *polling* a remote?

    b. Which one uses an address, and which one uses a TSC?

12. What is a self-healing ring network, and in which way is it better than a simple ring network?

13. a. How does the speed of a ring network compare with the speed of a star network?

    b. How does it compare with the speed of a bus network?

14. a. What are two advantages of the mesh network over other multipoint topologies?

    b. What disadvantage does the mesh network have?

15. Describe the structure of a hierarchical network.

16. What are the main components of the point-to-point communications system shown in Figure 4-8?

17. In which of the blocks of Figure 4-8 does the data originate?

18. What is the purpose of the interrupt line that connects the DTE to the terminal in Figure 4-8?

19. What are some other names by which the DTE may be known?

20. a. What four tasks does the DTE perform during transmission?

    b. What four tasks does it perform while receiving data?

21. a. What is the main purpose of the DCE?

    b. By what other name is the DCE known?

22. What technique does the DCE use to interface between the digital DTE and an analog communications medium such as a telephone line?

23. a. What type of circuit can be used as the modulator in an FSK modem?

    b. What type of circuit can be used as the demodulator?

24. Which organization published the RS-232C interface standard, and for what purpose is the standard intended?

25. a. How many conductors does the RS-232C standard specify?

    b. Are all of these conductors used in all installations?

26. What is meant by the term *negative logic?*

27. a. What voltage level does an RS-232 device output to represent a logic 1?

    b. What voltage level does it output to represent a logic 0?

28. a. What range of voltage levels should an RS-232 device which inputs logic signals recognize as a logic 1?

    b. What range of voltages should it recognize as a logic 0?

# Chapter 5

# CODES AND ERROR CORRECTION

## OBJECTIVES

After you have completed this chapter, you should be able to:

- Define the terms *code, encoding, parity bit, parity error, forward error correction (FEC), checksum,* and *cyclic redundancy check (CRC).*

- State how many bits are used in the Baudot, standard ASCII, extended ASCII, and EBCDIC codes.

- Use the ASCII and EBCDIC tables to convert between characters and the ASCII or EBCDIC codes that represent them.

- Describe how echoplex functions and state its advantages and disadvantages.

- Discuss the use of parity, checksums, and cyclic redundancy codes as a method of error detection.

- Discuss the difference between error detection and forward error correction.

## INTRODUCTION

We have defined data as information that is in digital format before it enters the communications system. Systems of binary numbers that represent information are called codes, and the process of putting information into digital format is called encoding. If communication is to take place, the transmitter and receiver must both use the same code. A number of standard codes have been developed, and this chapter discusses some of the more common ones.

Data must not only be communicated; it must be communicated accurately. Almost any communications medium subjects the data to noise which causes communications errors. Sophisticated data communications systems have methods of detecting and correcting those errors. This chapter discusses some of the more common methods used.

## 5-1     COMMON CODES

As mentioned in the introduction, before data can be communicated, or before it can even be manipulated by a computer, it must be put into the form of a code that computers can deal with. A **code** is a method of representing information by a system of symbols. When we were children, many of us made up a "secret code" that used the numbers *1* through *26* to represent letters of the alphabet. The number *1* stood for *A*, *2* for *B*, *3* for *C*, and so on. Codes used in data communications represent numbers, letters, punctuation marks, and control signals by combinations of 1s and 0s.

### 5-1-1     Morse Code

The first code to be widely used in electronic communications was the Morse code. There are two variations of the Morse code. The original Morse code was designed for communication over telegraph wires and is used today by a few operators solely in the interest of preserving it. The international Morse code was later developed for radio communication, and it is still used today by radio amateurs, by some ocean-going vessels, for transmitting the station identification of some radio transmitters, and for aeronautical beacons. It is not used for data communications.

**Morse code** uses combinations of short and long sounds to represent information. The short sounds are called dots, and the long sounds are called dashes. A dash is three times the length of a dot. Figure 5-1 gives the Morse code representations for the letters of the English alphabet, the digits *0* through *9* and a few common punctuation marks.

### 5-1-2     Baudot

Baudot was the first code to be designed to be sent and received by machine. Its official name is the CCITT Number 2 Code. **CCITT** stands for the **Comité Consulatif International Télégraphique et Téléphonique** (Consultative Committee for Interna-

**FIGURE 5-1**

International Morse code.

| | | | | | | |
|---|---|---|---|---|---|---|
| A | •— | N | —• | 0 | ————— | |
| B | —••• | O | ——— | 1 | •———— | |
| C | —•—• | P | •——• | 2 | ••——— | |
| D | —•• | Q | ——•— | 3 | •••—— | |
| E | • | R | •—• | 4 | ••••— | |
| F | ••—• | S | ••• | 5 | ••••• | |
| G | ——• | T | — | 6 | —•••• | |
| H | •••• | U | ••— | 7 | ——••• | |
| I | •• | V | •••— | 8 | ———•• | |
| J | •——— | W | •—— | 9 | ————• | |
| K | —•— | X | —••— | Period | •—•—•— | |
| L | •—•• | Y | —•—— | Comma | ——••—— | |
| M | —— | Z | ——•• | Question mark | ••——•• | |

tional Telegraph and Telephone in English), an international organization that publishes standards for telephone and telegraph communications. The code is better known in the United States as Baudot (pronounced bah-DOUGH) after J. M. E. Baudot who proposed the original version. In Great Britain it is called the Murray code after the person who developed the present version, and it is also known as the International Telegraph Alphabet Number 2. To avoid confusion, we will refer to it as Baudot.

As Figure 5-2 illustrates, all Baudot characters consist of 5 bits. A 5-bit code can have $2^5$ ($2 \times 2 \times 2 \times 2 \times 2$), or 32, possible combinations, which is insufficient for sending text. The English alphabet has 26 letters. Add to that 10 digits, a space, punctuation marks, and commonly used symbols, and far more than 32 characters are needed. The Baudot code solves that problem by assigning two meanings to most of the characters.

The first two columns of Figure 5-2 list the Baudot characters in binary and in hexadecimal. (A dollar sign [$] in front of a number is a commonly used method to indicate that the number in hexadecimal. That method is used throughout this book.) The LTRS (letters) column lists one set of meanings that the codes can have, and the FIGS (figures) column lists a second set of meanings. The FIGS column has not been standardized throughout the world, and the FIGS characters shown in Figure 5-2 are those most commonly used in the United States. The BELL code listed in the figures column is used to ring a bell on the receiving terminal to summon the attention of the operator.

If a Baudot terminal receives the character 11001, that character could represent either the letter *B* or a question mark. When the receiving terminal is turned on, it interprets all incoming characters as letters until it receives a figures shift (FIGS) character (11011). Then it interprets all subsequent incoming characters as figures until it receives a letters shift (LTRS) character (11111).

**FIGURE 5-2**
Baudot (CCITT-2) code as usually used in the United States.

| Baudot Code | HEX | LTRS | US FIGS |
|---|---|---|---|
| 00011 | $03 | A | $-$ |
| 11001 | $19 | B | ? |
| 01110 | $0E | C | : |
| 01001 | $09 | D | $ |
| 00001 | $01 | E | 3 |
| 01101 | $0D | F | ! |
| 11010 | $1A | G | & |
| 10100 | $14 | H | # |
| 00110 | $06 | I | 8 |
| 01011 | $0B | J | ' |
| 01111 | $0F | K | ( |
| 10010 | $12 | L | ) |
| 11100 | $1C | M | . |
| 01100 | $0C | N | , |
| 11000 | $18 | O | 9 |
| 10110 | $16 | P | 0 |
| 10111 | $17 | Q | 1 |
| 01010 | $0A | R | 4 |
| 00101 | $05 | S | BELL |
| 10000 | $10 | T | 5 |
| 00111 | $07 | U | 7 |
| 11110 | $1E | V | ; |
| 10011 | $13 | W | 2 |
| 11101 | $1D | X | / |
| 10101 | $15 | Y | 6 |
| 10001 | $11 | Z | " |
| 01000 | $08 | Carriage return (CR) | |
| 00010 | $02 | Line feed | |
| 11111 | $1F | Letters shift (LTRS) | |
| 11011 | $1B | Figures shift (FIGS) | |
| 00100 | $04 | Space bar (SP) | |
| 00000 | $00 | Blank | |

Baudot is not an ideal code for data communications, and it is very little used today. It was used on news and weather wires until about 1990, but those communications services now use the ASCII code (which is discussed in Section 5-1-4).

## 5-1-3  ARQ

One of the problems with Baudot is that it has no mechanism for detecting errors. For this reason the **automatic request for repetition (ARQ)** code was developed for

**FIGURE 5-3**
ARQ code.

| ARQ Code | HEX | LTRS | US FIGS |
|---|---|---|---|
| 0011010 | $1A | A | |
| 0011001 | $19 | B | ? |
| 1001100 | $4C | C | : |
| 0011100 | $1C | D | $ |
| 0111000 | $38 | E | 3 |
| 0010011 | $13 | F | ! |
| 1100001 | $61 | G | & |
| 1010010 | $52 | H | # |
| 1110000 | $70 | I | 8 |
| 0100011 | $23 | J | ' |
| 0001011 | $0B | K | ( |
| 1100010 | $62 | L | ) |
| 1010001 | $51 | M | . |
| 1010100 | $54 | N | , |
| 1000110 | $46 | O | 9 |
| 1001010 | $4A | P | 0 |
| 0001101 | $0D | Q | 1 |
| 1100100 | $64 | R | 4 |
| 0101010 | $2A | S | BELL |
| 1000101 | $45 | T | 5 |
| 0110010 | $32 | U | 7 |
| 1001001 | $49 | V | ; |
| 0100101 | $25 | W | 2 |
| 0010110 | $16 | X | / |
| 0010101 | $15 | Y | 6 |
| 0110001 | $31 | Z | " |
| 1000011 | $43 | Carriage return (CR) | |
| 1011000 | $58 | Line feed | |
| 0001110 | $0E | Letters shift (LTRS) | |
| 0100110 | $26 | Figures shift (FIGS) | |
| 1101000 | $68 | Space bar (SP) | |
| 0000111 | $07 | Blank | |

use over noisy transmission media, such as radio, where noise spikes cause many bit errors to occur. As shown in Figure 5-3, the ARQ code has the same system of letters and figures that Baudot has. But instead of 5 bits per character, ARQ uses 7. The code for each character contains exactly three binary 1s and four binary 0s. If an ARQ character is received with a different number of 1s and 0s, an error has occurred during transmission, and the receiving terminal sends a message back to the transmitting terminal requesting that the data be retransmitted. Hence the name automatic request for repetition.

### 5-1-4 ASCII

Figure 5-4 is a table of the ASCII code (pronounced AS-key). **ASCII** is an acronym for the **American Standard Code for Information Interchange.** ASCII is a 7-bit code. The international version of the code is called the CCITT Number 5 Code. ASCII has 7 bits, and it can therefore represent $2^7$, or 128, characters. An 8th bit, called a **parity bit,** is often added to the code for error checking. (The parity bit is discussed in Section 5-2-2.)

An extended 8-bit version of ASCII has also been developed. The extra bit gives the extended code twice as many characters as normal ASCII. The additional characters are mainly letters used in alphabets other than English and lines that can be used for drawing boxes, tables, and so on.

To find the ASCII code for a character in Figure 5-4, look up the number of the column and the number of the row in which the character is located. The column number is the most significant 3 bits and the row number is the least significant 4 bits of the ASCII code. The ASCII code can be expressed in either binary or hexadecimal.

---

■ **EXAMPLE 5-1**

What is the ASCII code for the letter *H* (uppercase) in binary and in hexadecimal?

**SOLUTION**

The letter *H* is located in column 4 and row 8. Therefore, the ASCII code for H is binary 100 1000, or $48. (*Note:* Writing 8-bit codes in 4-bit groups, called *nibbles,* makes them both easier to read and easier to convert to hexadecimal.

---

■ **EXAMPLE 5-2**

What is the ASCII code for the letter *k* (lowercase)?

**SOLUTION**

The letter *k* is located in row 6 and column B. Therefore, the ASCII code for the letter *k* is binary 110 1011, or $6B.

---

ASCII is still one of the most common codes used in data communications. It is also used to store data in personal computer memories and disks. One of ASCII's advantages over Baudot is that ASCII contains both upper- and lowercase letters of the alphabet. Another advantage is that ASCII contains **control codes,** which are located in columns 0 and 1 of the table. The control codes can be used as part of a protocol to direct certain operations in the receiving terminal. The purposes of some of those control codes are discussed in Chapter 11, the chapter on network protocols.

**FIGURE 5-4**
The ASCII code.

| MS Char → | 000 ($0) | 001 ($1) | 010 ($2) | 011 ($3) | 100 ($4) | 101 ($5) | 110 ($6) | 111 ($7) |
|---|---|---|---|---|---|---|---|---|
| **LS Char** | | | | | | | | |
| 0000 ($0) | NUL | DLE | SP | 0 | @ | P | ` | p |
| 0001 ($1) | SOH | DC1 | ! | 1 | A | Q | a | q |
| 0010 ($2) | STX | DC2 | " | 2 | B | R | b | r |
| 0011 ($3) | ETX | DC3 | # | 3 | C | S | c | s |
| 0100 ($4) | EOT | DCA | $ | 4 | D | T | d | t |
| 0101 ($5) | ENQ | NAK | % | 5 | E | U | e | u |
| 0110 ($6) | ACK | SYN | & | 6 | F | V | f | v |
| 0111 ($7) | BEL | ETB | ' | 7 | G | W | g | w |
| 1000 ($8) | BS | CAN | ( | 8 | H | X | h | x |
| 1001 ($9) | HT | EM | ) | 9 | I | Y | i | y |
| 1010 ($A) | LF | SUB | * | : | J | Z | j | z |
| 1011 ($B) | VT | ESC | + | ; | K | [ | k | { |
| 1100 ($C) | FF | FS | , | < | L | \ | l | | |
| 1101 ($D) | CR | GS | - | = | M | ] | m | } |
| 1110 ($E) | SO | RS | . | > | N | ^ | n | ~ |
| 1111 ($F) | SI | $\mu$S | / | ? | O | _ | o | DEL |

**FIGURE 5-5**
A partial EBCDIC table.

| Bits 4,5,6,&7 ↓ \ Bits 0,1,2,&3 → | 0000 ($0) | 0001 ($1) | 0010 ($2) | 0011 ($3) | 0100 ($4) | 0101 ($5) | 0110 ($6) | 0111 ($7) | 1000 ($8) | 1001 ($9) | 1010 ($A) | 1011 ($B) | 1100 ($C) | 1101 ($D) | 1110 ($E) | 1111 ($F) |
|---|---|---|---|---|---|---|---|---|---|---|---|---|---|---|---|---|
| 0000 ($0) | NUL | DLE | DS | | SP | & | - | | | | | | | | | 0 |
| 0001 ($1) | SOH | DC1 | SOS | | | | / | | a | j | | | A | J | | 1 |
| 0010 ($2) | STX | DC2 | FS | SYN | | | | | b | k | s | | B | K | S | 2 |
| 0011 ($3) | ETX | TM | | | | | | | c | l | t | | C | L | T | 3 |
| 0100 ($4) | PF | RES | BYP | PN | | | | | d | m | u | | D | M | U | 4 |
| 0101 ($5) | HT | NL | LF | RS | | | | | e | n | v | | E | N | V | 5 |
| 0110 ($6) | LC | BS | ETB | UC | | | | | f | o | w | | F | O | W | 6 |
| 0111 ($7) | DL | UIS | ESC | EOT | | | | | g | p | x | | G | P | X | 7 |
| 1000 ($8) | | CAN | | | | | | | h | q | y | | H | Q | Y | 8 |
| 1001 ($9) | | EM | | | | | | | i | r | z | | I | R | Z | 9 |
| 1010 ($A) | SMM | CC | SM | CU3 | ¢ | ! | ¦ | : | | | | | | | | |
| 1011 ($B) | VT | CU1 | CU2 | CU3 | . | $ | , | # | | | | | | | | |
| 1100 ($C) | FF | IFS | | DC4 | < | * | % | @ | | | | | | | | |
| 1101 ($D) | CR | IGS | ENG | NAK | ( | ) | _ | ' | | | | | | | | |
| 1110 ($E) | SO | IRS | ACK | | + | ; | > | = | | | | | | | | |
| 1111 ($F) | SI | IUS | BEL | SUB | \| | ¬ | ? | " | | | | | | | | |

### 5-1-5 EBCDIC

Another commonly used code for data communications is the **Extended Binary Coded Decimal Interchange Code** or **EBCDIC** (pronounced EB-sa-deck). The EBCDIC characters are shown in Figure 5-5.

IBM developed EBCDIC for use on its mainframe computer systems and is also used in IBM-compatible equipment. As shown in Figure 5-6, in EBCDIC, the bits are numbered in the reverse order from that of many other codes. In ASCII (and digital information in general) bit 0 is the least significant bit (LSB) and bit 7 is the most significant bit (MSB). In EBCDIC, bit 0 is the MSB, and bit 7 is the LSB.

With 8 bits, EBCDIC can represent $2^8$, or 256, different characters. Like ASCII, the EBCDIC code has both uppercase and lowercase letters of the alphabet, the digits *1* through *9,* and a large number of control codes. The control codes are located in columns 0 through 3 of the EBCDIC chart. You will learn the use of many of the EBCDIC control codes in Chapter 11.

---

■ **E X A M P L E   5 - 3**

Use Figure 5-5 to determine the EBCDIC code in both binary and hexadecimal for the lowercase letter *a*.

**SOLUTION**

Remember that EBCDIC bits are numbered from right to left and that bit 0 is the MSB. The column headings for the letter *a* in Figure 5-5 show that bits 0 through 3 are 1000. The row headings show that bits 4, 5, 6, and 7 are 0001. Putting the bits together yields the binary code 1000 0001, which can be written in hexadecimal as $81.

---

**FIGURE 5-6**
In EBCDIC, the bits are numbered in the reverse order from the system used in most binary codes.

| | | | **Normal Bit Numbering System** | | | | | | | |
|---|---|---|---|---|---|---|---|---|---|---|
| | b7 | b6 | b5 | b4 | b3 | b2 | b1 | b0 | | |
| MSB | 1 | 0 | 0 | 1 | 0 | 1 | 1 | 0 | | LSB |
| | | | **EBCDIC Bit Numbering System** | | | | | | | |
| | b0 | b1 | b2 | b3 | b4 | b5 | b6 | b7 | | |
| MSB | 1 | 0 | 0 | 1 | 0 | 1 | 1 | 0 | | LSB |

■ **EXAMPLE 5-4**

Use Figure 5-5 to look up the EBCDIC code, in both binary and hexadecimal, for the percent sign (%).

**SOLUTION**

From the column headings for the percent sign, bits 0 through 3 are 0110. Bits 4, 5, 6, and 7 are 1100. Putting the bits together, we have 0110 1100, or $6C.

■ **EXAMPLE 5-5**

Use the EBCDIC chart of Figure 5-5 to determine which character is represented by the hexadecimal code $4D.

**SOLUTION**

The character is in column $4 and row $D and is the left parenthesis or ( character.

## 5-2    ERROR DETECTION AND CORRECTION

If transmission media were perfect, we would not have to worry about errors in data communications. Unfortunately, that is not the case. Noise spikes and other types of interference can change 1s to 0s and 0s to 1s during transmission. A short 20-ms click on a telephone line may be annoying during a telephone conversation, but it is unlikely to disrupt voice communication. However, if data are being sent over the line at 4800 b/s, that same click may destroy 240 data bits. A number of techniques have been developed to detect and sometimes to correct errors.

All of the methods of detecting errors involve the transmission of redundant data. **Redundant data** are data that are not necessary to the information content of the transmission. Redundant data could be omitted and communication would still take place. Error checking schemes compare the redundant data to see if they agree. If they do agree, it is likely that no error has occurred. If they do not agree, it is almost certain that an error *has* occurred.

The simplest way to deal with errors is to let the receiving operator correct them. This method takes advantage of the fact that human language itself is redundant. For example, suppose the following sentence is sent over a news service communications system as part of a news story:

```
THE DOWNTOWN BRANCH OF THE BANK OF CENTERVILLE WAS
ROBBED OF MORE THAN $4000 LAST NIGHT.
```

If the transmission is sent in Baudot, and the first bit of the second *W* in the word *DOWNTOWN* is changed by a noise spike, the message will be received as:

THE DOWNTOAN BRANCH OF THE BANK OF CENTERVILLE WAS
ROBBED OF MORE THAN $4000 LAST NIGHT.

It would not be difficult for the receiving operator to realize that *DOWNTOAN* is
not a word and to make the necessary correction before publishing the story. There
is enough redundant information in the message to do that. However, if the character *4* in the sentence is affected by noise, and the message is received as:

THE DOWNTOWN BRANCH OF THE BANK OF CENTERVILLE WAS
ROBBED OF MORE THAN $&000 LAST NIGHT.

the receiving operator will know that there is an error in the message but will probably not know how to fix it. There is enough redundant information in the message to
detect the error, but there is not enough to correct it.

In most of today's data communications systems, the only types of errors that
humans are expected to correct are typing errors. Most communications systems
detect and correct errors that occur after the information leaves the keyboard.

## 5-2-1 Echoplex

**Echoplex** is a simple form of error detection that relies on redundant transmission
to help the sending operator make corrections. It is commonly used on full-duplex
communications systems in which each character is sent as it is typed into the transmitting terminal. Almost anyone who has used a computer and a modem has used
echoplex. As the receiving terminal receives each character, it retransmits or *echoes*
it back to the transmitting terminal where it appears on that terminal's screen. The
operator checks the character on the screen to see if it has been echoed correctly. If
there is an error, the operator presses the backspace key to erase the erroneous
character and then types the correct one.

The advantage of echoplex is its simplicity. It does not require complex circuitry,
and it is easy to implement. One disadvantage of echoplex is that it relies on a
human operator to detect and correct errors. Another disadvantage is that it makes
inefficient use of the communications channel, because the same information is
transmitted in both directions. Although echoplex is commonly used to correct typing errors in communications systems that transmit information as the operator
types it into a terminal, it is not used in other types of communications systems.

## 5-2-2 Parity

Parity is one of the simplest forms of automatic error detection and is frequently
used with the ASCII code. Although ASCII is a 7-bit code, a redundant bit, called a
parity bit, is often added to the ASCII character. The parity bit is placed in the most
significant bit (bit 7) position. There are two types of parity—odd and even. If even
parity is used, every 8-bit data word in a message contains an even number of binary
1s. If odd parity is used, every word has an odd number of 1s. As the parity bit is

added to the ASCII character by the sending terminal, it is either set or cleared to form the correct parity.

Neither type of parity has an advantage over the other in most communications systems, and both are widely used. However, the transmitting and receiving terminals must use the same type of parity, and all characters sent between those two terminals must have the same type of parity.

---

■ **EXAMPLE 5-6**

The following ASCII characters are sent: 110 0001, 111 0010, and 110 0101. If the characters are transmitted with odd parity, what parity bit is added to each character, a 1 or a 0? What is the ASCII code for each character in hexadecimal including the parity bit?

**SOLUTION**

For odd parity, the total number of binary 1s in each character, including the parity bit, is odd. The first character, 110 0001 has three 1s, which is already odd parity. Therefore, a parity bit of 0 is added in the MSB position to make the complete 8-bit data character 0110 0001, or $61. The second character, 111 0010 has an even number of 1s. The sending terminal adds a binary 1 as a parity bit to make the total number of 1s odd. The resulting ASCII character, including the parity bit, is 1111 0010, or $F2. The third character, 110 0101, also requires a 1 for odd parity, which makes the complete data character 1110 0101, or $E5.

---

The receiver checks the parity of each incoming ASCII character to see if it is correct. If the receiver is programmed to receive odd parity, every incoming data word must have odd parity. If it is programmed to receive even parity, every incoming data word must have even parity. If one bit in a data character gets changed by noise during transmission, the parity of the received character will be incorrect. When incorrect parity is received, it is called a **parity error.** For example, suppose a communications system uses even parity and that the ASCII character 1011 1000 is sent. If a noise spike changes bit 1, the character will be received as 1011 1010, which has odd parity. This is a parity error.

How a communications system responds to parity errors depends on how the terminals have been programmed. In a half-duplex or full-duplex system, the receiving terminal may send a message back to the transmitting terminal requesting that the entire message containing the error be retransmitted. In a simplex system, the receiving terminal cannot send messages back to the transmitting terminal, so there is no way for it to request retransmission. In such a case, the terminal may be programmed to print a star (*) on the screen to let the receiving operator know that an error has occurred.

A parity error is generated when an odd number of bits is changed during transmission, but no parity error is generated when an even number of bits is changed. For example, suppose 2 bits are changed by noise during transmission so that the character 1011 1000 is received as 1011 1110. Although the received character contains two errors, both the received character and the character that was originally sent have even parity. The receiving terminal does not generate a parity error, and the data error is not detected.

Like all methods of error detection, parity adds redundant information to the data stream. A disadvantage of parity is that it detects only errors that affect an odd number of bits in a data word. An advantage of parity is that it is simple to implement. Because of its simplicity, parity is widely used.

### 5-2-3  Horizontal and Vertical Parity Check

A better method of detecting errors involves using a combination of **horizontal and vertical parity checks.** The simple parity check discussed in Section 5-2-2 is a horizontal parity check. *Vertical parity* is calculated for all of the bits with the same bit number in a block of data. After a block of data has been sent, the transmitting terminal calculates a parity bit for bit 0 of all of the characters in the block, another parity bit for bit 1 of all of the characters, and so on. The vertical parity bits are transmitted as a **block check character (BCC)** at the end of the block of data.

Either even or odd parity may be used for both the horizontal and vertical parity bits. The same parity may be used for both, or one of them may have even parity, and the other may have odd parity. However, the transmitting and receiving terminals must use the same parity scheme. For illustration, the horizontal parity in Figure 5-7 is even, and the vertical parity is odd. Bits 0 through 6 in the figure are the

**FIGURE 5-7**
A short message using even character and odd column parity.

| P | b6 | b5 | b4 | b3 | b2 | b1 | b0 | ASCII Character |
|---|----|----|----|----|----|----|----|-----------------|
| 1 | 1 | 1 | 0 | 0 | 1 | 0 | 0 | d |
| 1 | 1 | 1 | 0 | 0 | 0 | 0 | 1 | a |
| 0 | 1 | 1 | 1 | 0 | 1 | 0 | 0 | t |
| 1 | 1 | 1 | 0 | 0 | 0 | 0 | 1 | a |
| 1 | 0 | 1 | 0 | 0 | 0 | 0 | 0 | SP |
| 0 | 1 | 1 | 0 | 0 | 0 | 1 | 1 | c |
| 0 | 1 | 1 | 0 | 1 | 1 | 1 | 1 | o |
| 1 | 1 | 1 | 0 | 1 | 1 | 0 | 1 | m |
| 1 | 1 | 1 | 0 | 1 | 1 | 0 | 1 | m |
| 1 | 1 | 0 | 0 | 0 | 0 | 1 | 1 | BCC |

ASCII code for the information transmitted. Notice that even the parity bit of the BCC passes both the vertical and horizontal parity check.

The receiver checks the horizontal parity of each character as it is received. The receiver also generates its own BCC and compares it with the check character received at the end of the block of data. The two should be identical. If they are not, an error has occurred, and the receiver can request that the sending terminal retransmit the block of data.

However, the combination of horizontal and vertical parity checking does more than detect errors. It also allows the receiver to correct single-bit errors without requesting further information from the transmitter, a process known as **forward error correction (FEC).** Figure 5-8 shows the data block of Figure 5-7, but bit 1 of the SP, or space, character has been altered by noise. Both the horizontal parity check for the space character and the vertical parity check for bit 1 fail. Therefore, bit 1 of the SP character must be in error. The receiver can correct the error by changing the 1 back to a 0.

Unfortunately, the combination of horizontal and vertical parity can reliably perform FEC only on single-bit errors. Errors that involve two or more bits cannot always be corrected. To illustrate, in Figure 5-9, both bit 1 of the SP character and bit 2 of the character *c* have been changed by noise. Both characters fail horizontal parity checks, and bits 1 and 2 fail their vertical parity checks, but the receiver cannot determine which bits are in error. The error could just as easily be bit 2 of the

**FIGURE 5-8**

Bit 1 of the SP character fails both character and column parity checks and is therefore in error.

| P | b6 | b5 | b4 | b3 | b2 | b1 | b0 | ASCII Character |
|---|----|----|----|----|----|----|----|-----------------|
| 1 | 1 | 1 | 0 | 0 | 1 | 0 | 0 | d |
| 1 | 1 | 1 | 0 | 0 | 0 | 0 | 1 | a |
| 0 | 1 | 1 | 1 | 0 | 1 | 0 | 0 | t |
| 1 | 1 | 1 | 0 | 0 | 0 | 0 | 1 | a |
| 1 | 0 | 1 | 0 | 0 | 0 | 1 | 0 | SP |
| 0 | 1 | 1 | 0 | 0 | 0 | 1 | 1 | c |
| 0 | 1 | 1 | 0 | 1 | 1 | 1 | 1 | o |
| 1 | 1 | 1 | 0 | 1 | 1 | 0 | 1 | m |
| 1 | 1 | 1 | 0 | 1 | 1 | 0 | 1 | m |
| 1 | 1 | 0 | 0 | 0 | 0 | 1 | 1 | BCC |

**FIGURE 5-9**
Two-bit errors can be detected by a combination of character and column parity checks, but they usually cannot be corrected.

| P | b6 | b5 | b4 | b3 | b2 | b1 | b0 | ASCII Character |
|---|----|----|----|----|----|----|----|-----------------|
| 1 | 1 | 1 | 0 | 0 | 1 | 0 | 0 | d |
| 1 | 1 | 1 | 0 | 0 | 0 | 0 | 1 | a |
| 0 | 1 | 1 | 1 | 0 | 1 | 0 | 0 | t |
| 1 | 1 | 1 | 0 | 0 | 0 | 0 | 1 | a |
| 1 | 0 | 1 | 0 | 0 | 0 | 1 | 0 | SP |
| 0 | 1 | 1 | 0 | 0 | 1 | 1 | 1 | c |
| 0 | 1 | 1 | 0 | 1 | 1 | 1 | 1 | o |
| 1 | 1 | 1 | 0 | 1 | 1 | 0 | 1 | m |
| 1 | 1 | 1 | 0 | 1 | 1 | 0 | 1 | m |
| 1 | 1 | 0 | 0 | 0 | 0 | 1 | 1 | BCC |

space character and bit 1 of the character *c*. Even though the receiving terminal cannot perform FEC, at least the receiving terminal can determine that a transmission error has occurred, and it can request that the sending terminal retransmit the entire block of data.

No system of error checking is 100% foolproof. Figure 5-10 contains 4 bit errors. Bits 1 and 2 of both the SP and c characters have been altered during transmission. Both characters pass their horizontal checks, and both bit positions pass vertical parity checks. Even the combination of horizontal and vertical parity checks has failed to detect the errors.

Parity bits can be generated by software routines in the sending terminal, and they can be checked by software routines at the receiving terminal. However, it is more efficient to generate and check parity bits in hardware. Figure 5-11 is the schematic of a circuit that can be used to generate horizontal parity bits. The 7 bits of the ASCII character are applied to the inputs labeled bit 0 through bit 6, and a bias bit is applied to the remaining input. If the bias bit is a 1, the correct horizontal parity bit will be generated to give the character odd parity. A bias bit of 0 will cause the circuit to generate the correct horizontal parity bit for even parity. Trace the circuit by assuming a set of inputs to assure yourself that it works.

Parity generator and checker circuits are part of the DTE circuit. They were once constructed from discrete, exclusive OR gates as shown in Figure 5-11, but today they are built into a larger integrated circuit that also performs other communications tasks, as will be discussed in Chapter 8.

**FIGURE 5-10**
Even the combination of character and column parity checks will not detect all errors.

| P | b6 | b5 | b4 | b3 | b2 | b1 | b0 | ASCII Character |
|---|----|----|----|----|----|----|----|-----------------|
| 1 | 1 | 1 | 0 | 0 | 1 | 0 | 0 | d |
| 1 | 1 | 1 | 0 | 0 | 0 | 0 | 1 | a |
| 0 | 1 | 1 | 1 | 0 | 1 | 0 | 0 | t |
| 1 | 1 | 1 | 0 | 0 | 0 | 0 | 1 | a |
| 1 | 0 | 1 | 0 | 0 | 1 | 1 | 0 | SP |
| 0 | 1 | 1 | 0 | 0 | 0 | 1 | 1 | c |
| 0 | 1 | 1 | 0 | 1 | 1 | 1 | 1 | o |
| 1 | 1 | 1 | 0 | 1 | 0 | 1 | 1 | m |
| 1 | 1 | 1 | 0 | 1 | 1 | 0 | 1 | m |
| 1 | 1 | 0 | 0 | 0 | 0 | 1 | 1 | BCC |

## 5-2-4   Checksums

As illustrated in Figure 5-12, a **checksum** is the least significant byte of the arithmetical sum of the binary data transmitted. As the data is sent, the transmitting terminal sums it. At the end of the data block, it sends the least significant byte of the sum as an extra character, called the checksum. The receiver generates its own checksum by summing the data as it is received. At the end of the block, it compares the checksum it generated with the checksum it receives from the transmitter. If the

**FIGURE 5-11**
A parity generator circuit.

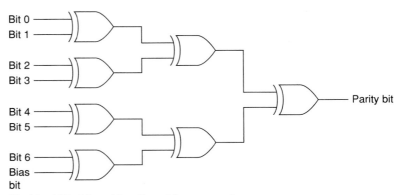

Bit 0
Bit 1
Bit 2
Bit 3
Bit 4
Bit 5
Bit 6
Bias bit

Parity bit

The bias bit is 1 for odd parity or 0 for even parity.

**FIGURE 5-12**
The checksum is the least significant byte of the sum of the coded data.

| Character | EBCDIC |
|-----------|--------|
| T | $E3 |
| e | $85 |
| r | $99 |
| r | $99 |
| i | $89 |
| b | $82 |
| l | $93 |
| e | $85 |
| Checksum | $BD |

two are identical, it is likely that no error occurred. If the two checksums are different, an error has occurred, and the receiver requests that the block of data be resent.

### 5-2-5 Cyclic Redundancy Check (CRC)

One of the more effective methods of error detection is the **cyclic redundancy check (CRC).** A circuit that can be used to generate a 16-bit CRC character is shown in Figure 5-13. Identical CRC circuits are used in the transmitting and the receiving terminals to generate a check character which is highly dependent on all the data that were sent in the block. We will use the CRC circuit in the receiving terminal as our example.

**FIGURE 5-13**
A CRC circuit.

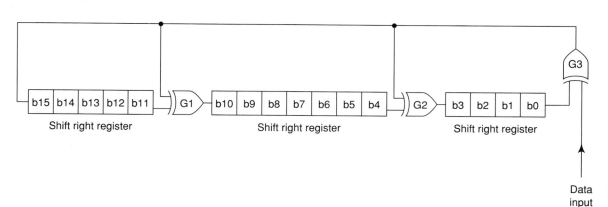

The CRC circuit is initialized with all 0s in the shift registers. Each time a bit is received, every bit in the shift registers is shifted right. Assume that the first bit received is a 1. It is exclusively ORed in G3 with a 0 shifted out of b0 of the shift register to produce a logical 1 which is in turn shifted into the b15 position of the shift register and continues to shift right as each subsequent bit is received. Four received bits later, it will have been shifted to the b11 position where it will influence the output of exclusive OR gate G1. The output of G1 is shifted to the right until it arrives at the b4 position and influences the output of G2. The G2 output in turn shifts right to the b0 position where it is exclusively ORed with a received bit of data to influence the output of G3 and thereby the input to the CRC circuit.

The important thing to recognize is that once a bit is received, it continues to influence the contents of the shift registers in the CRC circuit. If one bit is received incorrectly, it will cause the contents of the CRC shift registers to be different than they would have been if all bits had been received correctly.

As mentioned, the transmitting terminal has a CRC circuit identical to the CRC circuit in the receiver. As each bit is transmitted, a copy of that bit is input into the CRC circuit. At the end of the block of data, the sending terminal transmits the contents of its CRC registers. When the receiver receives the CRC character, it compares it with the contents of its own CRC registers. The two CRC characters should be identical. If they are not, an error has occurred in transmission, and the receiver can request that the sending terminal retransmit the block of data.

Although Figure 5-13 shows a circuit that generates a 16-bit CRC, 32-bit CRCs are also common in many data communications systems. Twelve-bit and 24-bit CRCs are used in some systems. Like the parity checker circuit, CRC generators are usually not separate circuits as shown in the figure. They are included in a larger integrated circuit that also performs other data communications functions.


■  **SUMMARY**

In this chapter we have looked at codes used in data communications and methods used to detect and sometimes correct errors. Of the codes presented in this chapter, the two that are most commonly used in data communications are ASCII and EBCDIC. Baudot is a 5-bit code, and it was the first code to be widely used for data communications. Baudot has two modes, a letters mode and a figures mode, each with its own character set. The LTRS and FIGS characters are used to shift back and forth between the two modes. Communications systems that once used Baudot have now almost all switched to the ASCII code.

ASCII is a 7-bit code, although a redundant 8th bit, called a parity bit, is sometimes added to detect errors. There is also an 8-bit version of ASCII which is called extended ASCII. ASCII is used both in data communications and to store data in personal computer memories and disks.

EBCDIC is an 8-bit code that was developed by IBM Corporation for use in its larger computers. EBCDIC is also used in equipment that was designed to be compatible with those IBM computers.

Errors inevitably occur in data transmission. In some systems, those errors are tolerated, and nothing is done to correct them. However, a number of schemes have been developed to detect and sometimes correct errors. All of these methods use redundant information. In echoplex, the receiving terminal echoes each received character back to the sending terminal where it appears on the terminal screen. The terminal operator visually inspects each character to make sure that it is correct. Echoplex's main use is to correct typing errors.

Parity is an extra bit that is added to each data character in the MSB position. The parity bit is set or cleared to ensure that each character either contains an even number of 1s or that each character contains an odd number of 1s. Parity is frequently used with the ASCII code.

A combination of horizontal and vertical parity checks can not only detect errors, but also allow the receiver to correct single-bit errors, a process known as forward error correction (FEC). This system, in addition to having a parity bit for each character, uses a binary check character (BCC) which is transmitted at the end of a block of data.

A checksum is no more than the least significant byte of the arithmetical sum of all the binary characters transmitted in a block of data. Both the transmitter and the receiver calculate a checksum, and at the end of a transmission, the sending terminal transmits the checksum which the receiver then compares with its own checksum.

A cyclic redundancy check (CRC) character can be formed by circulating transmitted data through a system of shift registers and exclusive OR gates. Identical circuits are used at the transmitter and receiver. At the end of a block of data, the sending terminal transmits its CRC character, and the receiver compares it with the CRC character that it has generated. If the two CRC characters are different, an error has occurred.

## ■ QUESTIONS

1. Define the term *code*.
2. a. How many bits are used in the Baudot code to represent each character?
   b. Explain the purpose of Baudot's LTRS and FIGS characters.
3. What feature does ARQ add to the Baudot code?
4. What does the acronym ASCII stand for?
5. a. How many bits does the standard ASCII code have?
   b. How many characters can standard ASCII represent?
6. a. How many bits does extended ASCII have?
   b. How many characters can extended ASCII represent?
7. Name two advantages that ASCII has compared to Baudot.
8. Which company developed the EBCDIC code?
9. a. How many bits does the EBCDIC code have?

b.   How many characters can the EBCDIC code represent?

10. What is meant by the term *redundant information?*

11. Why does a noise spike on a telephone line disrupt data communications more than it disrupts voice communications?

12. a.   How does echoplex work?

b.   What is the advantage of echoplex?

c.   What are two disadvantages of echoplex?

d.   What type of error is echoplex designed to correct?

13. a.   Explain how adding a parity bit to ASCII characters helps to detect errors.

b.   What type of errors cannot be detected by checking parity?

14. What is forward error correction?

15. Explain how a combination of horizontal and vertical parity checks can be used to perform forward error correction on single-bit errors.

16. Sketch the parity generator circuit of Figure 5-11 on a piece of paper. Assume that the bias bit is a 0 and that the other inputs come from the ASCII character for the lowercase letter *a*. At the output of each gate, indicate whether the gate outputs a logic 1 or a logic 0.

17. a.   Explain how an 8-bit checksum is generated.

b.   When is the checksum transmitted?

18. Explain how the CRC circuit of Figure 5-13 is used to detect errors.


■  **PROBLEMS**

1.   Use Figure 5-4 to look up the ASCII code for each of the following characters and control codes. Give your answer in hexadecimal.

| | | |
|---|---|---|
| a. R | d. T | g. 3 |
| b. Q | e. DEL | h. q |
| c. d | f. a | i. L |

2.   What character is represented by each of the following ASCII codes?

| | |
|---|---|
| a. $32 | d. $03 |
| b. $73 | e. $39 |
| c. $19 | |

3.   Use Figure 5-5 to look up the EBCDIC code for each of the following characters and control codes. Give your answer in hexadecimal.

| | | |
|---|---|---|
| a. A | d. 0 (zero) | g. N |

    b. PRE          e. HT          h. #

    c. M           f. EOB        i. a

4. Use Figure 5-5 to look up the following EBCDIC codes and convert them to characters and control codes.

    a. $C1         d. $A5        g. $26

    b. $E5         e. $00        h. $E2

    c. $81         f. $26        i. $D6

# Chapter 6

# SERIAL INTERFACES

**OBJECTIVES**

After you have completed this chapter, you should be able to:

- Identify three levels in which the interfaces of two pieces of equipment must be compatible if those two pieces of equipment are to communicate with each other.

- Describe the 20-mA loop and state its advantages and disadvantages when compared with interfaces that use voltage signals.

- State the ranges of voltages that an RS-232 interface may use to assert and to sense both a logic 1 and a logic 0.

- Name the five groups into which the RS-232 circuits are divided.

- Identify the following RS-232 control circuits and briefly describe the function of each: (a) RTS, (b) CTS, (c) DCD, (d) DSR, and (e) DTR.

- Briefly describe the characteristics of each of the following serial interface standards: (a) RS-449, (b) RS-422, and (c) RS-423.

- Explain the difference between RS-449 category I and category II circuits.

## INTRODUCTION

In previous chapters, we have discussed the problems involved in communicating serial data over long distances. This chapter deals with serial communications over short distances, for example, between two pieces of equipment located in the same building or even side-by-side in the same room.

For communications over standard telephone lines, serial data are modulated onto an analog carrier. However, for short-distance serial communications, no carrier is needed, and data are sent unmodulated. A signal that consists of unmodulated information is called a **baseband** signal.

The **communications port** of a piece of electronic equipment is where data are input or output. An *interface* connects the communications ports of two pieces of equipment and carriers information between them. The two pieces of equipment could be a computer and a printer, a keyboard and a computer, or a DTE and a DCE. For communication to take place, the communications ports of the two pieces of equipment must be compatible at three levels: mechanical, electrical, and protocol. At the mechanical level, both pieces of equipment must have compatible plugs, sockets, pins, and cables. Two pieces of equipment cannot be interfaced if the plug of one piece of equipment will not fit into the socket of the other.

Both pieces of equipment must use the same electrical signals. If one piece of equipment uses TTL signaling levels and the other uses RS-232 levels, they cannot be directly connected to each other and expected to communicate. Most serial interfaces use control signals, called handshaking signals, to coordinate the transfer of data. The handshaking signals of both pieces of equipment must be compatible.

Finally, both must use the same protocol. Remember that a **protocol** is a system of rules that govern the operation of a communications system. A protocol includes rules that stipulate such things as the code, speed of communication, and system of control codes. If one piece of equipment uses 2400 b/s asynchronous ASCII and the other uses 9600 b/s synchronous EBCDIC, they will not communicate.

Many serial interface standards have been developed to enable different pieces of equipment to communicate with each other. The serial interface standards covered in this chapter address only electrical and mechanical compatibility. Standard protocols are discussed in Chapter 11.

## 6-1   CURRENT LOOP INTERFACES

Most serial interface standards use two different voltage levels—one of them to represent a mark and the other to represent a space—but there are also standards that use current flow instead of voltage. Two current flow standards are the 80-mA loop and the 20-mA loop. The **80-mA loop** uses a current of 80 mA to represent a mark and 0 mA (no current flow) to represent a space. The **20-mA loop** (as you have probably assumed) uses 20 mA to represent a mark and 0 mA to represent a space. The 20-mA loop is the more common of the two, so it is the one discussed in the following paragraphs.

### 6-1-1 The 20-mA Loop

Figure 6-1 illustrates a simplex 20-mA loop. The transmitter contains a 20-mA constant current source in series with a switch. Although the switch shown in the diagram is mechanical, modern circuits would use a solid-state device such as a FET. To send a mark, the switch is closed, which allows the 20-mA current to flow around the loop. To send a space, the switch is opened, which stops current flow. At the receiver, the current flows through a resistor and produces a voltage drop across the resistor that is amplified by an op amp.

The single current loop shown in Figure 6-1 allows only simplex transmission. Duplex communication requires two 20-mA loops as shown in Figure 6-2. Simplex transmission requires only two conductors, whereas duplex requires three or four conductors. (If three conductors are used, there is a conductor to carry current in each direction plus a common or ground conductor that acts as a return current path for both loops.) As we shall see, the number of conductors required for simplex transmission is far fewer than the number required by other serial interfaces.

### 6-1-2 Advantages of Current Interfaces

Historically, the main use of the 20-mA loop was as an interface to mechanical teletype terminals. When electronic terminals came into being, they continued to use the 20-mA loop in order to be compatible with the teletype equipment that they replaced. The 20-mA loop was commonly used through the 1970s to interface mainframe computers to their remote terminals.

Even for newer applications, current loops offer advantages over interfaces that use voltage signals, especially when the distance between the two pieces of equipment to be connected is more than about 50 ft. Current loops are less susceptible to noise; they allow higher communications speeds and longer cable runs; and they use fewer conductors. Some of these advantages are discussed in more detail in the following paragraphs.

In high-impedance voltage-based interfaces, noise is often a problem. Noise spikes can easily reach voltages that override 5 V TTL signals. However, it is

**FIGURE 6-1**

In a 20-mA loop, the presence or absence of current indicates a mark or a space respectively.

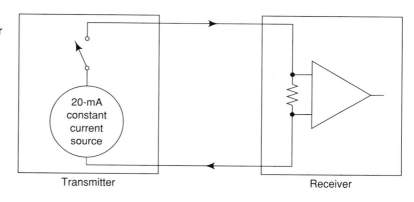

Transmitter

Receiver

**FIGURE 6-2**
Duplex transmission requires two 20-mA loops and four conductors.

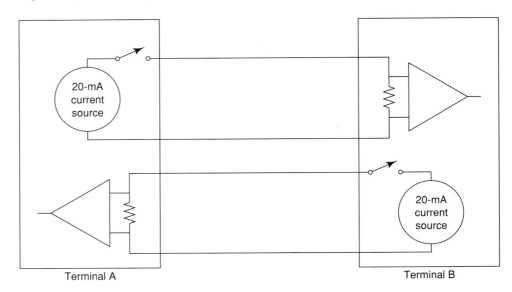

Terminal A                                              Terminal B

unlikely that a noise spike will contain enough energy to produce 20 mA of current flow. Current loops can be several thousand feet long and still carry data at well over 10,000 b/s without undue noise interference. The RS-232 voltage-based interface standard, in contrast, begins to degrade if the cable run is much longer than 50 ft (about 15 m).

As we have seen, current loops require only two conductors for simplex operation and three or four conductors for duplex. This is a real advantage when the two pieces of equipment are located at a substantial distance from each other. Most voltage-based interfaces use numerous conductors to carry handshaking signals that coordinate the transfer of data. A fully implemented RS-232 interface uses 25 conductors. Cables with a large number of conductors can be very expensive.

### 6-1-3  Optically Isolated Current Loops

Figure 6-3 illustrates how an inexpensive optocoupler (optical coupler) can be used to electrically isolate the transmitter from the receiver in a current-loop interface. The optocoupler itself consists of a light-emitting diode (LED) and a photodetector transistor both sealed inside the same integrated circuit package. The LED emits light whenever current is passed through it, and the photodetector transistor conducts when its base region is illuminated.

Input data alternately turn the LED on and off. The light from the LED then switches the photodetector transistor on and off, which in turn switches the current on and off in the 20-mA loop. Data are carried between the LED and the photodetector by light waves. There is no electrical connection between the data input and

**FIGURE 6-3**
An optocoupler allows electrical isolation between the transmitter and receiver in a current loop.

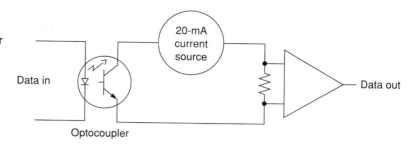

the data output. Commonly available optocouplers can withstand voltages in excess of 1000 V between the input and the output without breaking down. Optically isolated interfaces are used in medical equipment, where strict safety regulations demand that any sensors attached directly to a patient be electrically isolated from electronic equipment.

### 6-1-4 Disadvantages of Current Loop Interfaces

A disadvantage of the 20-mA loop is that there is no standardization of the mechanical interface, and the only electrical standardization is that 20 mA represents a mark and that 0 mA represents a space. The current supply can be located anywhere in the loop, either in the transmitter or in the receiver. There is no protocol standardization either. This lack of standardization means that there is no guarantee that two devices that use 20-mA loops can be connected and that communication will take place.

The 20-mA loop was developed during the teletype days and was so widely used that it came to be regarded as a "standard," even though it has never been officially recognized as such. Later, electronic computer terminals also used the 20-mA loop. Because there was no published standard, each terminal manufacturer used its own judgment to implement the loop. As a result, some versions of the 20-mA loop are incompatible with each other. But as we will soon see in our discussion of RS-232, even the existence of an officially published standard does not prevent equipment manufacturers from developing their own variations.

## 6-2 THE RS-232 INTERFACE

The RS-232 standard was published by the Electronic Industries Association (EIA) in the 1960s to describe an interface between a DTE and a DCE. The document which describes the RS-232 standard bears the title *Interface Between Data Terminal Equipment and Data Communication Equipment Employing Serial Binary Data Interchange.* The CCITT also publishes an international version of RS-232, which it calls **V.24** (pronounced V dot 24). RS-232 covers the electrical and mechanical portions of interface. It says nothing about protocol except to limit the maximum data transfer rate to 20 kb/s.

As mentioned in Chapter 4, the letters *RS* stand for *recommended standard,* and 232 is the number assigned the standard. A letter placed after the standard number indicates the latest revision. For example, RS-232-C is the C revision of the standard. For simplicity, we will not use the revision letter and will refer to the interface simply as RS-232.

RS-232 has been called the "non-standard standard," because so many variations of it have evolved. Over the years RS-232 has been modified to connect all manner of equipment in addition to the terminal and modem for which it was originally designed. The serial ports on the back of many personal computers are called RS-232 ports and are used to connect the computer to a mouse, printer, modem, or other peripheral. Devices as diverse as home security system controllers, test equipment, data acquisition system, and shortwave radio receivers often have an RS-232 port to allow them to communicate with a computer.

Variations of RS-232 have evolved to meet these interfacing needs, and the variations are often incompatible with each other. An engineer or technician cannot assume that two devices with RS-232 ports can be plugged into each other and will communicate. However, someone who understands the standard is better prepared to analyze the variations of RS-232 that are encountered in the field and to select the cables, connectors, and so on that are necessary to make it work.

### 6-2-1 Review of the Data Communications System Model

Figure 6-4 is a simplified block diagram of the interface between a data terminal and a telephone line. Between the terminal and the telephone line are a DTE (data terminal equipment) and a DCE (data communications equipment). The word *terminal* means the end. Just as a bus terminal is the end of a bus route, a communications terminal is the end of a communications system. A communications terminal may be as simple as a keyboard and a video display, or it may be a large and complex computer. The terminal is where transmitted data originates, and it is the destination of received data.

Technically, the terminal is considered part of the DTE, but the functions that the terminal performs are so important that we will consider it to be a separate block in the communications system. The main purpose of the DTE is to convert

**FIGURE 6-4**
Simplified block diagram of the interface between a data terminal and a telephone line.

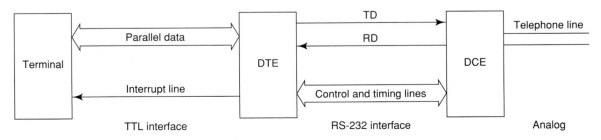

between the parallel data format used inside the terminal and the serial format used to transmit and receive data over a telephone line. If the communications system uses parity, the DTE generates the correct parity bit during transmission, and the DTE checks parity during reception. As we will discuss in Chapter 8, if the communications system uses a format called asynchronous transmission, the DTE also generates start and stop bits to mark the beginning and end of each byte of data during transmission, and it checks for the presence of start and stop bits during reception.

The DCE is a modem that accepts serial baseband data from the DTE during transmission. It modulates that data onto a carrier, and sends the data over the telephone line. During reception, the DCE demodulates the incoming carrier and passes the demodulated serial baseband data on to the DTE.

The majority of modern terminals use either 3 V or TTL logic levels internally, and they manipulate data in parallel. To be compatible with the terminal, the interface between the terminal and the DTE also uses either 3 V or TTL logic levels and a parallel data format. The interface's parallel data lines are bidirectional. The same data lines carry data from the terminal to the DTE during transmission from the DTE to the terminal during reception. The interrupt line allows the DTE to get the terminal's attention when the DTE is ready to have the terminal write data to it or read from it.

The RS-232 interface between the DTE and DCE is quite complex as we will soon see. It has been simplified in Figure 6-4. The TD or transmit data line carries transmit serial data from the DTE to the DCE, and the RD, or receive data line, carries received serial data from the DCE to the DTE. The control and timing lines shown in the diagram coordinate the transfer of data between the DTE and the DCE.

## 6-2-2  RS-232 Logic Levels

As we saw in Chapter 4, the RS-232 interface that connects the DTE and the DCE uses negative logic levels. A negative voltage represents a logic 1 or mark, and a positive voltage represents a logic 0 or space.

Figure 6-5 shows the signal levels output by and recognized by an RS-232 compatible serial port. When a device outputs a logic signal, we say that the signal is *asserted*. When a device inputs a logic signal, we say the signal is *sensed*. To assert a logic 1, an RS-232 line may output any voltage in the range of −5 V to −15 V. To assert a logic 0, it may output any voltage in the range of +5 V to +15 V.

**FIGURE 6-5**
RS-232 electrical signal levels use negative logic.

| Binary State | Output Voltage | Recognized Voltage | Control Line | Data Line |
|:---:|:---:|:---:|:---:|:---:|
| 0 | +5 V to +15 V | +3 V to +25 V | On | Space |
| 1 | −5 V to −15 V | −3 V to −25 V | Off | Mark |

The RS-232 specification states that when a device senses an RS-232 logic signal, it must recognize a wider range of voltage levels. Any voltage between –3 V and –25 V must be sensed as a logic 1, and any voltage between +3 V and +25 V must be sensed as a logic 0. This wider range of voltages allows power supply variations and noise.

A logic 0 makes a control line active or asserts it, and a logic 1 makes a control line inactive or turns it off. Voltages between –3 V and +3 V are undefined, and they should not be present on the interface. If they are present, it is a sign of a malfunction. Voltages more negative than –25 V or more positive than +25 V should also not be present on the interface, because such extremes in voltage could cause equipment damage.

### 6-2-3   The RS-232 Circuits

The RS-232 standard specifies the pin number of each conductor, but it does not specify the connectors to be used at the ends of the cable. By custom, the DB-25 (D-type with 25 pins) plug and socket are often used with the RS-232 interface. A DB-25 connector is pictured in Figure 6-6.

The conductors of the RS-232 interface are called *circuits.* The circuits are divided into five groups: ground, data, control, timing, and secondary channel. Figure 6-7 shows, in numerical order, which circuit is assigned to each pin of the connector. The RS-232 specification assigns a two- or three-letter designation to each circuit. The first letter of each designation indicates the group to which the circuit belongs. Ground designations begin with the letter *A,* data circuits with the letter *B,* control circuits with the letter *C,* timing circuits with the letter *D,* and secondary circuits with the letter *S.* The EIA designation can be confusing, so unofficially each conductor also has been assigned a mnemonic. A **mnemonic** is an abbreviation that is designed to be easy to remember. For example, the mnemonic for the request-to-send circuit is RTS, which is much easier to remember than the EIA designation, CA. As you might imagine, the mnemonics are much more frequently used than are the official EIA circuit names.

Each of the individual circuits carries its signal in one direction only, either from the DTE to the DCE or from the DCE to the DTE. For example, pin 2, the transmitted data circuit carries the serial data to be transmitted from the DTE to the

**FIGURE 6-6**
Front view of a D-type connector, frequently used with the RS-232 interface.

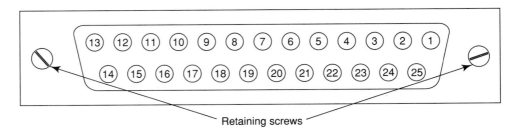

Retaining screws

**FIGURE 6-7**

RS-232 circuit assignment by pin number.

| Pin | EIA Name | Mnemonic | Description | Direction |
|-----|----------|----------|-------------|-----------|
| 1 | AA | PG | Protective ground | |
| 2 | BA | TD | Transmitted data | DTE to DCE |
| 3 | BB | RD | Received data | DCE to DTE |
| 4 | CA | RTS | Request to send | DTE to DCE |
| 5 | CB | CTS | Clear to send | DCE to DTE |
| 6 | CC | DSR | Data set ready | DCE to DTE |
| 7 | AB | SG | Signal ground or common return | |
| 8 | CF | DCD | Received line signal detector (data carrier detect) | DCE to DTE |
| 9 | | | (reserved for data set testing) | |
| 10 | | | (reserved for data set testing) | |
| 11 | | | (not assigned) | |
| 12 | SCF | SDCD | Secondary received line signal detector | DCE to DTE |
| 13 | SCB | SCTS | Secondary clear to send | DCE to DTE |
| 14 | SBA | STD | Secondary transmitted data | DTE to DCE |
| 15 | DB | TSET or TC | Transmitter signal element timing (transmit clock) | DCE to DTE |
| 16 | SBB | SRD | Secondary received data | DCE to DTE |
| 17 | DD | RSET or RC | Receiver signal element timing (receive clock) | DCE to DTE |
| 18 | | | (not assigned) | |
| 19 | SCA | SRTS | Secondary request to send | DTE to DCE |
| 20 | CD | DTR | Data terminal ready | DTE to DCE |
| 21 | CG | SQ | Signal quality detector | DCE to DTE |
| 22 | CE | RI | Ring indicator | DCE to DTE |
| 23 | CH or CI | None | Data rate selector (CH = DTE to DCE, CI = DCE to DTE) | See Description. |
| 24 | DA | TSET or TC | Transmitter signal element timing (transmit clock) | DTE to DCE |
| 25 | | | (not assigned) | |

**FIGURE 6-8**
RS-232 circuit assignment by group.

| Pin | EIA Name | Mnemonic | Description | Direction |
|-----|----------|----------|-------------|-----------|
| 1 | AA | PG | Protective ground | |
| 7 | AB | SG | Signal ground or common return | |
| 2 | BA | TD | Transmitted data | DTE to DCE |
| 3 | BB | RD | Received data | DCE to DTE |
| 4 | CA | RTS | Request to send | DTE to DCE |
| 5 | CB | CTS | Clear to send | DCE to DTE |
| 6 | CC | DSR | Data set ready | DCE to DTE |
| 20 | CD | DTR | Data terminal ready | DTE to DCE |
| 22 | CE | RI | Ring indicator | DCE to DTE |
| 8 | CF | DCD | Received line signal detector (data carrier detect) | DCE to DTE |
| 21 | CG | SQ | Signal quality detector | DCE to DTE |
| 23 | CH or CI | None | Data rate selector (CH = DTE to DCE, CI = DCE to DTE) | See Description. |
| 24 | DA | TSET or TC | Transmitter signal element timing (transmit clock) | DTE to DCE |
| 15 | DB | TSET or TC | Transmitter signal element timing (transmit clock) | DCE to DTE |
| 17 | DD | RSET or RC | Receiver signal element timing (receive clock) | DCE to DTE |
| 14 | SBA | STD | Secondary transmitted data | DTE to DCE |
| 16 | SBB | SRD | Secondary received data | DCE to DTE |
| 19 | SCA | SRTS | Secondary request to send | DTE to DCE |
| 13 | SCB | SCTS | Secondary clear to send | DCE to DTE |
| 12 | SCF | SDCD | Secondary received line signal detector | DCE to DTE |

110

mitted data circuit carries the serial data to be transmitted from the DTE to the DCE. The DTE outputs data on pin 2, and the DCE inputs this same data on its pin 2.

## Grounds

Figure 6-8 lists the RS-232 circuits grouped according to their EIA circuit names. There are two ground conductors, protective ground and signal ground, whose EIA circuit names are AA and AB respectively. Protective ground is sometimes called frame ground (FG), and it is often left unconnected. When it is used, it is connected to the frame or chassis of both the DTE and DCE. Its purpose it to guarantee that the chassis of the DTE and the DCE are at the same electrical potential. Signal ground is the reference line for all signals in the interface.

## Data Circuits

Lines BA and BB are the transmitted and received data lines (TD and RD). The transmit data line carries serial data from the DTE to the DCE, and the receive data line carries data from the DCE to the DTE.

## Control Circuits

The RS-232 interface has eight control lines, which are shown in Figure 6-9. A NOT bar above a mnemonic indicates that the control line is active when it is in the logic 0 state and has a positive voltage on it.

The Telco name for a modem or DCE is a **data set.** When the data set ready (DSR or CC) control line is active, it notifies the DTE that the DCE is turned on, connected to a telephone line, and ready to receive or transmit data. In a similar

**FIGURE 6-9**
Eight control lines connect the DTE and DCE.

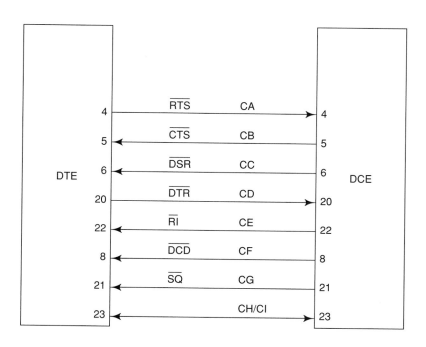

manner, when the data terminal ready (DTR or CD) line is active, it notifies the DCE that the DTE is turned on and ready to send or receive data.

The ring indicator (RI or CI) circuit is made active by the DCE whenever it receives a ringing voltage from the telephone line. The data carrier detect (DCD or CF) line is active whenever the DCE is locked onto a carrier received over the telephone line. The DCD line is also called the received line signal detector (RLSD).

The two remaining control lines, request to send (RTS or CA) and clear to send (CTS or CB) are handshaking lines. The term **handshaking** refers to an exchange of control signals between two devices in which one device outputs a control signal to request that the second device perform some action. The second device performs the requested action and returns another control signal to confirm that the action has been performed. The second control signal is the *handshake response* to the first.

In the RS-232 interface, request to send is a signal from the DTE to the DCE requesting that the DCE output a carrier onto the telephone line in preparation for transmitting data. Clear to send (CTS or CB) is a handshake response from the DCE to the DTE that confirms that a carrier has been placed on the telephone line. RTS and CTS are used for half-duplex operation. To permit half-duplex, the modem carrier is turned on to transmit and turned off to receive.

Figure 6-10 illustrates this RTS/CTS handshake sequence. Assume that the terminal connected to the DTE has a message to send and that the DTR and DSR control lines have already been asserted to indicate that the DTE and DCE are both functioning. In preparation for data transmission, the DTE makes RTS active. The DCE responds by placing a carrier on the line and delaying for a short time (perhaps 250 ms) to allow the DCE on the other end of the telephone line time to lock onto the carrier. (No check is made to ensure that the other DCE actually *does* lock onto the carrier.) Then the DCE makes CTS active, which completes the handshake and gives the DTE permission to send data.

When the transmission is complete, the DTE returns RTS to the inactive state. The DCE responds by removing the carrier from the telephone line and returning CTS to its inactive state.

**FIGURE 6-10**

Before sending a message (1) the DTE makes RTS active, (2) the DCE responds by outputting a carrier onto the telephone line, and (3) the DCE makes CTS active.

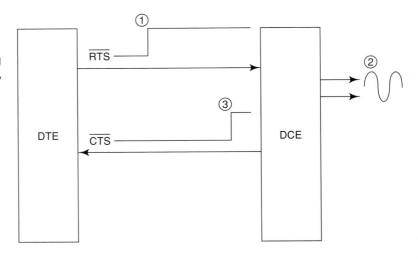

Two of the control lines, the signal quality detector (SQ or CG) and the data signal rate selector (CH/CI) are rarely used. The SQ circuit was designed to allow the DCE to notify the DTE when there is a high probability of an error in the received data caused by poor quality reception of the analog signal from the telephone line. An "on" condition indicates that the received signal quality is good and that there is a low probability of errors. An "off" condition indicates that the received signal quality is poor and that there is a high probability of errors in the received data caused by poor quality reception.

The data signal rate selector is used in synchronous communications systems that are capable of transmitting and receiving at two different speeds. When the line is in the "on" condition, the higher of the two rates is selected. When it is in the "off" condition, the lower rate is selected. The circuit can be set up to allow either the DTE or the DCE to be in control. If the DTE is in control, the circuit is designated CH, and if the DCE is in control, it is designated CI.

In a typical application, most of the RS-232 control circuits are not used. The three most commonly used control circuits are RTS, CTS, and DCD. The least used control circuits are SQ and CH/CI.

## Timing Circuits

The RS-232 interface has three timing circuits that can be used to carry clock signals between the DTE and DCE. Two of the circuits are for the transmit clock (one circuit in each direction) and one of the circuits is for the receive clock.

Both of the transmit clock circuits have been given the name *transmitter signal element timing,* although they are more commonly known as the *transmit clock (TC)* circuits. Circuit DA is used in those rare cases in which the transmit clock oscillator is located in the DTE, and it carries the transmit clock signal from the DTE to the DCE. It is much more common for the transmit clock oscillator to be located in the DCE, in which case circuit DB is used to communicate the clock signal to the DTE.

As you will see when you read the chapters on modems, the DCE can recover a clock signal from the received data stream. Circuit DD, known as the *receiver signal element timing* or more simply as the *receive clock (RC),* can be used to communicate this recovered clock signal from the DCE to the DTE.

## Secondary Circuits

Some DCEs have a low-speed **reverse channel** that is used to carry signaling information from the receiving modem back to the transmitting modem. The reverse channel is also called the **backward channel** or the **supervisory channel.** The reverse channel operates at low speed, in the opposite direction from that in which data is being sent. Its purpose is to allow the receiving terminal to communicate control codes (also known as *supervisory signals*) to the transmitting terminal. A control code might request the sending terminal to retransmit a block of data when a parity error has occurred.

The secondary circuits in the RS-232 interface support the reverse channel and include secondary transmitted data (SBA), secondary received data (SBB), secondary request to send (SCA), secondary clear to send (SCB), and secondary data carrier detect (SCF). The secondary circuits perform the same functions for the reverse channel that their primary counterparts perform for the main communications channel.

### 6-2-4 RS-232 in the Real World

The main disadvantage of the RS-232 interface is that the engineer or technician cannot connect two pieces of equipment with RS-232 ports and assume that they will work. There are too many variations of the interface. Not all equipment uses the same control lines. If the two pieces of equipment are something other than a terminal and a modem, the engineer or technician must decide which of them functions as the DTE and which functions as the DCE. A rule of thumb is, if it outputs data on the transmit data line, it is a DTE. If it outputs data on the received data line, it is a DCE.

Sometimes both pieces of equipment function as DTEs as is the case when data are transferred from the serial port of one computer to the serial port of a second computer. If two pieces of equipment that function as DTEs are connected using a standard RS-232 interface cable, both of them output data on the transmitted data line, and both of them attempt to input data on the received data line. The result of such a connection is that no communication will take place.

A **null modem cable** is used to interface two DTEs. Certain pairs of conductors are swapped in the cable to "fool" each DTE into behaving as if it were communicating with a DCE as is illustrated in Figure 6-11. For example, the transmitted and received data lines are crossed so that when one DTE outputs data on its TD line, those data are input on the RD line of the other DTE. Control signals are also rewired to function properly. When one DTE outputs a DTR signal, that signal is received as a DSR by the other DTE. When one DTE outputs an RTS, that signal is looped back to the same DTE's CTS line, and the DTE behaves as if it had received the proper handshake response. The second DTE receives the signal on its RTS line.

Although RS-232 continues to be the most popular serial interface standard, RS-232's 20,000 b/s limit on data transfer is too slow for many applications. RS-232 also requires two power supplies to provide its positive and negative voltages, whereas most equipment manufacturers would prefer to use a single power supply. Although the 50-ft limit to the length of RS-232 cables can be extended by using low capacitance cables or lower data speeds, there is a need for an interface that will carry data at higher speeds over longer distances. RS-232 is also criticized for being too complicated. Many of its circuits are seldom used. Some, but not all, of the disadvantages of RS-232 have been addressed in the development of a newer family of serial interface standards, RS-449.

### 6-3 THE RS-449 FAMILY OF INTERFACES

The RS-449 interface standard was published by the EIA in November of 1977. **RS-449** specifies the functional circuits and mechanical interface between a DTE and a

**FIGURE 6-11**
A null modem cable allows two DTEs to be interfaced by means of their RS-232 ports.

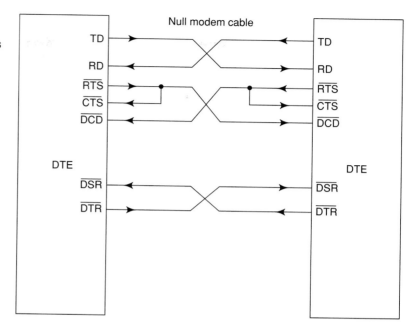

DCE. The electrical interface is specified in separate standards such as **RS-422** and **RS-423.** RS-449 specifies a DB-37 connector (D-type connector with 37 pins) for the primary channel. The reverse channel, if implemented, uses a separate DB-9 connector.

Figure 6-12 lists the circuits of the RS-449 interface. RS-449 is designed to be compatible with and to replace RS-232, so most of the RS-232 circuits are present in RS-449. The circuit names have been changed slightly. For example, transmitted data and received data have been renamed *send data* and *receive data,* and data terminal ready has been renamed *terminal ready.*

The confusing RS-232 system of classifying circuits A, B, C, and so on has been eliminated in the RS-449 standard. RS-449 primary channel circuit abbreviations are two-letter mnemonics, and the secondary channel circuit abbreviations are two-letter or three-letter mnemonics.

A big change from RS-232 to RS-449 is that more return signal paths have been added. In RS-232, all data and signal levels are referenced to signal ground. The RS-449 not only has a signal ground (pin 19), but it also has a receive common (pin 20) and send common (pin 37). The secondary channel connector has its own signal ground (pin 5), receive common (pin 6), and send common (pin 9) circuits. RS-449 also makes available a separate return signal path for each of the high-speed circuits (pin numbers 22 through 27, 29 through 31, and 35). These return circuits are used with the RS-422 electrical specification to allow their associated circuits to operate at higher speeds and be less sensitive to noise. RS-423 does not use the return circuits and references digital signal levels to the common circuits.

**FIGURE 6-12**

RS-449 circuits.

## Primary Channel Connector

| Pin | Function | Abbreviation | Direction | RS-232 Equivalent Function |
|-----|----------|--------------|-----------|----------------------------|
| 1 | Shield | — | — | Frame ground |
| 2 | Signaling rate indicator | SI | DTE to DCE | Data signal rate selector |
| 3 | Unused | | | |
| 4 | Send data | SD | DTE to DCE | Transmitted data |
| 5 | Send timing | ST | DCE to DTE | Transmit clock (DCE source) |
| 6 | Receive data | RD | DCE to DTE | Received data |
| 7 | Request to send | RS | DTE to DCE | Request to send |
| 8 | Receive timing | RT | DCE to DTE | Receive clock |
| 9 | Clear to send | CS | DCE to DTE | Clear to send |
| 10 | Local loopback | LL | — | None |
| 11 | Data mode | DM | DCE to DTE | Data set ready |
| 12 | Terminal ready | TR | DTE to DCE | Data terminal ready |
| 13 | Receiver ready | RR | DCE to DTE | Data carrier detect |
| 14 | Remote loopback | RL | DTE to DCE | None |
| 15 | Incoming call | IC | DCE to DTE | Ring indicator |
| 16 | Select frequency | SF | DTE to DCE | Data signal rate selector |
|    | Signaling rate selector | SR | DCE to DTE | Data signal rate selector |
| 17 | Terminal timing | TT | DTE to DCE | Transmit clock (DTE source) |
| 18 | Test mode | TM | DCE to DTE | None |
| 19 | Signal ground | SG | — | Signal ground |
| 20 | Receive common | RC | DCE to DTE | None |
| 21 | Unused | | | |
| 22 | Send data return | SD | DTE to DCE | None |
| 23 | Send timing return | ST | DCE to DTE | None |
| 24 | Receive data return | RD | DCE to DTE | None |
| 25 | Request to send return | RS | DTE to DCE | None |
| 26 | Receive timing return | RT | DTE to DCE | None |
| 27 | Clear to send return | CS | DCE to DTE | None |
| 28 | Terminal in service | IS | DTE to DCE | None |
| 29 | Data mode return | DM | DCE to DTE | None |
| 30 | Terminal ready return | TR | DTE to DCE | None |
| 31 | Receiver ready return | RR | DCE to DTE | None |
| 32 | Select standby | SS | DTE to DCE | None |
| 33 | Signal quality | SQ | DCE to DTE | Signal quality detector |
| 34 | New signal | NS | DTE to DCE | None |
| 35 | Terminal timing return | TT | DTE to DCE | None |
| 36 | Standby indicator | SB | DCE to DTE | None |
| 37 | Send common | SC | DTE to DCE | Signal ground |

**FIGURE 6-12,** *continued*

**Secondary Channel Connector**

| Pin | Function | Abbreviation | Direction | RS-232 Equivalent Function |
|-----|----------|--------------|-----------|----------------------------|
| 1 | Shield | — | — | Frame ground |
| 2 | Secondary receiver ready | SRR | DCE to DTE | Secondary data carrier detect |
| 3 | Secondary send data | SDD | DTE to DCE | Secondary transmitted data |
| 4 | Secondary receive data | SRD | DCE to DTE | Secondary receive data |
| 5 | Signal ground | SG | — | Signal ground |
| 6 | Receive common | RC | DCE to DTE | Signal ground |
| 7 | Secondary request to send | SC | DCE to DTE | Secondary request to send |
| 8 | Secondary clear to send | SCS | DCE to DTE | Secondary clear to send |
| 9 | Send common | SC | DTE to DCE | Signal ground |

### 6-3-1 Balanced and Unbalanced Circuits

RS-422 is an electrical specification that allows communications speeds of up to 10 Mb/s at distances up to 40 ft (12 m) or communications at speeds of 100 kb/s at distances up to 4000 ft (1222 m). These high speeds are possible because RS-422 specifies balanced circuits. Figure 6-13 illustrates the difference between balanced and unbalanced circuits. As we know (but sometimes forget when we are working with digital), electrical signals require a closed circuit. For a signal current to flow through a conductor, there must be a return path to complete the circuit. Figure 6-13(a) shows that unbalanced interfaces such as RS-232 and RS-423 use a common signal ground conductor to complete the circuit, whereas in balanced interfaces, such as RS-422, each circuit has its own return path.

Unbalanced circuits are susceptible to two types of noise—voltage drops across the resistance in the common return path and stray signals induced in the conductors by magnetic and electrical fields. All electrical conductors have a certain

**FIGURE 6-13**
(a) Unbalanced interfaces reference all signals to a common ground. (b) Balanced interfaces use a separate return path for each signal.

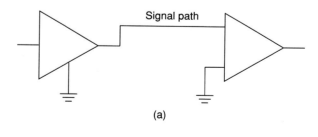

(a)

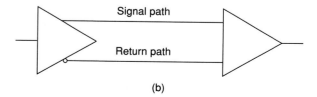

(b)

amount of resistance. Figure 6-14 illustrates the resistance in the common signal return path of three unbalanced circuits. Each of the currents that flows through the common return causes a voltage drop across the resistance. These voltage drops cause the voltage difference between the ground references at the DTE and DCE to vary and thereby couple signals from one circuit to another.

Figure 6-15 illustrates what happens when stray signals are induced into communications circuits by electric or magnetic fields. In the unbalanced circuit of Figure 6-15(a), noise induced in the circuit is not canceled. If the noise is strong enough, it can interfere with the digital information carried by the circuit. In the balanced circuit of Figure 6-15(b), the same noise signal is induced into both the signal path and the return path. This type of noise is called **common-mode noise.** The sense amplifier on the right of the diagram amplifies the differential voltage that appears across its inputs. Because the common-mode noise is the same on both inputs to the amplifier, it presents no differential voltage to the amplifier, and it is not amplified.

### 6-3-2  Category I and Category II Circuits

RS-449 circuits are divided into two classes—category I and category II. There are 10 category I circuits, which consist of the data circuits, the timing circuits, and 5 of the control circuits. Specifically, the category I circuits are send data (SD), receive data (RD), send timing (ST), receive timing (RT), terminal timing (TT), request to

**FIGURE 6-14**
When a single return path is used, the signals interfere with each other by causing different voltage drops across the resistance in the return path.

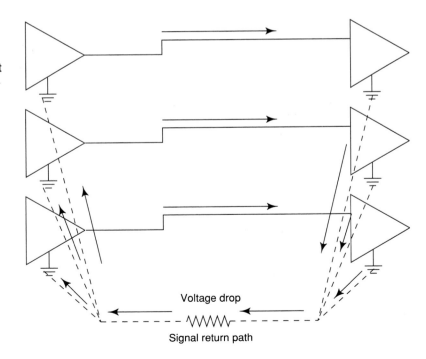

Voltage drop

Signal return path

**FIGURE 6-15**
(a) Induced signals in unbalanced circuits cause noise. (b) Induced signals in balanced signals are canceled.

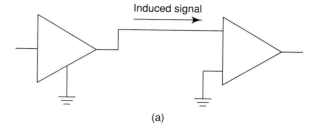

(a)

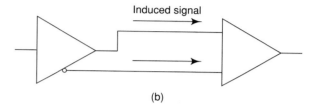

(b)

send (RS), clear to send (CS), receiver ready (RR), terminal ready (TR), and data mode (DM). Each of these category I circuits is assigned its own return path in the RS-449 interface. All other RS-449 circuits are category II.

Category I circuits may use either the RS-422 balanced or the RS-423 unbalanced electrical specification. Interfaces designed for slower speeds usually use the unbalanced RS-423 specification, whereas high-speed interfaces use the balanced RS-422 interface. Category II circuits always use RS-423. This means that RS-422 and RS-423 circuits may both be present in the same RS-449 cable.

## 6-3-3 RS-422 and RS-423 Voltage Levels

The RS-422 and RS-423 standards have been designed so that their assert and sense voltage levels overlap the range of voltages used by RS-232. RS-423 asserts a logic 1 or a mark by outputting any voltage between –3.6 V and –6 V. It asserts a logic 0 or a space by outputting any voltage between +3.6 V and +6 V. RS-422 asserts a logic 1 by outputting any voltage between –2 V and –6 V and asserts a space by outputting a voltage between +2 V and +6 V. Both RS-422 and RS-423 can sense a logic 1 at voltages more negative than –200 mV and a logic 0 at voltages more positive than +200 mV.

To smooth the transition from RS-232 to the newer standards, the EIA designed RS-423 to be compatible with RS-232. Both are unbalanced standards, and it is possible to connect an RS-232 port with an RS-423 port using a special cable. The RS-232 voltage levels are padded down to bring them within the sense voltage range of RS-423. RS-423 voltage levels can be directly sensed by RS-232. RS-422 ports cannot be connected to RS-232 ports.

### 6-3-4 **Advantages and Disadvantages of RS-449**

The main advantage of the RS-449 mechanical interface and the RS-422 and RS-423 electrical interfaces are that they permit higher communications speeds over longer distances. Another advantage, not previously mentioned, is that both RS-422 and RS-423 permit up to 10 receivers to be installed in each circuit. RS-232 permits only one receiver.

However, the new standards have been slow to be accepted by the industry, and most serial communications ports continue to use some variation of the RS-232 standard. If RS-232 is unnecessarily complicated for most applications, then RS-449 is even more so. The RS-449 connector is expensive, and very few applications need all of its capabilities. RS-232 continues to be the serial port of choice.

### ■ SUMMARY

This chapter has discussed several common serial interfaces that are used to communicate data between pieces of equipment located relatively short distances apart, generally in the same room with each other. A number of standards have evolved to make it easier to connect equipment from different manufacturers, However, each of the standards discussed in this chapter is often modified in practice, so there is no guarantee that two pieces of equipment which are said to use a given interface standard can in fact communicate with each other.

For two pieces of equipment to communicate, their interfaces must have three levels of compatibility: mechanical, electrical, and protocol. Mechanical compatibility means that both devices use the same types of pins, plugs, sockets, and cables. Electrical compatibility means that they must both use the same system of electrical signals. Protocol compatibility means that both devices must use the same system of rules for communication. The standards discussed in this chapter specify the electrical interface and all or some of the mechanical interface, but they do not resolve the protocol issue.

Current loops use a constant current flow to represent a mark and no current flow to represent a space. The most common current loop is the 20-mA loop. The most common serial interface is RS-232, which uses a negative voltage to represent a mark and a positive voltage to represent a space. In addition to circuits for carrying data in each direction, RS-232 includes numerous control and timing circuits.

The RS-449 mechanical interface and the RS-422 and RS-423 electrical interfaces were designed to replace RS-232. RS-422 is a balanced interface, which is designed for high-speed data transfers. RS-423 is an unbalanced interface that is compatible with RS-232.

### ■ QUESTIONS

1. What is the name given to a signal that consists of unmodulated information?
2. What is a communications port?

3. How is the word *interface* defined in this chapter?

4. At what three levels must the communications ports of two pieces of equipment be compatible for communication to take place between them?

5. a. What does the word *protocol* mean when it is applied to data communications?

   b. Name three things that are stipulated by the rules of a data communications protocol?

6. a. What is the most common current loop interface?

   b. How does this interface represent a mark?

   c. How does this interface represent a space?

7. List three advantages that current loop interfaces have compared with interfaces that use voltage signals?

8. What is an optocoupler?

9. Can *any* two pieces of equipment that use 20-mA loops be interfaced with each other? Give reasons for your answer.

10. What organization published the RS-232 interface standard?

11. In the designation RS-232-C:

    a. what do the letters *RS* stand for?

    b. what does the number *232* stand for?

    c. what does the letter *C* stand for?

12. a. Why have so many variations of RS-232 evolved?

    b. If there are so many variations of RS-232, what is the purpose of studying the standard?

13. a. What is the main purpose of the DTE in a communications system?

    b. What is the main purpose of the DCE in a communications system?

14. a. What do we mean when we say that a communications port *asserts* a logic signal?

    b. What do we mean when we say that a logic signal *senses* a logic signal?

15. a. What range of voltage levels may an RS-232 port use to assert a logic 1?

    b. What range of voltage levels may it use to assert a logic 0?

16. a. What range of voltage levels must an RS-232 port sense as a logic 1?

    b. What range of voltage levels must it sense as a logic 0?

17. a. What logic level (1 or 0) is used to assert an RS-232 control line?

    b. What voltage level (positive or negative) do control lines have on them when they are asserted?

18. Name the five groups into which the RS-232 circuits are divided.

19. a. In which direction does the RS-232 TD line carry data? (DTE to DCE or DCE to DTE?)

  b.  In which direction does the RS-232 RD line carry data?

20. What is the Telco name for a modem?

21. Name the five groups into which RS-232 circuits are divided.

22. What is the full name and the purpose of each of the following RS-232 control lines?

  a. DSR    d. DCD

  b. DTR    e. RTS

  c. RI    f. CTS

23. What is another name for the data carrier detect line?

24. a.  What is the meaning of the term *handshaking?*

  b.  Briefly describe the RTS/CTS handshaking sequence.

25. Which three RS-232 control signals are the most commonly used?

26. a.  What are two other names for *reverse channel?*

  b.  What is the purpose of a *reverse channel* in a communications link?

27. Why can the engineer or technician not connect two pieces of equipment with RS-232 ports and assume that they will work?

28. What is the purpose of a null modem cable?

29. List three disadvantages of the RS-232 interface that make it less than ideal as a serial interface.

30. a.  Which standard discussed in Section 6-3 describes the *mechanical* interface between a DTE and a DCE?

  b.  Which two separate standards describe the *electrical* interface?

31. a.  What is the maximum communications speed of an RS-422 interface that is 40 ft long?

  b.  What is the maximum communications speed if the interface is 4000 ft long?

32. a.  Why are balanced circuits less susceptible to noise pickup than are balanced circuits?

  b.  Are RS-422 circuits balanced, or are they unbalanced?

  c.  Are RS-423 circuits balanced, or are they unbalanced?

33. a.  Which RS-449 circuits (category I or category II) can be either RS-422 or RS-423?

  b.  Which circuits are always RS-423?

34. a.  What range of voltages may be *asserted* by RS-423 circuits to output a logic 1?

  b.  What range of voltages may be *asserted* by RS-423 circuits to output a logic 0?

35. a.  What range of voltages may be *asserted* by RS-422 circuits to output a logic 1?

 b. What range of voltages may be *asserted* by RS-422 circuits to output a logic 0?

36. a. What is the minimum voltage *sensed* by both RS-422 and RS-423 as a logic 1?

 b. What is the minimum voltage *sensed* by both RS-422 and RS-423 as a logic 0?

37. a. What are two advantages of the RS-449 family of interfaces compared with RS-232?

 b. Despite those advantages, why does RS-232 continue to be more widely used than RS-449?

# Chapter 7

# PARALLEL INTERFACES

**OBJECTIVES**

After you have completed this chapter, you should be able to:

- List the two advantages of parallel interfaces over serial interfaces for short-distance communications.

- Name the three types of circuits (lines) used in the Centronics interface and the function of each.

- Describe the handshaking sequence that takes place each time a byte of data is transferred from the computer to the printer by means of the Centronics interface.

- Describe the function of the controller, the talker, and the listeners in the IEEE 488 interface.

- Name the two IEEE 488 operating modes and briefly describe the purpose of each mode.

- Name the three types of circuits in the IEEE 488 interfaces and briefly describe the purpose of each type.

- Describe the handshake sequence that takes place each time a byte of data is transferred from the talker to the listeners over the IEEE 488 interface.

## INTRODUCTION

Chapter 6 discussed serial interfaces that communicate data one bit at a time. This chapter deals with parallel interfaces, which generally transfer at least 8 bits at a time. Parallel interfaces are commonly used to transfer data between two or more devices located in the same room. Special control signals, sometimes called handshaking signals, coordinate the transfer of data over a parallel interface. Each time a byte of data is sent over the interface, the sending device outputs a control signal to inform the receiving device that the data are available. The receiving device sends a handshake response back to the transmitting device when it is ready for another byte of data.

Parallel interfaces have two advantages over serial transfer for short-distance communications. First, most terminals process data in parallel form. It is simpler to leave the data in parallel form than to convert them from parallel to serial at the sending terminal and later from serial back to parallel at the receiving terminal. Second, because parallel interfaces transfer several data bits simultaneously, they work more rapidly than comparable serial interfaces.

## 7-1 THE CENTRONICS PARALLEL INTERFACE

The **Centronics parallel interface** was designed to communicate data from a microcomputer to a printer. Centronics was one of the first companies to design printers specifically for use with desktop personal computers. Earlier printers used 20-mA loops or RS-232 serial interfaces. Centronics simplified the interface by having its printers accept data in the format used by personal computers—8-bit parallel with TTL logic levels. Manufacturers of desktop computers began to add a Centronics-compatible parallel port to their machines to accommodate the printers. Other printer manufacturers adopted the Centronics interface, and it became a de facto standard. Today the Centronics interface is the most-used parallel standard for interfacing personal computers to printers and other peripheral devices.

If you read the interfacing section of manuals of printers made by different manufacturers (and I suggest that you do), you will find slight variations in the names of some of the control lines and in the minimum timing of some of the control signals. However, the interface is standard enough that almost any printer with a Centronics port can be connected to almost any computer that also has a Centronics port.

Figure 7-1 shows the connector used on a Centronics-compatible printer. It is a 36-pin Amphenol 57-30360 connector or its equivalent, also called a **champ connec-**

**FIGURE 7-1**
36-pin Centronics interface printer connector.

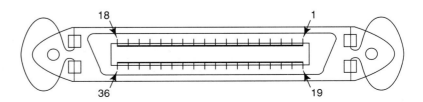

**tor.** Some of the pins are not assigned in the Centronics specification. Unassigned pins are available to carry special-purpose signals that are used by some computer and printer manufacturers.

If the printer is interfaced to an IBM-compatible personal computer, the Centronics interface has a DB-25 connector at its computer end. Because a DB-25 connector has 11 fewer pins than the Amphenol connector, some of Centronics interface lines must be left out. We will discuss the DB-25 connector pin assignments shortly. First we will look at the complete Centronics interface.

Figure 7-2 lists the Centronics printer interface lines and the pins to which they are connected on the Amphenol connector. The lines can be divided into three

**FIGURE 7-2**
The Centronics printer interface lines.

| Pin Number | Return Pin | Signal | Abbreviation | Active | Type | Direction |
|---|---|---|---|---|---|---|
| 1 | 19 | Strobe | $\overline{STB}$ | Low | Control | To printer |
| 2 | 20 | Data bit 0 | d0 | | Data | To printer |
| 3 | 21 | Data bit 1 | d1 | | Data | To printer |
| 4 | 22 | Data bit 2 | d2 | | Data | To printer |
| 5 | 23 | Data bit 3 | d3 | | Data | To printer |
| 6 | 24 | Data bit 4 | d4 | | Data | To printer |
| 7 | 25 | Data bit 5 | d5 | | Data | To printer |
| 8 | 26 | Data bit 6 | d6 | | Data | To printer |
| 9 | 27 | Data bit 7 | d7 | | Data | To printer |
| 10 | 28 | Acknowledge | $\overline{ACK}$ | Low | Status | To computer |
| 11 | 29 | Busy | BUSY | High | Status | To computer |
| 12 | | Paper out | PO | High | Status | To computer |
| 13 | | Select | SLCT | High | Status | To computer |
| 14 | | Auto feed | $\overline{AF}$ | Low | Control | To printer |
| 15 | | Unused | — | — | — | — |
| 16 | | Signal ground | SG | — | — | — |
| 17 | | Frame ground | FG | — | — | — |
| 18 | | +5 V | — | — | — | — |
| 31 | 30 | Prime | $\overline{PRIME}$ | Low | Control | To printer |
| 32 | | Error | $\overline{ERROR}$ | Low | Status | To computer |
| 33 | | Signal ground | SG | — | — | — |
| 34 | | Unused | — | — | — | — |
| 35 | | Unused | — | — | — | — |
| 36 | | Select in | $\overline{SLCTIN}$ | Low | Control | To printer |

**FIGURE 7-3**
In addition to the data lines, the Centronics interface has three control lines and five status lines.

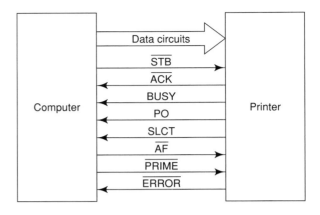

groups: data, control, and status. All of the data lines and several of the control and status lines have individual returns. There are also several ground lines and one line that carries +5 V. Figure 7-3 shows how the data, control, and status lines of the Centronics interface connect between the computer and the printer.

### 7-1-1  The Data Lines

The Centronics interface uses 8 parallel data circuits, pins 2 through 9. In Figure 7-2, the data bits are numbered d0 through d7, but they may be numbered d1 through d8 in some printer manuals. D0 (or d1) is the least significant bit. Each of the data lines has a dedicated return circuit. The data circuits operate in only one direction and carry the information to be printed from the computer to the printer.

When text is printed, each character is sent to the printer in the form of a 7-bit ASCII character, sometimes with an 8th parity bit, or more frequently in the newer personal computers, in the form of an 8-bit extended ASCII character.

### 7-1-2  The Control Lines

The Centronics interface has four control circuits, which the computer uses to control the operation of the printer. The *strobe* ($\overline{STB}$) line is active low. The computer outputs a negative pulse on $\overline{STB}$ to direct the printer to accept the data from the interface's data lines. $\overline{STB}$ is discussed in more detail in Section 7-1-5 on handshaking.

The *auto feed* ($\overline{AF}$) control line determines whether or not the printer automatically performs a line feed when it receives a carriage return signal. In the ASCII code, carriage return and line feed are separate characters ($0D and $0A respectively). The carriage return character causes the print head to return to the left side of the paper, and the line feed causes the paper to advance to the next line. Normally, the computer sends both characters to the printer at the end of each line of text. Some software may send a carriage return only. If the computer holds $\overline{AF}$ low, the printer responds to the carriage return character by performing both a carriage return and a line feed.

Most modern printers are programmable devices that contain memory. They can be programmed to print a variety of fonts and different numbers of characters per inch. They also have a memory buffer that can hold at least a full line of text before printing it. When the computer makes the $\overline{\text{PRIME}}$ (some printer manufacturers call it the *initialize* line) control line low, the printer clears its memory including the printer programming and the print buffer. The printer returns to the condition it was in when it was turned on. One use of the $\overline{\text{PRIME}}$ control line is to abort a print job in progress.

A fourth control line, called select in ($\overline{\text{SLCTIN}}$), is part of the Centronics interface, but it is seldom used. The computer must make the $\overline{\text{SLCTIN}}$ control line low so that the printer will accept data from the computer. Some printers have an internal switch that can be set to permanently ground the $\overline{\text{SLCTIN}}$ line.

### 7-1-3  The Status Lines

The status lines tell the computer what the printer is doing. All of the status lines carry signals from the printer to the computer. The *acknowledge* ($\overline{\text{ACK}}$) status line is an active-low handshake response to $\overline{\text{STB}}$. The printer pulses $\overline{\text{ACK}}$ low to signal the computer that it has processed a byte of data that it received by way of the interface and that it is ready for another. The $\overline{\text{ACK}}$ signal is discussed further in Section 7-1-5 on handshaking.

The *BUSY* status line is an active-high signal. It is normally in the low state, and it goes high anytime the printer is busy and therefore unable to accept data from the computer. Four conditions can cause the printer to indicate that it is busy:

1.  When the printer is inputting data from the data lines or when the printer's data buffer is full and unable to accept more data.
2.  When the printer is printing or otherwise processing data.
3.  When the printer is turned off or is *off line.* Most printers have an off-line switch that disables their ability to accept and print data. The operator can switch the printer off line to replace the paper supply, change the ribbon, or clear a jammed printer. Most printers automatically go on line when they are turned on. The printer also goes on line when it receives a $\overline{\text{PRIME}}$ control signal or when it is manually switched on line by the operator. The printer goes off line when it is manually switched off line or when it is out of paper.
4.  When the printer's $\overline{\text{ERROR}}$ line is low.

The BUSY signal is further discussed in Section 7-1-5 on handshaking.

The *paper out* (PO) line is normally in the low state and goes high when the printer is out of paper. Any time the printer makes the PO line high, it also makes the $\overline{\text{ERROR}}$ status line active.

*Select* (SLCT) is an active-high status line that indicates whether the printer is selected (on line). It is high when the printer is on line, and it is low when the printer is off line.

The $\overline{\text{ERROR}}$ status line is active low and indicates that there is some difficulty with the printer. It is high during normal operation. The following conditions can cause $\overline{\text{ERROR}}$ to go low:

1. The printer is off line.
2. The printer is out of paper.
3. Some other error condition in the printer prevents it from operating normally.

### 7-1-4 Miscellaneous Lines

Pins 20 through 27 are the return signal lines for data pins d0 through d7 respectively. Pin 19 is the return signal path for $\overline{\text{STB}}$, and pins 28, 29, and 30 are the return lines for $\overline{\text{ACK}}$, BUSY, and $\overline{\text{PRIME}}$. Pins 16 and 33 are signal ground (SG) lines and serve as a common return path for those signals that do not have their own returns. Pin 17 is frame ground (FG). FG electrically connects the chassis of the computer and the printer so that they are at the same potential and do not constitute a shock hazard. Pin 18 supplies a +5 V-V signal from the computer to the printer. This +5 V is sufficient to power the printer's status circuits (BUSY, for example) when the printer is turned off, but it is not designed to power the printer's operation. Pin 18 is not used in most applications.

### 7-1-5 Handshaking

Figure 7-4 is a timing diagram of the handshaking signals that the computer and the printer exchange each time the computer sends a byte of data to the printer. The computer outputs data to the printer only when the printer's BUSY status line is low as it is at t1 in the figure. After the computer outputs the data on the data circuits, it delays 1 $\mu$s to give the electrical signals on the data circuits time to stabilize. Then it outputs a negative pulse on the $\overline{\text{STB}}$ line (t2) to tell the printer that the data are available.

The $\overline{\text{STB}}$ pulse width is at least 1 $\mu$s in duration. After the end of the $\overline{\text{STB}}$ pulse (t4), the computer must hold the data on the data lines for at least one additional microsecond to give the printer time to accept the data. The computer removes the data from the data lines at t5.

**FIGURE 7-4**
The exchange of signals between the computer and the printer over the Centronics parallel interface.

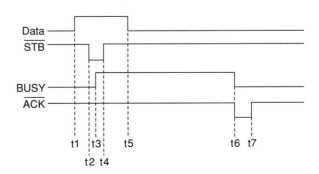

The printer responds to $\overline{STB}$ by making BUSY high (t3). The printer then processes the byte of data by printing it or by placing it in an internal buffer. When the printer is again ready to accept data, it returns the BUSY line to its low state (t6) and also outputs a negative pulse on the $\overline{ACK}$ line. The width of the $\overline{ACK}$ pulse (t6 to t7) may be up to 5 $\mu$s. The low level of the BUSY status line and the negative pulse on $\overline{ACK}$ tell the computer that the printer is ready for the next byte of data. The handshake sequence repeats until the computer has output all the data to be printed.

### 7-1-6 Connecting Centronics to the Computer

Although the Centronics interface is designed to use a 36-pin connector, when IBM designed the first personal computer, it decided to use a DB-25 connector for the printer port. That meant that 11 pins of the Centronics interface had to be left out. Other IBM-compatible personal computer manufacturers continue to follow the original IBM printer port standard. Today, a standard printer cable for a personal computer uses a 36-pin Amphenol connector on the printer end of the cable and a DB-25 connector on the computer end.

Figure 7-5 shows the pin assignments on both the Amphenol and the DB-25 connector. The unused Centronics circuits and the +5 V supply are not connected. Some of the return signal paths (grounds) are also not used. For example, signal ground and frame ground are not connected to the DB-25 connector. Of the eight individual return signal paths for the data bits, only four are connected to the DB-25 connector. The acknowledge return path is also not connected. Because printers are relatively slow mechanical devices, even with some of its ground paths removed, the personal computer version of the Centronics interface is more than adequate for sending data to a printer.

### 7-1-7 Advantages and Disadvantages of the Centronics Interface

The Centronics interface has at least three advantages. It is an inexpensive method of connecting a small computer to a printer. It uses the same TTL logic levels that most computers use, so it does not require additional power supplies. The system of control and status lines is fairly simple and easy to deal with.

A disadvantage of the Centronics interface is that it is slower than many other parallel interfaces. However, as mentioned above, its speed is more than adequate for most printers, which are slow, mechanical devices.

## 7-2 THE IEEE 488 PARALLEL INTERFACE

The **IEEE 488 interface** is a parallel interface that is designed to connect communications and computer equipment to test and measurement devices such as signal generators, voltmeters, and frequency counters. The IEEE 488 interface is also known as the **General Purpose Interface Bus (GPIB)** and the **Hewlett-Packard Interface Bus (HP-IB),** in honor of the company that developed the standard.

**FIGURE 7-5**

Connecting a Centronics cable to a DB-25 connector.

| Amphenol Connector | Signal | DB-25 Connector |
|---|---|---|
| 1 | Strobe | 1 |
| 2 | Data bit 0 | 2 |
| 3 | Data bit 1 | 3 |
| 4 | Data bit 2 | 4 |
| 5 | Data bit 3 | 5 |
| 6 | Data bit 4 | 6 |
| 7 | Data bit 5 | 7 |
| 8 | Data bit 6 | 8 |
| 9 | Data bit 7 | 9 |
| 10 | Acknowledge | 10 |
| 11 | Busy | 11 |
| 12 | Paper out | 12 |
| 13 | Select | 13 |
| 14 | Auto feed | 14 |
| 15 | Unused | Not connected |
| 16 | Signal ground | Not connected |
| 17 | Frame ground | Not connected |
| 18 | +5 V | Not connected |
| 19 | Strobe return | 19 |
| 20 | Data bit 0 return | Not connected |
| 21 | Data bit 1 return | 20 |
| 22 | Data bit 2 return | Not connected |
| 23 | Data bit 3 return | 21 |
| 24 | Data bit 4 return | Not connected |
| 25 | Data bit 5 return | 22 |
| 26 | Data bit 6 return | Not connected |
| 27 | Data bit 7 return | 23 |
| 28 | Acknowledge return | Not connected |
| 29 | Busy return | 24 |
| 30 | Prime return | 25 |
| 31 | Prime | 16 |
| 32 | Error | 15 |
| 33 | Signal ground | 18 |
| 34 | Unused | Not connected |
| 35 | Unused | Not connected |
| 36 | Select in | 17 |

First published as a standard in April 1975, the original version of IEEE 488 specified the electrical and mechanical portions of the interface, but it did not cover the protocol. The standard was slightly revised in November 1978. In June 1987 it was renamed IEEE 488.1, and at the same time a second standard was published, IEEE 488.2. IEEE 488.2 specifies a set of codes, formats, protocols, and commands to be used with the interface. However, the original standard is still generally referred to as IEEE 488, and that is the name we shall use for it in this book.

### 7-2-1  Overview of IEEE 488

The IEEE 488 bus has 8 parallel bi-directional data lines, and it can connect up to 15 devices. The maximum allowable distance between two adjacent devices is 2 m (about 6.5 ft), and the maximum total length of the bus is 20 m (about 65.5 ft). The various pieces of equipment that it interfaces are often located in the same or adjoining equipment racks. A cable with a 24-pin ribbon connector at each end connects adjacent pieces of equipment. These characteristics are summarized in Figure 7-6.

Equipment connected to the interface's data bus may use either open-collector or tristate drivers. When open-collector drivers are used, the maximum bus speed is 250,000 bytes per second. If tristate drivers are used, the maximum speed is increased to 1 million bytes per second. Because a byte is 8 bits, that amounts to 8 million bits per second, which makes the IEEE 488 bus the fastest interface discussed so far in this book. The IEEE 488 bus uses standard TTL logic levels.

### 7-2-2  The Talker, the Listeners, and the Controller

Hewlett-Packard's tutorial on the IEEE 488 bus likens the bus to the operation of a committee in which the chairman decides who talks and who listens. In a well-run committee meeting, only one person talks at a time while the other members listen. The chairman can relinquish control of the committee to another member, who then becomes the new chairman. The "chairman" of the IEEE 488 is the *controller*. The controller can select one device to send data over the bus. The device selected to

**FIGURE 7-6**
A summary of IEEE 488 bus characteristics.

| Logic levels | TTL |
|---|---|
| Data lines | 8, bi-directional |
| Maximum number of devices | 15 |
| Distance between adjacent devices | 2 m maximum |
| Maximum total length | 20 m |
| Connector | 24-pin ribbon |
| Maximum speed with open-collector drivers | 250 kilobytes per second |
| Maximum speed with tristate drivers | 1 megabyte per second |

**FIGURE 7-7**
The four types of IEEE 488 devices.

| Controller | In charge of bus. Specifies which devices are programmed as the talker, as listeners, or are in the standby mode. There can be only one controller at a time. |
|---|---|
| Talker | Sends data over the bus to the listeners. There can be only one talker at a time. |
| Listeners | Receive data from the talker. There can be many listeners. |
| Standby | All devices that are not programmed as a controller, talker, or listener are in the standby mode. |

send data is called a **talker.** There can be only one talker at any given time. A number of devices, called **listeners,** can be selected to receive the data. Devices that are not programmed as the talker, the controller, or listeners are placed in a *standby mode.* The characteristics of the four types of devices are summarized in Figure 7-7.

Like the committee chairman, the controller can change the function of the devices under its supervision. The talker can be reprogrammed to become a listener, and another device can be reprogrammed to be the new talker. The controller can even relinquish control of the bus to another device, in which case that device becomes the new controller, and the former controller becomes the talker, a listener, or is placed in the standby mode.

### 7-2-3 Operating Modes

The IEEE 488 interface has two modes of operation: *command* and *data.* The controller uses the attention ($\overline{\text{ATN}}$) bus management control line to switch the interface between the two modes. When the controller asserts $\overline{\text{ATN}}$ by pulling it low, all devices connected to the interface switch into the command mode. When the controller makes $\overline{\text{ATN}}$ high, all devices switch to the data mode.

In the command mode, the controller can program the other devices connected to the interface. For example, the controller could use the command mode to program the frequency of a frequency generator or the voltage range for a digital voltmeter, or the controller could program a device to operate as either the talker or a listener. Each device connected to the bus has an address, which a technician can set by means of dip switches or jumpers. In the command mode, the controller directs commands to a specific device by first sending its address over the data bus. When the interface is in the command mode, all information that passes over the data bus is either commands or addresses. In the data mode, the only information that passes over the data bus is data that are sent from the talker to the listeners.

### 7-2-4 The IEEE 488 Interface Lines

Figure 7-8 is a list of the circuits that make up the IEEE 488 interface. The circuits may be divided into three groups: data circuits, handshake circuits (sometimes called *byte transfer lines*), and interface management circuits.

**FIGURE 7-8**
Pin assignment of the IEE 488 interface.

| Pin | Line Name | Abbreviation | Type |
|-----|-----------|--------------|------|
| 1 | Data bit 1 (LSB) | DI01 | Data |
| 2 | Data bit 2 | DI02 | Data |
| 3 | Data bit 3 | DI03 | Data |
| 4 | Data bit 4 | DI04 | Data |
| 5 | End or identify | $\overline{EOI}$ | Interface mgt. |
| 6 | Data available | $\overline{DAV}$ | Handshake |
| 7 | Not ready for data | $\overline{NRFD}$ | Handshake |
| 8 | Not data accepted | $\overline{NDAC}$ | Handshake |
| 9 | Interface clear | $\overline{IFC}$ | Interface mgt. |
| 10 | Service request | $\overline{SRQ}$ | Interface mgt. |
| 11 | Attention | $\overline{ATN}$ | Interface mgt. |
| 12 | Shield (earth ground) | | |
| 13 | Data bit 5 | DI05 | Data |
| 14 | Data bit 6 | DI06 | Data |
| 15 | Data bit 7 | DI07 | Data |
| 16 | Data bit 8 (MSB) | DI08 | Data |
| 17 | Remote enable | $\overline{REN}$ | Interface mgt. |
| 18 | Ground return for DAV | | |
| 19 | Ground return for NRFD | | |
| 20 | Ground return for NDAC | | |
| 21 | Ground return for IFC | | |
| 22 | Ground return for SRQ | | |
| 23 | Ground return for ATN | | |
| 24 | Signal ground | | |

## Data Circuits

The 8 data circuits are numbered DI01 through DI08. DI08 is the most significant bit. The purpose of the data circuits is to carry 8-bit parallel data from the talker to the listeners or to carry addresses and commands from the controller to the other devices connected to the interface. The data circuits are bi-directional.

## Handshake Circuits

The IEEE 488 bus has three handshake circuits: not ready for data ($\overline{NRFD}$), data not accepted ($\overline{NDAC}$), and data valid ($\overline{DAV}$). These handshake circuits coordinate the transfer of data from the talker to the listener. $\overline{NRFD}$ is an active-low control line that is asserted by a listener when it is not ready to accept data from the data lines. The $\overline{NRFD}$ output pins of the devices are wire-ORed together so that any listener connected to the bus can pull the $\overline{NRFD}$ line low. If there is more than one listener, the wired-OR configuration also ensures that the $\overline{\text{NRFD}}$ line will remain low as long as the slowest listener is not ready to accept data.

Not data accepted ($\overline{\text{NDAC}}$) is another active-low line that is controlled by the listener or listeners. It signals the talker that the listeners have not yet accepted data and that the talker should continue to hold the data on the bus. Like $\overline{\text{NRFD}}$, $\overline{\text{NDAC}}$ is wire-ORed to all of the devices on the interface so that any listener can hold it low. $\overline{\text{NDAC}}$ is not released until the slowest listener has accepted the data from the interface bus.

Data available ($\overline{\text{DAV}}$) is an active-low control line that is used by the talker in the data mode or by the controller in the command mode to signal the other devices on the bus that there is a data byte, address, or command available on the data bus.

Figure 7-9 illustrates the sequence of handshake signals that is exchanged each time a byte of data is sent from the talker to one or more listeners. The steps in the handshake sequence are as follows:

t1    The talker places a byte of data on the interfaces data bus and waits for the listeners to be ready to accept it.

t2    The listeners release the $\overline{\text{NRFD}}$ bus to indicate that they are ready to receive data.

t3    The talker responds to the inactive $\overline{\text{NRFD}}$ signal by asserting $\overline{\text{DAV}}$. $\overline{\text{DAV}}$ informs the listeners that a byte of data is available to them on the data bus.

t4    The listeners assert $\overline{\text{NRFD}}$ to signal the talker that they are processing the data byte and are unavailable to accept additional data.

**FIGURE 7-9**
The handshaking sequence on the IEEE 488 bus.

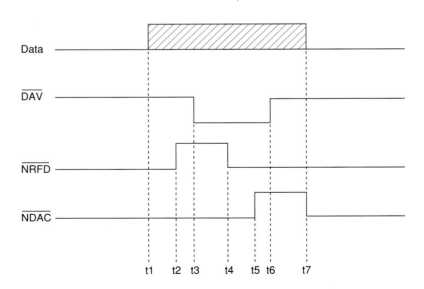

t5          When the listeners have accepted the byte of data, they release $\overline{NDAC}$ to inform the talker that it is no longer necessary for it to hold the data on the bus.

t6          The talker responds to the inactive $\overline{NDAC}$ by releasing $\overline{DAV}$.

t7          The listeners assert $\overline{NDAC}$ and the talker removes the data byte from the bus.

The cycle then repeats for each data byte transfer.

### Interface Management Circuits

The IEEE 488 interface has five bus interface management circuits that are used to control certain operations of the devices connected to the interface and to manage the flow of information among them. Each of the interface management circuits is briefly discussed in the following paragraphs:

**Attention ($\overline{ATN}$).**  As mentioned in Section 7-2-3, the controller uses $\overline{ATN}$ to switch the bus between the data and command modes. When the controller makes $\overline{ATN}$ high, the interface is in the data mode, and the talker can send data over the data bus to the listeners. When the controller asserts $\overline{ATN}$ by pulling it low, the IEEE 488 interface is in the command mode, and the controller can send addresses and commands over the data bus. The controller can use the command mode, for example, to address an individual device and program it to operate as the talker, as a listener, or it can put the device into the standby mode. It can also program features, such as the range of a voltmeter, the output voltage of a programmable power supply or the frequency of a signal generator.

**Interface clear ($\overline{IFC}$).**  When the controller asserts $\overline{IFC}$, all devices connected to the interface suspend operations. The bus is placed into an idle state, and no communication takes place. $\overline{IFC}$ can be thought of as a "reset" line.

**Remote enable ($\overline{REN}$).**  The controller uses $\overline{REN}$ to switch the devices connected to the interface between local and remote operation. When $\overline{REN}$ is asserted by the controller, all devices are placed into remote operation and operate under the command of the controller. When the controller makes $\overline{REN}$ high, all devices are under local control and respond to the control knobs on their front panels. Remember that these devices are usually computer-controlled pieces of test equipment. When they are under local control, and operator can use their front panel controls to operate them directly without having to program them by means of the computer.

**Service request ($\overline{SRQ}$).**  Any device can assert the $\overline{SRQ}$ line to interrupt the normal operation of the interface and signal the controller that it needs attention. When the controller senses an active $\overline{SRQ}$, it first determines which device requested service and why. It does this by placing the interface in the command mode and addressing the devices one at a time in a process called **polling.** When it addresses the device that asserted $\overline{SRQ}$, that device responds by sending codes over the data bus that notify the controller of the action that it should take. For example, if the device has information to send, it will request that the controller reprogram it as the talker.

**End or identify ($\overline{EOI}$).**    The $\overline{EOI}$ circuit has two purposes. When the interface is in the data mode, the talker has control of $\overline{EOI}$ and asserts it when it sends the last byte of a data message. In this case the control line means *end of message*. In the command mode, the controller can assert $\overline{EOI}$ to perform a *parallel poll* to obtain information from several devices simultaneously. For example, the controller could perform a parallel poll of the listeners to ask them if they are ready to receive data. If all of them respond that they are, the controller programs the talker to send data and then places the interface in the data mode so that the communication can begin.

### 7-2-5  Advantages and Disadvantages of IEEE 488

The IEEE 488 interface bus is designed specifically as an interface for computer-controlled test equipment, and it functions well in that environment. It allows up to 15 devices to be connected to the same bus, and it allows data transfer rates of up to 1 million bytes per second. It uses standard TTL logic levels, and it is not very susceptible to noise. A disadvantage, however, is that it not designed for general data communications among computers, terminals, and printers.

### ■  SUMMARY

This chapter has discussed two standard parallel interfaces. Parallel interfaces usually transfer 8 or more bits at a time by means of parallel electrical paths. Parallel data transfer is more rapid than serial data transfer, but it is usually limited to communication over short distances, most often between devices located in the same room. Parallel data transfer uses handshaking signals to coordinate the transfer of data between sending and receiving devices.

Parallel data transfer has two important advantages when compared with serial transfer. First, because the data in most terminals (such as computers) are in parallel form to begin with, it is simpler to leave the data in that form. Serial transfer, in contrast, requires that the data be converted from parallel to serial at the sending device and that it be converted from serial back to parallel at the receiver. The second advantage is that parallel data transfer is usually more rapid than serial.

Two parallel interfaces were discussed in this chapter. The Centronics parallel interface was designed to transfer data from a microcomputer to a printer. It has an 8-bit unidirectional data path as well as several control and status lines. The control lines enable the computer to manage the operation of the printer, and the status lines report the condition of the printer to the computer. The Centronics interface uses standard TTL logic levels.

The IEEE 488 interface bus is used to connect communications and computer equipment to test and measurement devices. Like the Centronics interface, it has an 8-bit data bus and uses TTL logic levels. The IEEE 488 bus can interface up to 15 devices. Under normal operation, one of the devices is programmed to function as the controller, and this device supervises the other devices connected to the interface. One device is programmed to function as the talker and send data over the bus. Up to 14 devices may be programmed as listeners to receive data from the bus. Any device that is not programmed as the controller, the talker, or a listener is placed in the standby mode. Devices may be reprogrammed by the controller. A device that is programmed to function as the talker at one moment, may be reprogrammed to function as the listener at a later time, and a listener may be reprogrammed to function as the talker.

## ■ QUESTIONS

1. What is the general term for the control signals that coordinate the transfer of data over a parallel interface?

2. Name two advantages of parallel interfaces compared to serial interfaces.

3. How many bits does the Centronics interface transfer in parallel?

4. What logic levels does the Centronics interface use?

5. a. What type of connector is used to connect a printer to a Centronics interface?

   b. What type of connector is used to connect an IBM-compatible personal computer to a Centronics interface?

6. a. How many control lines does the Centronics interface have?

   b. List these control lines and briefly describe the purpose of each.

7. What is the purpose of the $\overline{\text{ACK}}$ status line?

8. a. What is the purpose of the BUSY status line?

   b. What four conditions can cause the printer to indicate that it is busy?

9. List three conditions that can cause the printer to make the Centronics interface $\overline{\text{ERROR}}$ status line active.

10. Briefly describe the handshaking sequence that takes place between the computer and the printer each time a byte of data is transferred over the Centronics interface.

11. How is the Centronics 36-conductor interface adapted to a DB-25 connector for use with an IBM-compatible computer?

12. What are three advantages of the Centronics interface?

13. a. What disadvantage does the Centronics interface have?

    b. Why is this disadvantage not serious for a printer interface?

14. a. For what purpose was the IEEE 488 interface designed?

  b. By what other names is the IEEE interface known?

15. a. How many parallel data lines does the IEEE 488 bus have?

  b. Are the IEEE 488 data lines unidirectional or bi-directional?

16. a. How many bytes of data can be transferred each second over the IEEE 488 bus if open-collector drivers are used?

  b. How many bytes can be transferred each second if tristate drivers are used?

17. a. What is the function of the controller in the IEEE interface?

  b. What is the function of the talker?

  c. What is the function of the listeners?

18. a. What are the names of the two IEEE 488 operating modes?

  b. Which control line does the controller use to switch the IEEE 488 interface between the two modes?

19. a. What is the purpose of the IEEE 488 command mode?

  b. What is the purpose of the data mode?

20. Into which three groups can the IEEE interface circuits be divided?

21. a. What are the names of the three IEEE handshake circuits?

  b. State briefly the function of each of the handshake circuits.

22. Briefly describe the handshake sequence that takes place each time a byte of data is transferred from the talker to the listeners by means of the IEEE 488 interface.

# ■ Chapter 8

# DATA TERMINAL EQUIPMENT

## OBJECTIVES

After you have completed this chapter, you should be able to:

- ■ Define the terms *synchronous communications, asynchronous communications, SYN character, start bit, stop bit,* and *framing error.*
- ■ List the two main functions of a DTE.
- ■ List the three main types of integrated circuits used to perform the DTE function and state the differences among them.
- ■ Name the three main sections of a DTE and the function of each section.
- ■ Name the six ACIA internal registers that can be accessed by the terminal, and name the function of each.
- ■ Discuss the electrical connections between the ACIA and the terminal and between the ACIA and the DTE.

## INTRODUCTION

It is critical for effective data communications that the transmitter and receiver operate in synchronization. That is to say, both of them must operate at the same speed, and both must agree where one bit ends and the next bit begins and where

**FIGURE 8-1**
The interface between a terminal and a telephone line.

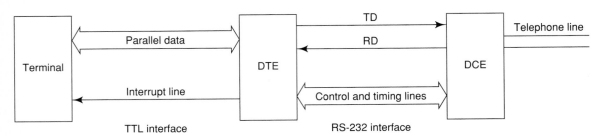

one data word ends and the next data word begins. Two methods are used to obtain this synchronization. In **synchronous communications,** both the transmitter and receiver operate from the same clock signal. **Asynchronous communications** allows the transmitter and receiver to have separate clocks that are very close to each other in frequency, but do not have to be exactly equal with each other. This chapter discusses both synchronous and asynchronous communications.

Figure 8-1 is the diagram of the interface between the terminal and an analog link in a basic data communications system. Although the communications link shown in the diagram is a telephone line, it could be any analog communications medium, for example, a radio channel. The diagram has been presented previously in this book. As you may remember, the system consists of three main parts: the terminal, the data terminal equipment (DTE), and the data communications equipment (DCE). The terminal, which is often a computer, introduces the data into the communications system for transmission and is the destination for received data.

The two main functions of the DTE are to convert transmitted data from the parallel format used by the terminal to the serial format that is used for communication over the analog communications link and to convert received data from the serial format of the communications link to the parallel format used by the terminal.

The DCE, which is also known as a **modem** or **data set,** modulates the serial digital data onto an analog carrier for transmission, and it demodulates the received analog carrier to recover the serial digital data.

The terminal and DTE generally use TTL logic signals to communicate with each other, although they can also use other logic levels. This chapter discusses in detail a DTE that uses TTL signals. The DTE and DCE often communicate with each other by means of an RS-232 interface.

Several types of devices can perform the DTE function. Because the devices are similar in their operation, this chapter concentrates on a specific chip, the **asynchronous communications interface adapter (ACIA).** Learning the ACIA well will make it easier for you to understand other DTE devices when you encounter them in the field.

## 8-1 SYNCHRONOUS AND ASYNCHRONOUS COMMUNICATIONS

Serial data may be sent either synchronously or asynchronously. In data communications, the word *synchronous* means occurring in time with a clock signal. When data

**FIGURE 8-2**

In synchronous serial data, there is no way to tell where one character ends and the next begins except by counting bits.

0  0  1  0  1  1  1  0  1  0  1  0  0

are sent synchronously, the clock of the receiver must be perfectly in step with (synchronized to) the clock of the transmitter. *Asynchronous* means not occurring in time with a clock signal. When data are sent asynchronously, the clock frequencies of the transmitter and receiver can be slightly different.

When synchronous data are sent, one character immediately follows another in an unbroken string of 1s and 0s with no separation between data words. Figure 8-2 shows a synchronous ASCII waveform. By looking at the waveform, there is no way to tell where one ASCII character stops and the next begins. The receiver counts bits to stay in synchronization. If the data use the ASCII code, each ASCII character, including its parity bit, is 8 bits long, and the receiver recognizes a new character every 8 bits. If the receiver somehow gets out of step, it receives all of the following data incorrectly until it can be resynchronized. When the receiver loses synchronization, it is said to be *out of frame*. Errors that occur because the receiver is out of frame are called **framing errors.**

Data, especially ASCII data, are sometimes sent as they are typed into a computer by a human operator. Such transmissions are often asynchronous. Because a human can strike a key and cause a character to be sent at any time, the receiver must be notified when a character is about to arrive. Asynchronous characters are *framed* by a start bit and one or more stop bits. The **start bit** is sent at the beginning of the character to notify the receiver that ASCII data are about to follow. The **stop bit** (or bits) is sent at the end of a character to notify the receiver that the character has ended. A start bit is always a space, and a stop bit is always a mark.

## 8-1-1 Asynchronous Communications

Figure 8-3 shows the waveform of two asynchronous ASCII characters at normal TTL logic levels as they might appear at the input of the DTE at the receiving terminal if viewed on an oscilloscope screen. A mark is +5 V and a space is 0 V. The first

**FIGURE 8-3**

Asynchronous characters are "framed" by a start bit and a stop bit.

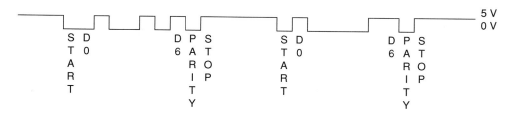

bits transmitted are shown at the left side of the waveform. The mark level at the far left side of the waveform indicates that no data are being received at the moment.

When the first space occurs, the receiving DTE recognizes it as the start bit, and it shifts in the 8 bits that follow. The first 7 bits following the start bit are the ASCII character. These ASCII data bits are labeled D0 through D6 in the figure, and they are sent and received least significant bit (LSB) first. After the data bits comes the parity bit, followed by a mark which is the stop bit. After the stop bit, if the next data word does not immediately follow, the line remains at the mark level until the start bit of the next character is received. The bits of asynchronous ASCII characters are always sent and received in the order shown in the figure.

As mentioned earlier, in asynchronous transmission it is not necessary that the clocks of the transmitting and receiving DTEs be *exactly* the same frequency, but their frequencies must be within a few percent of each other. The receiving DTE synchronizes itself to the start bit at the beginning of each character. Once it detects a start bit, its clock need only be accurate enough to clock in the following 9 bits without losing synchronization.

If the receiver does somehow get out of synchronization while it is receiving a character and does not receive a mark when it expects the stop bit, a framing error occurs. The receiver cannot tell the difference between a stop bit and any other mark, so it is possible for the receiver to be out of frame without generating a framing error.

Although asynchronous data transmission first came into wide use with the Baudot code, which was designed to be transmitted by an electromechanical terminal, asynchronous transmission is also used today with computer-sent data. For example, most DTEs that are used with personal computers operate asynchronously.

A disadvantage of asynchronous communications is that the start and stop bits carry no data. Because these 2 extra bits are added to each 8-bit data character, they slow communication speed by 20%.

## 8-1-2 Synchronous Communications

Because synchronous communication does not use start and stop bits, it is faster than asynchronous communication. Synchronous communication is preferred for high-speed data communications. However, the absence of start and stop bits means that some other method must be used to inform the receiver where one data character ends and the next one begins.

When synchronous communication is used, the receiver is synchronized to the incoming data stream by a series of special synchronizing, or **SYN**, characters. If you consult the ASCII chart in Chapter 5, you will find that the ASCII code for a SYN character is $16. In the EBCDIC chart, also located in Chapter 5, the code for SYN can be found to be $32.

At the beginning of each synchronous transmission, a minimum of two SYN characters are sent. Other groups of two or more SYN characters may be sent during a message to help the receiver stay in synchronization. Two SYN characters are sent because random data could cause the bit pattern of a single SYN character to

**FIGURE 8-4**
This circuit detects two consecutive ASCII SYN characters with even parity.

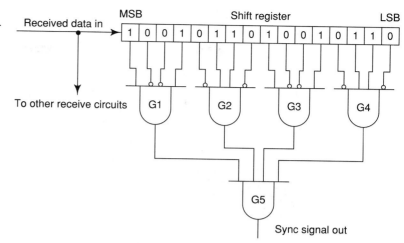

occur in a data stream, but it is unlikely that a random data stream will mimic two consecutive SYN characters.

Figure 8-4 is a diagram of a circuit that monitors the incoming bit stream in the receiving DTE of a synchronous communications system in order to detect a series of ASCII SYN characters. As data bits are received, they are shifted into the shift register. Random bit patterns will cause the output of one or more of the AND gates, G1 through G4, to be low, and therefore the output of AND gate G5 will remain low. When two sequential SYN characters with even parity are shifted into the register, the outputs of AND gates G1 through G4 all go high, which in turn causes the output of G5 to go high. A high on the output of G5 synchronizes the receiver so that it recognizes the next received bit as the beginning of a data word.

As has already been mentioned, in synchronous communications the clock frequencies of the transmitting and receiving DTE must be exactly the same. With modern technology, it might be possible to build two clock circuits that operated at exactly the same frequency, but they would be prohibitively expensive to build, and they would require constant calibration. As Figure 8-5 illustrates, clock synchroniza-

**FIGURE 8-5**
In synchronous communications, the modem recovers the clock signal from the incoming carrier.

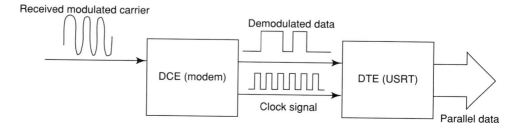

tion is usually maintained by recovering the clock signal from the incoming bit stream. In the figure, the DCE is a modem, and the DTE is a universal synchronous receiver/transmitter (USRT). When the modem demodulates the incoming signal, it also recovers the clock signal from the incoming signal and passes the clock signal on to the USRT. A more detailed explanation of clock recovery is presented in a later chapter on synchronous modems.

## 8-2 PARALLEL-TO-SERIAL CONVERSION

As mentioned in the introduction, one of the DTE's functions is to convert the transmitted data from the parallel format that the terminal uses to the serial format that the DCE uses. The DTE also converts received data from the serial format of the DCE to the parallel format that the computer uses. If the communication is asynchronous, the DTE adds start and stop bits. The DTE can also add the correct and parity bit to each byte of the transmitted data and check for start and stop bits and the correct parity of the received data. All of the DTE functions can be performed by a single integrated circuit.

### 8-2-1 Serial Communication Interface Chips

As also mentioned in the introduction, some of the devices that can be used as a DTE are:

1.  The **universal asynchronous receiver/transmitter (UART).** As its name implies, the UART is used for asynchronous serial data communications.

2.  The **universal synchronous receiver/transmitter (USRT).** The USRT is used for synchronous serial data communication.

3.  The **universal synchronous/asynchronous receiver/transmitter (USART).** The terminal can program a USART to handle either synchronous or asynchronous data communication.

Figure 8-6 is a simplified block diagram of a DTE. The diagram shows the DTE's three main sections: (1) *the transmit section,* which converts data from the parallel format used by the terminal to the serial format required by the DCE, (2) *the receive section,* which converts the serial data from the DCE to the parallel format required by the terminal, and (3) *the status and control section,* which regulates and monitors the operation of the other two sections.

### 8-2-2 The Transmit Section

The transmit section contains two registers: a parallel-input, parallel-output buffer register and a parallel-input, serial-output shift register. To transmit a byte of data, the terminal sends the data over the parallel data bus to the *transmit (TX) buffer register.* The DTE then transfers the data in parallel from the TX buffer register into the *TX shift register.* If asynchronous communication is being used, the DTE also

**FIGURE 8-6**
The three sections of a DTE.

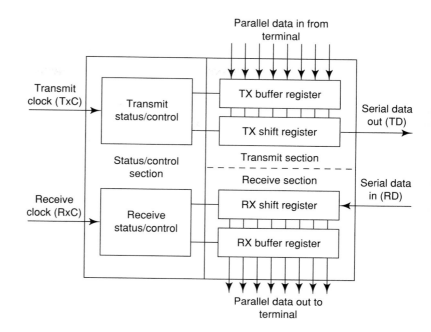

adds start, stop, and parity bits to the data at this time. The TX shift register shifts the data out over the transmit data line (TD) to the DCE at a speed determined by an external *transmit clock signal (TxC)*. While the data are being shifted out of the TX shift register, the terminal places the next byte of data to be transmitted into the TX buffer register, so that it will be ready for transmission as soon as the shift register is empty.

### 8-2-3 The Receive Section

The receive section also contains two registers, a serial-input, parallel-output shift register and a parallel-input, parallel-output buffer register. Data received from the DCE over the receive data line (RD) are shifted into the *receive (RX) shift register* at a rate determined by an external *receive clock signal (RxC)*. After a byte of data is shifted into the RX shift register, it is checked for framing and correct parity. If asynchronous communication is being used, the start, stop, and parity bits are removed, and the data byte is transferred in parallel into the *RX buffer register,* where it is held for the terminal. The terminal then reads the data from the RX data register by means of the parallel data bus.

### 8-2-4 The Status and Control Section

The status and control section performs two main functions: it controls the operation of the transmit and receive sections, and it reports the status of the transmit and receive sections to the terminal. As a controller, it determines the parity of the data that the transmitter sends and that the receiver accepts. The transmit and receive clock signals also pass through the status and control section, which may contain a programmable frequency divider to allow the DTE to operate at different communications speeds.

The status and control section reports the status of the TX and RX buffer registers to the terminal. It notifies the terminal when the data in the TX buffer register have been transferred into the TX shift register so that the terminal can output the next byte of data to be transmitted. It notifies the terminal when data have been received and transferred into the RX buffer register so that the terminal can input the data. It also notifies the terminal when there has been a framing or parity error in the received data.

## 8-3    OVERVIEW OF THE ASYNCHRONOUS COMMUNICATIONS INTERFACE ADAPTER

The 6850 **ACIA** is a UART built into a single integrated circuit. The ACIA was designed by Motorola, although other semiconductor companies are also licensed to manufacture it. It was meant to be a serial interface between computers based on Motorola's 6800 family of microprocessors (MPUs) and a serial peripheral such as a DCE, although it has been widely used with other MPUs. Like most UART and USRT integrated circuits, the ACIA uses TTL logic levels, which means that it may require external circuity to interface it to the RS-232 logic levels that many DCEs use. Figure 8-7 shows the ACIA's external pins and its internal registers.

### 8-3-1    The ACIA Registers

As Figure 8-7 illustrates, the ACIA has six important internal registers. Two of these registers are located in the transmit section; two are located in the receive section; and two are located in the status and control section.

#### The Transmit Registers

The ACIA transmit section is *double buffered,* which means that the transmit section can hold 2 bytes of data at the same time. While 1 byte of data is being shifted out of the transmit shift register toward the DCE, the next byte to be sent is held in the *transmit data register* **(TDR).** The TDR is an 8-bit, write-only buffer. That means that the terminal can place data into the TDR, but later there is no way for the terminal to examine the register. The terminal writes data to the TDR in parallel form through the ACIA's 8 data pins (D0 through D7). Data written to the TDR are transferred in parallel to the *transmit shift register,* where start, stop, and parity bits are added and the data are shifted to the transmit data (TxD) line in serial form in time with the transmit clock signal (TxC).

#### The Receive Registers

The receive section of the ACIA is also double buffered. It contains two registers, the *receive shift register* and the *receive data register* **(RDR).** Data are shifted into the receive shift register from the receive data (RxD) line in time with the receive clock

**FIGURE 8-7**
Registers and pinout of the
asynchronous communications
interface adapter.

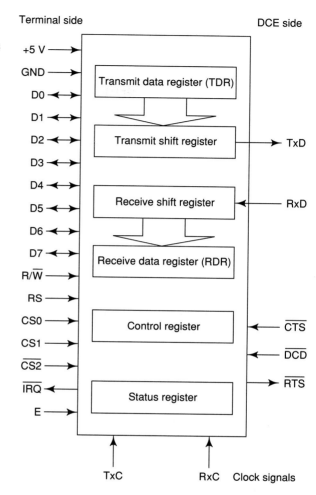

signal (RxC). The ACIA strips off the start, stop, and parity bits. When a complete
data word has been shifted into the receive shift register, the ACIA passes the data
in parallel from the shift register to the RDR. The terminal then reads the data in
parallel from the RDR by means of the ACIA's 8 data pins.

The RDR is a read-only register, which means that the terminal can read data
from the RDR, but it cannot write data to it. The RDR shares an address with the
TDR. If the terminal writes data to that address, the data go into the TDR. If it
reads data from that address, the data are read from the RDR.

## The Control Register

The **control register (CR)** is an 8-bit write-only register. The terminal must write a
data byte to the control register to configure the ACIA before it can send or receive
data. In the diagram of the control register shown in Figure 8-8, the rectangles
labeled CR0 through CR7 represent the individual bit positions in the register. CR0,

**FIGURE 8-8**

The ACIA control register fields.

| CR7 | CR6 | CR5 | CR4 | CR3 | CR2 | CR1 | CR0 |
|-----|-----|-----|-----|-----|-----|-----|-----|
| RCV IRQ | Transmit control | | Word select | | | Clock divide | |

for example, is an abbreviated way of saying "control register bit zero"; CR1 stands for "control register bit one," and so on. The control register bits are divided into four groups or *fields: clock divide, word select, transmit control,* and *receiver interrupt request (RCV IRQ).* Each of these fields controls a different function of the ACIA. We will discuss the operation of each of the control register bit fields shortly.

### The Status Register

Figure 8-9 is a diagram of the ACIA's status register **(SR).** In the diagram, the status register bits are numbered SR0 through SR7, which stands for "status register bit zero" through "status register bit seven." The status register is an 8-bit read-only register. Its function is to report on the operation of the ACIA. The status register shares an address with the control register, and like the control register, it is divided into four bit fields: *transmit and receive (TX/RX) status, modem, receiver error,* and *interrupt request (IRQ).* We will discuss the status register operation in detail later in this chapter.

### 8-3-2   The ACIA Pinout

The pins of the ACIA integrated circuit can be divided into three classes as shown in Figure 8-7: pins that connect to the terminal, pins that connect to the DCE, and pins that connect to the ACIA's clock.

### The Terminal Interface Pins

The *data pins,* D0 through D7, connect to the terminal's data bus and are bi-directional. The terminal uses them to write information into the ACIA's control and transmit data registers and to read information from the ACIA's status and receive data registers.

The *chip select lines* (CS0, CS1, and $\overline{CS2}$) and the *enable* line (E) must all be active when the terminal reads from or writes to one of the ACIA's four addressable registers. The chip select lines are connected through an address decoder to the

**FIGURE 8-9**

The ACIA status register fields.

| SR7 | SR6 | SR5 | SR4 | SR3 | SR2 | SR1 | SR0 |
|-----|-----|-----|-----|-----|-----|-----|-----|
| IRQ | Receiver error | | | Modem | | TX/RX status | |

address bus of the terminal's MPU, and the enable line is connected to the terminal's internal clock signal. When the terminal's MPU outputs one of the ACIA's two addresses, the address decoder makes the ACIA's CS pins active, so that the MPU can communicate with it. Data transfers between the MPU and the ACIA take place during the brief periods when the MPU's clock signal is high.

The ACIA's *register select* (RS) pin is connected to the least significant bit of the address bus of the terminal, and the ACIA's *READ/$\overline{WRITE}$* ($R/\overline{W}$) pin is connected to the terminal's READ/$\overline{WRITE}$ line. When the terminal addresses the ACIA, the logic state of these two pins acting together determines the specific internal register to which the terminal writes data or from which the terminal reads data. Figure 8-10 is a truth table that shows how the ACIA internal registers are selected. When the terminal reads data from the ACIA, it places a logic 1 on the R/$\overline{W}$ line. The terminal can read data only from the ACIA's status and receive data registers. When the terminal writes data to the ACIA, it places a logic 0 on the R/$\overline{W}$ line. The terminal can write data only to the ACIA's control and transmit data registers.

When the terminal addresses the ACIA, it places either a 0 or a 1 on the RS pin. When it places a 0 on the RS pin, the terminal can either write data to the ACIA's CR or read data from the SR. When it places a 1 on the RS pin, it can either write data to the TDR or read data from the RDR.

---

### ■ EXAMPLE 8-1

The terminal outputs a binary 0 on the RS line and a binary 1 on the R/$\overline{W}$ line when it addresses the ACIA. Which ACIA internal register does it address?

### SOLUTION

From Figure 8-10, when the RS line is in the binary 0 state and the R/$\overline{W}$ line is in the binary 1 state, the ACIA's status register (SR) is addressed.

---

The ACIA's **interrupt request ($\overline{IRQ}$)** line is connected to an interrupt pin of the terminal's MPU and allows the ACIA to interrupt the MPU's operations when the ACIA needs attention. For example, the ACIA can be programmed to output a logic 0 on the $\overline{IRQ}$ line each time it receives a byte of data. The terminal's MPU, in turn, can be programmed to respond to the $\overline{IRQ}$ line by temporarily interrupting whatever program it might be executing and switching to a special program called an

**FIGURE 8-10**
Addressing the ACIA internal registers.

| RS | R/$\overline{W}$ | Register Selected |
|----|------|-------------------|
| 0  | 0    | CR                |
| 0  | 1    | SR                |
| 1  | 0    | TDR               |
| 1  | 1    | RDR               |

*interrupt service routine.* The interrupt service routine causes the terminal's MPU to read the received data byte from the ACIA's RDR into the terminal's memory. The MPU then returns to the main program and resumes execution at the point where it left off when the interrupt occurred.

### The Peripheral Interface Pins

The ACIA uses the TxD pin to transmit serial data toward the DCE, and it uses the RxD pin to receive serial data from the DCE. The ACIA also supports three of the RS-232 handshake lines. The clear to send ($\overline{\text{CTS}}$), data carrier detect ($\overline{\text{DCD}}$), and request to send ($\overline{\text{RTS}}$) lines are RS-232 handshake lines that coordinate data transfers between the ACIA and the DCE. Drivers must be used to interface between the ACIA's TTL logic levels and the RS-232 logic levels that many modems use.

### The Clock Pins

The ACIA's transmit and receive clock pins (TxC and RxC) are connected to an external clock generator. These two clock lines determine how fast the ACIA transmits and receives data. Although it is possible to operate the transmitter and receiver at different clock speeds, the two clock pins are almost always tied to a common clock signal as shown in Figure 8-11.

## 8-4 USING THE ACIA

Standard telephone circuits and other analog communications channels are designed to carry alternating current signals, not the direct current digital logic signals that the ACIA outputs. Before the ACIA's serial output can be transmitted over a telephone circuit, a DCE must modulate the data onto an audio sine-wave carrier.

The most common standard interface between a DTE and a DCE in the United States is the Electronic Industries Association (EIA) standard RS-232, which was

**FIGURE 8-11**
The TxC and RxC lines of the ACIA are usually tied to a common clock signal.

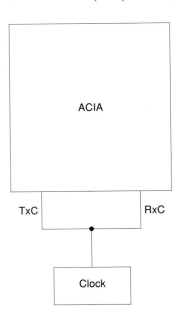

discussed in Chapter 6. Remember that a device that uses the RS-232 standard asserts a logic 1 by outputting a voltage in the range of –5 V to –15 V and that it asserts a logic 0 by outputting a voltage in the range of +5 V and +15 V. The RS-232 standard specifies many more control signals than the three handshake lines that the ACIA supports. You should also remember from the discussion of RS-232 in Chapter 6 that equipment manufacturers commonly use only a fraction of the RS-232 lines available.

Because the ACIA, like most other single-chip UARTs, uses TTL logic levels and supports only a fraction of the RS-232 control signals, it is not directly compatible with the RS-232 interface. But it is a simple matter to adapt the ACIA to the RS-232 standard by using driver circuits to convert between the RS-232 and TTL logic levels and by using only those RS-232 control lines that the ACIA supports.

### 8-4-1 Interfacing the ACIA and the Modem

Figure 8-12 shows how the ACIA is connected to a terminal and a modem. On the terminal side of the ACIA, data pins D0 through D7 connect to the data bus of the terminal's MPU. The ACIA's RS pin connects to the least significant bit of the MPU's address bus. The MPU's other address lines connect to an address decoder, and the outputs of the address decoder connect to the ACIA's chip select (CS) pins. Whenever the MPU outputs the ACIA's address, the address decoder makes the ACIA's CS pins active, and the MPU can write data to or read data from one of the ACIA's internal registers.

The R/$\overline{\text{W}}$ pin of the ACIA connects to the R/$\overline{\text{W}}$ pin of the MPU, and the enable (E) pin of the ACIA connects to the MPU's clock signal. The E clock synchronizes parallel data transfers between the MPU and the ACIA. The parallel transfers can occur only when the E clock is high. The TxC and RxC clocks are completely independent of the E clock. The TxC clock synchronizes serial transfers from the DTE to the DCE, and the RxC clock synchronizes serial data transfers from the DCE to the DTE.

**FIGURE 8-12**
The ACIA showing the connections to the terminal and the modem.

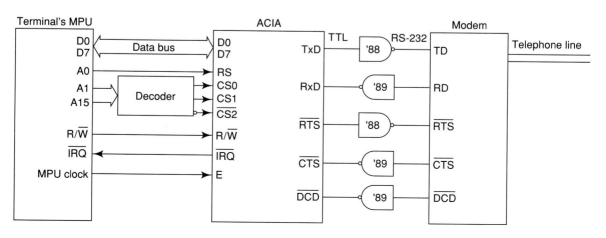

The interrupt request ($\overline{\text{IRQ}}$) pin of the ACIA connects to the interrupt pin of the MPU. The $\overline{\text{IRQ}}$ line is usually connected through a nominal 3000-$\Omega$ pull-up resistor (not shown in the figure) to the +5-V power supply. The ACIA can use $\overline{\text{IRQ}}$ to signal the terminal's MPU that the ACIA needs attention.

Interface chips are used to convert between the ACIA's TTL logic levels and the RS-232 logic levels used by many modems. The device in the TxD line that looks like a one-input NAND gate is a line driver (such as the Motorola MC1488) that accepts TTL logic levels and outputs RS-232 logic levels. The device in the RxD line is a line receiver (such as Motorola's MC1489) that accepts RS-232 logic levels at its input and converts them to TTL logic levels at its output. If the ACIA outputs a mark at a +5-V logic level on its TxD line, the line driver converts it to a voltage between –5 V and –15 V, which represents a mark in RS-232 logic levels. Frequently, –12 V is used for a mark and +12 V is used for a space, because they are common power supply voltages.

The transmit data (TxD) line carries serial data from the ACIA to the modem, where they are modulated onto an analog carrier and sent over the telephone line. The modem also receives incoming data from the telephone line, demodulates them from the carrier, and passes them along to the ACIA in serial form over the RxD line.

The request to send ($\overline{\text{RTS}}$), clear to send ($\overline{\text{CTS}}$), and data carrier detect ($\overline{\text{DCD}}$) control lines coordinate the operation of the ACIA and the modem. When the ACIA is configured to transmit data, it makes $\overline{\text{RTS}}$ active. The modem responds to $\overline{\text{RTS}}$ by putting a carrier on the telephone line and delaying for a short period (perhaps 250 ms) to allow the receive modem to lock onto the carrier. This time delay is called **modem turnaround time.** At the end of the modem turnaround time, the modem makes $\overline{\text{CTS}}$ active. $\overline{\text{CTS}}$ is a handshake response to $\overline{\text{RTS}}$ and allows the ACIA to transmit. In fact, the ACIA will not output serial data on its TxC line unless $\overline{\text{CTS}}$ is active.

In the meantime, the modem at the receiving end should have received the carrier and should have locked onto it. When the receiving modem locks onto the carrier, it makes its $\overline{\text{DCD}}$ pin active to notify the receiving ACIA that it is about to receive data. A receiving ACIA will not input serial data from its RxC line unless $\overline{\text{DCD}}$ is active.

## 8-4-2 The ACIA Status Register

Figure 8-13 shows the individual bits of the ACIA's status register. As we saw in Figure 8-9, these bits are grouped into fields. Each field reports on a specific aspect of the ACIA's operation. We will now look at the function of the individual bits within each field.

**FIGURE 8-13**
The ACIA status register bits.

| SR7 | SR6 | SR5 | SR4 | SR3 | SR2 | SR1 | SR0 |
|------|------|------|------|------|------|------|------|
| IRQ | PE | OVRN | FE | $\overline{\text{CTS}}$ | $\overline{\text{DCD}}$ | TDRE | RDRF |

### The Transmit and Receive Status Bits

The two least significant bits of the status register, bits SR0 and SR1, report the status of the receiver and transmitter sections of the ACIA. Bit SR0 is the *received data register full (RDRF)* bit. The ACIA sets this bit each time a received data word is transferred from the receive shift register to the RDR. The RDRF bit signals the terminal that it should read the received data. The ACIA clears the RDRF bit when the terminal reads the data from the RDR.

Bit SR1 is the *transmit data register empty (TDRE)* bit. The ACIA sets the TDRE bit each time data is transferred from the TDR to the transmit shift register. The TDRE bit signals the terminal that it can write the next byte of data to be transmitted to the TDR. The ACIA clears the TDRE bit when the terminal writes data to the TDR.

Figure 8-14 is the flowchart of a program that the terminal's MPU can execute to receive data by way of the ACIA. The MPU reads (copies) the contents of the

**FIGURE 8-14**
The terminal can poll the RDRF bit to determine when data have been received.

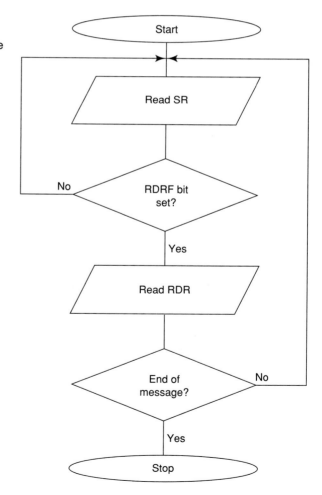

ACIA's status register into one of its own internal registers. Then it polls (examines) the RDRF bit to determine if the ACIA has a byte of received data ready to transfer to the terminal. If the RDRF bit is not set, the MPU repeats the procedure and reads the SR again. When the RDRF bit is finally set, the MPU reads the received data byte from the RDR. Reading the RDR clears the RDRF status bit. If the end of the received message has been reached, the program ends. If there are more data to be received, the MPU branches back to the beginning of the program and resumes polling the RDRF bit.

Figure 8-15 is a flowchart of a similar program that the terminal's MPU can execute to transmit data through the ACIA. In this case, the MPU repeatedly polls the status register's TDRE bit until it is set. Then it writes the next byte of data in the transmitted message to the ACIA's TDR. Writing data to the TDR clears the TDRE status bit. If the end of the message has been reached, the program ends. If there

**FIGURE 8-15**
The terminal can poll the TDRE bit to determine when the ACIA is ready to transmit more data.

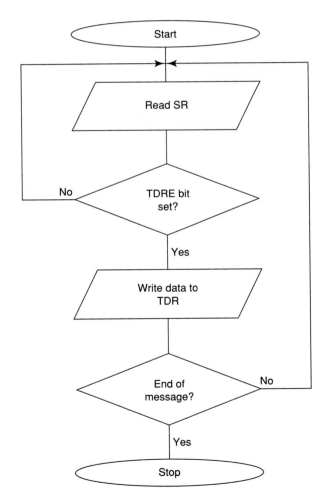

are more data to send, the MPU resumes polling the TDRE bit until it sets, indicating that the ACIA is ready for the next byte of data.

The advantage of repeated polling of the RDRF or TDRE bit to coordinate parallel data transfers between the terminal's MPU and the ACIA is that it is a simple operation, and it is easy to write a program to do it. The disadvantage is that the time the MPU spends repeatedly polling a status bit could be used to perform some other function in the terminal. Most modern microprocessors can execute a program instruction every few hundred nanoseconds. Serial data transmission speeds over analog telephone lines, in contrast, are limited to one data byte every several milliseconds. Polling a status bit repeatedly forces the MPU to wait for the ACIA to catch up. A more efficient use of MPU time is to allow the MPU to execute another program when the ACIA does not require attention. The ACIA can be configured to assert its $\overline{IRQ}$ pin each time the RDRF or TDRE bit sets, and the $\overline{IRQ}$ signal can be used to interrupt the MPU's execution of the program for the few microseconds it takes to read the RDR or write to the TDR.

### The Modem Status Bits

Referring back to Figure 8-13, bits SR2 and SR3 are the modem status bits. They report the status of the control lines coming from the modem. Bit SR2 is the $\overline{DCD}$ status bit. While the modem is receiving data, it holds the $\overline{DCD}$ line at a logic 0 level to indicate that it is locked onto a received carrier from the telephone line. This logic 0 on the ACIA's $\overline{DCD}$ pin causes the status register $\overline{DCD}$ bit to reset. If the modem loses the incoming carrier, it places a logic 1 on the $\overline{DCD}$ line, which in turn causes the ACIA to set the $\overline{DCD}$ bit in the status register. If the receiver portion of the ACIA has been configured to generate interrupt requests, this will also cause the ACIA to assert its $\overline{IRQ}$ pin.

Bit SR3 is the $\overline{CTS}$ status bit. The modem holds its $\overline{CTS}$ pin at a logic 0 level during transmission to give the ACIA permission to send, which in turn makes the $\overline{CTS}$ status bit low. If the $\overline{CTS}$ line goes to a logic 1 level for any reason, the $\overline{CTS}$ status bit also sets, which in turn disables the ACIA's ability to transmit. The terminal's MPU can poll the $\overline{DCD}$ and $\overline{CTS}$ status bits to determine if they are at the correct level.

### The Receive Error Status Bits

Bits SR4, SR5, and SR6 are the receiver error bits. Each of these bits, when set, indicates a different type of error in the received data. Bit SR4 is the framing error (FE) bit. The ACIA sets the FE bit when it receives a space in the position where it expected to find the stop bit. (Remember that the stop bit is always a mark.) The ACIA clears the FE status bit when it receives another byte of data with proper framing. If the FE status bit is set, it indicates that the byte of data currently in the RDR had a framing error when it was received.

Bit SR5 is the overrun (OVRN) error status bit. An **overrun error** indicates that one or more bytes of data were lost because the terminal failed to read them from the RDR. For example, suppose one character is received into the receive shift register and then transferred to the RDR. Then a second character is shifted into the receive shift register. This second character should also be transferred into the RDR, but if the MPU has not yet read the first character from the RDR, the second character will not be transferred. It will be lost as a third character is received into the receive shift register over the top of it. This is an overrun error.

Now assume that the terminal reads the first character from the RDR while the third character is being received. When the third character is completely shifted in, it is transferred into the RDR. At the same time, the ACIA sets the OVRN status bit to indicate that one or more data words received before this byte were overrun and therefore lost. The ACIA resets the OVRN bit when the terminal reads the RDR.

Bit SR6 is the parity error (PE) status bit. The ACIA sets the PE bit when a data byte that was received with incorrect parity is transferred from the receive shift register to the RDR. It clears the PE bit when a byte that was received with correct parity is transferred into the RDR.

The receiving terminal can be programmed to poll the error bits each time it reads a byte of data from the RDR. If one of them is set, there is an error in the received data, and the receiving terminal can be programmed to send a message back to the originating terminal to request a retransmission.

### The Interrupt Request Bit

Bit 7 is the interrupt request (IRQ) bit, which is set when either the transmit or receive section of the ACIA asserts the $\overline{IRQ}$ pin. If the transmit section of the ACIA caused the interrupt, the ACIA clears the interrupt (releases its $\overline{IRQ}$ pin and clears the IRQ bit) when the terminal writes data to the TDR. If the receiver caused the interrupt, the ACIA clears the interrupt when the terminal reads the RDR.

## 8-4-3   The ACIA Control Register

Before the ACIA can be used, it must be configured to send and receive the proper number of data bits, the proper number of stop bits, the desired parity, and so on. Configuring the ACIA is a two-step process. In step one the terminal resets the ACIA to clear any previous programming. In step two the terminal writes a control word to the control register. The table in Figure 8-16 can be used to calculate the required control word.

### Receive Interrupt Enable

Control register bit 7 (CR7) is the receive interrupt enable bit. If bit CR7 is set, the receive section of the ACIA can generate interrupt requests. If CR7 is clear, it cannot. When the receiver is interrupt enabled, it generates an interrupt request by asserting the ACIA's $\overline{IRQ}$ line every time the RDRF status bit sets when a received data word is transferred from the receive shift register into the receive data register. The interrupt is cleared when the terminal's MPU reads the ACIA's RDR and thereby clears the RDRF status bit.

**FIGURE 8-16**

Truth table of the bits in the ACIA control register fields.

| CR7 | Receive Interrupt Bit |
|-----|-----------------------|
| 0 | Receive interrupt disabled |
| 1 | Receive interrupt enabled |

| CR6 | CR5 | Transmit Control |
|-----|-----|------------------|
| 0 | 0 | $\overline{\text{RTS}}$ asserted, transmit interrupt disabled |
| 0 | 1 | $\overline{\text{RTS}}$ asserted, transmit interrupt enabled |
| 1 | 0 | $\overline{\text{RTS}}$ not asserted, transmit interrupt disabled |
| 1 | 1 | $\overline{\text{RTS}}$ asserted, transmit a break (constant space) on TxD pin, transmit interrupt disabled |

| CR4 | CR3 | CR2 | Data Word Select |
|-----|-----|-----|------------------|
| 0 | 0 | 0 | 7 data bits, even parity, 2 stop bits |
| 0 | 0 | 1 | 7 data bits, odd parity, 2 stop bits |
| 0 | 1 | 0 | 7 data bits, even parity, 1 stop bit |
| 0 | 1 | 1 | 7 data bits, odd parity, 1 stop bit |
| 1 | 0 | 0 | 8 data bits, no parity bit, 2 stop bits |
| 1 | 0 | 1 | 8 data bits, no parity bit, 1 stop bit |
| 1 | 1 | 0 | 8 data bits, even parity, 1 stop bit |
| 1 | 1 | 1 | 8 data bits, odd parity, 1 stop bit |

| CR1 | CR0 | Clock Divide |
|-----|-----|--------------|
| 0 | 0 | $\div 1$ |
| 0 | 1 | $\div 16$ |
| 1 | 0 | $\div 64$ |
| 1 | 1 | Master reset |

## Transmit Control

Bits CR6 and CR5 make up the transmit control field, which configures the $\overline{RTS}$ handshake line and determines the ability of the ACIA transmit section to generate interrupt requests. $\overline{RTS}$ is normally asserted when the ACIA is configured to transmit data. The transmit section can be either interrupt enabled or interrupt disabled. If the terminal is going to repeatedly poll the TDRE bit to determine when it should write transmit data to the TDR, the ACIA's transmit section should be interrupt disabled. If the transmit section is interrupt enabled, the ACIA asserts the $\overline{IRQ}$ line to interrupt the terminal's MPU each time the TDRE status bit is set. Remember that the TDRE bit sets when a data word is transferred from the transmit data register into the transmit shift register. The interrupt is cleared when the terminal's MPU writes a byte of data to the TDR and thereby clears the TDRE bit.

The transmit control bits can also be configured to cause the ACIA to output a **break** on its TxD line. A break is a constant space level that is sent in some communications systems to signal the terminal at the other end of the circuit to stop sending data.

## Data Word Select

Bits CR4, CR3, and CR2 select the configuration of the data word that the ACIA transmits and receives. The data word can be either 7 or 8 bits long. Seven data bits are used to send standard ASCII code, and 8 data bits are used to send extended ASCII or to send uncoded digital data directly from the computer's memory. The data word can be programmed for either even or odd parity or no parity bit at all. If even or odd parity is selected, the ACIA will automatically add the correct parity bit to the transmitted data and check the received data for proper parity. One or two stop bits can be selected. Modern asynchronous communications systems use one stop bit.

## Clock Divide

The ACIA divides the external TxD and TxC clock signals to obtain the ACIA transmit and receive bit rates. Bits CR1 and CR0 select clock divide by 1, 16, or 64. For example, if the ACIA clock frequency is 9600 Hz and the control register clock divide bits are configured to divide by 16, the bit rate is 9600/16 or 600 b/s. The divide-by-1 option is seldom used for reasons that will be discussed shortly.

The clock divide field is also used to reset the ACIA. As mentioned earlier, before the ACIA is configured, it must be reset. The terminal resets the ACIA by writing binary 0000 0011 (hexadecimal 03) to the ACIA's control register. Then the terminal writes a second data word to the control register to configure it to the desired transmission and reception conditions.

■ **E X A M P L E  8 - 2**

Calculate the control word that should be placed in the ACIA's control register to configure the ACIA to disable its receive interrupt capability, assert the $\overline{RTS}$ line, enable the transmit interrupt, select 7 data bits with even parity and 1 stop bit, and divide the clock frequency by 64. Use the truth tables in Figure 8-16 to calculate the bits.

## SOLUTION

From the truth tables in Figure 8-16, the control register bits are configured as follows:

CR7 = 0 to disable the receive interrupt.

CR6 = 0 and CR5 = 1 to assert the $\overline{\text{RTS}}$ line and enable the transmit interrupt feature.

CR4 = 0, CR3 = 1, and CR2 = 0 to select 7 data bits, even parity and 1 stop bit.

CR1 = 1 and CR0 = 0 to select clock divide by 64.

To summarize the control register bits:

| CR7 | CR6 | CR5 | CR4 | CR3 | CR2 | CR1 | CR0 |
|-----|-----|-----|-----|-----|-----|-----|-----|
| 0 | 0 | 1 | 0 | 1 | 0 | 1 | 0 |

which is the equivalent of hexadecimal 2A.

## 8-5    ACIA TIMING

When it is receiving data, the ACIA synchronizes itself to the incoming bit stream at the beginning of each data word. It does this by detecting the 1-to-0 transition at the leading edge of each start bit. Remember that the stop bit of an asynchronous data word is always a mark or logic 1. After the stop bit, a device sending asynchronous data maintains the communications line in the mark condition until the next data word begins. It switches the line to the space or logic 0 condition when it begins sending the start bit of the next character. The start bit is always a space.

After it receives the stop bit of one character, the ACIA monitors the receive data line, looking for the 1-to-0 transition that could be the leading edge of the start bit of the next data word. However, a negative edge could also be a noise spike. Noise spikes are common on communications lines and in computer equipment. The ACIA can differentiate between a start bit and a noise spike by measuring the duration of the pulse. A noise spike has a short duration, often measured in microseconds. A low that lasts for at least half a bit time is probably the start bit.

When it is waiting for a start bit, the ACIA monitors the receive data line on the rising edge of each RxC clock pulse, as illustrated in Figure 8-17. As long as the received data line is high, the start bit has not yet arrived. When the ACIA detects a low, it monitors the receive data line for 8 *additional* clock pulses, if it is configured for clock divide by 16 or 32 *additional* clock pulses, if it is configured for clock divide

**FIGURE 8-17**
With a clock divide by 16, when the ACIA detects a negative edge on the received signal, it checks it 8 more times to be sure it is the start bit.

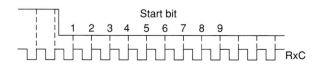

by 64. If the received data line is low each time it is monitored, the ACIA assumes that it has received a start bit. If the data line returns high in a shorter period of time, the ACIA assumes it has received a negative-going noise spike, and it begins looking for the start bit again.

Monitoring the start bit repeatedly not only prevents the ACIA from mistaking a noise spike for the start bit, but it also causes the ACIA to delay one-half bit time to make its last check of the start bit at its approximate center. Received bits are not clean signals. They are usually noisy, and more important, slow rise and fall times cause the bits to have rounded edges. At the edge of a bit, the receive data line is in transition between logic states, and it is not clear whether a mark or a space is being received. For this reason, it is important that the ACIA monitor the received bits near their centers. Once the start bit has been confirmed, the ACIA delays 1 bit time (16 clock cycles for clock divide by 16 or 64 clock pulses for clock divide by 64) before checking the received data line again. This puts it in the approximate center of the first data bit. It checks the logic level of the data bit, and then it delays an additional bit time before it checks the next bit, and so on until it receives the stop bit. This ensures that each bit is checked near its center.

If the ACIA is programmed for clock divide by 1, the ACIA can sample the start bit only one time, and there is no guarantee that it will sample the start bit and the following data bits near their centers. It may sample the bits near their edges, causing errors. Therefore, the clock divide by 1 option is seldom used for receiving data, although it can be used for transmission.

## ■ SUMMARY

This chapter explained that serial data may be sent either synchronously or asynchronously. In synchronous data communications, the clock signals of the transmitter and receiver must be of the same frequency, and the receiver derives its clock signal from the incoming data stream. Synchronous transmission uses synchronization (SYN) characters to synchronize the receiver to the incoming characters. Thereafter, the receiver counts bits. Every 8 bits, a new character begins. If the receiver somehow loses count, it is said to be out of frame.

In asynchronous transmission, a character can be sent at any time. When no character is being sent, a continuous stream of binary 1s (marks) is transmitted. Each character begins with a start bit, which is always a logic 0 (space). The receiver synchronizes on the mark-to-space transition at the beginning of the start bit. Each character ends with a stop bit, which is always a mark. If the receiver does not receive a mark when it expects a stop bit, it generates a framing error. In general, synchronous data are used for high-speed communications, and asynchronous communications is used for lower-speed communications.

This chapter also covered the data terminal equipment (DTE) used in many data communications systems. The DTE is the interface between the terminal and the data communications equipment (DCE). The two main purposes of the DTE are to convert transmitted data from the parallel format used by the terminal to the serial format required to send data over an analog communications link such as a telephone line and to convert received data from the serial format of the communications link to the parallel format used by the terminal. Three types of integrated circuits may be used as a DTE: the universal asynchronous receiver/transmitter (UART), the universal synchronous receiver/transmitter (USRT), and the universal synchronous/asynchronous receiver/transmitter (USART). The three main sections of a DTE are the transmit section, which converts transmitted data from parallel to serial; the receive section, which converts received data from serial to parallel; and the status and control section, which controls the operation of the transmit and receive sections and reports on their status to the terminal.

The chapter has discussed in detail the asynchronous communications interface adapter (ACIA) integrated circuit, which is a type of UART. The ACIA has six internal registers. In its receive section, it has a serial-input, parallel-output receive shift register and a parallel-input, parallel-output receive data register (RDR). Because these two registers enable the receive section of the ACIA to hold two bytes of data, the receive section is said to be double buffered. Received data is first shifted from the ACIA's receive data line or RxD into its receive shift register, and then it is transferred in parallel into the RDR where it is held until it is read into the terminal by means of the ACIA's data pins. The receive section also checks the received data for framing and proper parity.

The transmit section is also double buffered. The terminal writes data to be transmitted into the parallel-input, parallel-output transmit data register (TDR). From there, the data are transferred in parallel to the parallel-input, serial output transmit shift register, where start, stop, and parity bits are added. The data are then shifted out over the ACIA's transmit data line or TxD.

The ACIA's control register is used to configure the ACIA to transmit and/or to receive data. The 8-bit control register is divided into four bit fields, each of which controls a specific aspect of the ACIA's operation. Before sending or receiving data, the terminal configures the ACIA by writing the correct bit pattern to the control register.

The ACIA's status register is an 8-bit register that reports to the terminal on the operation of the ACIA. It is also divided into four bit fields, each of which reports on a specific aspect of the ACIA's operation.

The ACIA pins can be divided into three groups: terminal interface pins, modem interface pins, and clock pins. One of the ACIA's terminal interface pins that was discussed in detail is the interrupt request or $\overline{\text{IRQ}}$ pin. The $\overline{\text{IRQ}}$ pin can be used to interrupt the terminal's microprocessor to get its attention when the ACIA has a byte of data in its RDR that the terminal should read or when the ACIA is ready for the terminal to write a byte of data into its TDR for transmission.

The ACIA's modem interface pins are the TxD pin, which carries transmitted serial data from the ACIA to the DCE; the RxD pin, which carries received serial data from the DCE to the ACIA; and three RS-232 handshake lines: $\overline{\text{RTS}}$, $\overline{\text{CTS}}$, and $\overline{\text{DCD}}$. Because the ACIA uses TTL logic levels, the modem interface lines may require level converters to interface them to the RS-232 logic levels used by many modems.

■ **QUESTIONS**

1. What is the basic difference between synchronous and asynchronous serial communications?

2. Which is faster, synchronous communications or asynchronous communications, and why is it faster?

3. What type of error occurs if the receiving terminal loses track of where one character ends and the next character begins?

4. a. What is the purpose of the SYN character used with synchronous communications?

   b. Once a synchronous receiver has detected a series of SYN characters, how does it remain in frame until the next SYN characters are received?

5. Explain in your own words how the circuit of Figure 8-4 works.

6. a. What is the purpose of the start and stop bits used with asynchronous communications?

   b. Is the start bit a mark, or is it a space?

   c. Is the stop bit a mark, or is it a space?

7. Name the three types of devices that can perform the DTE function.

8. a. What are the three main sections of a DTE?

   b. State the function of each of these sections.

9. a. What two registers are located in the transmit section of a DTE?

   b. What is the purpose of each of these registers?

10. a. What two registers are located in the receive section of a DTE?

    b. What is the purpose of each of these registers?

11. What are the two main functions of the status and control section of a DTE?

12. What type of logic levels does the ACIA use?

13. What does the term *double buffered* mean as it applies to the transmit section of the ACIA?

14. a. How many bits of data can the ACIA's TDR hold?

    b. Can the terminal both write data to and read data from the TDR?

    c. Into which register are data placed when they leave the TDR?

15. a. What are the names of the two registers in the receive section of the ACIA?

    b. What is the purpose of each of these registers?

16. Can the terminal both write data to and read data from the RDR?

17. With which other ACIA register does the RDR share an address?

18. a. What are the names of the four fields into which the ACIA's control register is divided?

    b. Can the terminal both write data to and read data from the control register?

19. a. What are the names of the four fields into which the ACIA's status register is divided?

    b. Can the terminal both write data to and read data from the status register?

    c. With which other ACIA register does the status register share an address?

20. Into which three classes can the pins of the ACIA be divided?

21. What is the purpose of the ACIA's data pins?

22. Which four ACIA pins must be active in order for the terminal to read data from or write data to one of the ACIA's internal registers?

23. When the terminal addresses the ACIA, which two ACIA pins determine the specific ACIA register to which the terminal writes data or from which it reads data?

24. What is the purpose of the ACIA's $\overline{\text{IRQ}}$ pin?

25. a. Which three RS-232 handshake lines does the ACIA support?

    b. Does the ACIA use RS-232 logic levels on these lines?

26. a. What range of voltages is asserted on an RS-232 circuit to represent a mark or logic 1?

    b. What range of voltages is asserted on an RS-232 line to represent a space or logic 0?

27. a. Which clock signals are used to transfer serial data between the ACIA and the DCE?

    b. Which clock signal is used to transfer parallel data between the ACIA and the terminal's MPU?

28. a. Which modem interface line must be active to enable the ACIA to output serial data on its TxC line?

    b. Which modem interface line must be active to enable the ACIA to input data from its RxC line?

29. a. Which status register bit does the ACIA set each time it transfer a byte of received data from the receive shift register to the RDR?

    b. What action causes the ACIA to clear this status bit?

30. a. Which status register bit does the ACIA set each time the ACIA transfer a byte of data from the TDR to the transmit shift register?

    b. What action causes the ACIA to clear that bit?

31. a. What is the advantage of having the terminal's MPU repeatedly poll the ACIA's RDRF or TDRE bit when it is sending or receiving data?

    b. What is the disadvantage?

    c. What is a more efficient method for the ACIA to inform the terminal's MPU when the RDRF or TDRE bit sets?

32. a. What are the names of the ACIA's two modem status bits?

    b. What is the function of each of the modem status bits?

33. a. What are the names of the ACIA's three receive error status bits?

    b. Describe what type of receive error causes each of these bits to set.

34. a. If the transmit section of the ACIA generates an interrupt, how is that interrupt cleared?

    b. If the receive section of the ACIA generates an interrupt, how is that interrupt cleared?

35. What two steps must be performed to configure the ACIA to send or receive data?

36. a. Which ACIA control register bit determines whether or not the ACIA receive section can generate interrupt requests?

    b. If the ACIA receive section is interrupt enabled, what action causes it to generate an interrupt request?

37. a. Which two bits in the ACIA's control register field make up the transmit control field?

    b. If the ACIA transmit section is interrupt enabled, what causes it to generate an interrupt request?

38. a. Which three control register bits make up the data word select field?

    b. How many bits can the ACIA transmit or receive in each data word?

    c. What type of parity can the ACIA be programmed to send and receive?

39. a. Which two control register bits make up the clock divide field?

    b. How is the clock divide field used to reset the ACIA?

40. When the ACIA receives data, how does it synchronize itself to the incoming bit stream?

41. Explain how the ACIA distinguishes between a start bit and a negative-going noise spike when it is receiving data.

42. Why is it important that the ACIA check received data bits near their centers instead of near their edges?

43. Why is it best not to use the ACIA's clock-divide-by-1 feature for receiving data?

# ■ Chapter 9

# INTRODUCTION TO MODEMS

**OBJECTIVES**

After you have completed this chapter, you should be able to:

- ■ List the basic functions that a modem performs.
- ■ State the effect that the bandwidth of a communications circuit has on the circuit's maximum communications speed as predicted by Shannon's Law.
- ■ Explain the difference between bits per second and baud as measurements of communications speed.
- ■ Describe the differences among frequency-shift keying, phase-shift keying, and quadrature amplitude modulation.
- ■ Explain how a phasor diagram and a constellation diagram represent the output conditions of a phase-shift keyed modem.
- ■ Explain how data compression can increase the apparent speed of a modem.
- ■ Explain the difference between a synchronous modem and an asynchronous modem.

## INTRODUCTION

Figure 9-1 is a diagram of the interface between the terminal and an analog link, such as a telephone line, in a basic data communications system. The diagram has been presented several times earlier in this book. In past chapters, we discussed the RS-232C interface and the data terminal equipment (DTE). This chapter and Chapter 10 discuss the data communications equipment (DCE) part of the diagram. You may remember that the DCE is also called a **modem** (short for modulator/demodulator) or a **data set.** The most common term is *modem.* This chapter provides an overview of the function of the modem in a communications system, and Chapter 10 discusses some of the most important modem standards.

The modem performs five basic functions:

1. It accepts transmitted serial digital data that the DTE sends, often by means of an RS-232 transmit data (TD) line.
2. It modulates the data onto an analog carrier and transmits the data over an analog communications medium such as a radio channel or a telephone line.
3. It demodulates the analog carrier that it receives from the analog communications medium to recover the received digital data.
4. It passes the demodulated serial data to the DTE, often by means of an RS-232 receive data (RD) line.
5. In synchronous systems, the DCE supplies a clock signal to the DTE.

## 9-1    AN OVERVIEW OF MODEMS

Early modems were built from discrete electronic components and simple integrated circuits such as balanced modulators, voltage-controlled oscillators, and phase-locked loops. In those days, a modem manufacturer also had to know how to design a modem.

The electronic circuitry of a modern modem is contained in one, two, or three very complex integrated circuits called **chipsets,** which are designed and produced

**FIGURE 9-1**
The interface between a terminal and a telephone line.

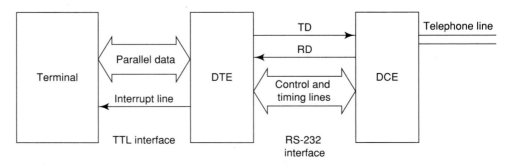

by semiconductor manufacturers. A chipset contains all or most of the electronics needed to build a piece of electronic equipment. Many different modem manufacturers purchase the same chipset from a semiconductor manufacturer and produce modems that have almost identical features. The resulting competition among semiconductor manufacturers to sell their chipsets and among modem manufacturers to sell their modems has caused modem prices to fall drastically in recent years. For example, a 9600-b/s full-duplex modem, which would have been prohibitively expensive for the average home computer user not too many years ago, can now be purchased for less than $40.

One of the consequences of the high integration of modem chipsets is that the small group of designers of today's modems, who work for semiconductor manufacturers, are almost the only people who understand in detail how the electronics inside a modern modem really work. The semiconductor supplier may even design the circuit board and supply the software that the modem manufacturer resells to the end customer. Today's modem manufacturer is often a company that is efficient at assembling electronic equipment, but may have little expertise in electronic design. The modem manufacturer is more interested in *what* the chipset does than in *how* the chipset functions.

### 9-1-1 The Physical Form of Modems

Modems are built in three physical forms. Some computer manufacturers build the modem chipset onto the motherboard (main circuit board) of computers and terminals. These **built-in modems** use the same logic levels as the computer itself. The advantages of built-in modems are that they are inexpensive and are an integral part of the computer. The disadvantage of built-in modems is that it is difficult to upgrade them when newer and faster models are introduced.

The most popular type of modem for desktop computers is a small add-in circuit board that plugs into the computer's motherboard. **Plug-in modems** include the DTE, and they use the same logic levels as the computer. Built-in and plug-in modems connect directly to the computer's internal parallel bus. They are therefore in intimate communication with the computer and are easily controlled by the computer's software. This fact, plus their low price, is what makes them so popular.

The third type of modem is a stand-alone unit built into a box and located outside the computer or terminal. The **stand-alone modem** connects to the terminal by means of an RS-232 interface. Stand-alone modems do not include the DTE. The DTE is located within the terminal. Stand-alone modems usually have their own internal power supplies, although some pocket-sized models that are designed to be used with portable computers derive their power from the RS-232 interface signals supplied by the terminal.

### 9-1-2 Simplex, Half-Duplex, and Full-Duplex Modems

Modems can be simplex, half-duplex, or full-duplex. Simplex modems are used in applications such as weather wires and news service wires, which send data from a central location to the newsrooms of newspapers and radio and television stations over leased telephone circuits. Because simplex communications is in one direction only, simplex modems can use the full bandwidth of the telephone circuit.

Half-duplex modems transmit only in one direction at a time, so they can also use the full bandwidth of the telephone circuit. A disadvantage of half-duplex communication is that each time the direction of communication is reversed, the telephone circuit must be "turned around." The modem that was transmitting is switched to the receive mode, and the modem that was receiving is switched to the transmit mode. Turning a circuit around can take several hundred milliseconds, a waste of valuable communications time.

Another disadvantage of half-duplex communication is that the receiving terminal cannot provide immediate feedback in case of errors. As mentioned previously in this book, some half-duplex modems have a low-speed back channel that is too slow for data communications, but which is adequate to allow the receiving terminal to signal the transmitter that a block of data was either received correctly or was received in error.

Full-duplex modems transmit and receive at the same time. When a full-duplex modem communicates over a four-wire leased telephone circuit (which is really two telephone circuits, one for communication in either direction), it can use the full bandwidth of the communications channel. For full-duplex communications over two-wire telephone circuits, technology once required modems to use one carrier frequency to transmit and a different carrier frequency to receive. Figure 9-2 illustrates how these modems divide the telephone line into two communications channels, which are labeled east-to-west and west-to-east in the figure. Each channel uses half the bandwidth of the telephone line.

The maximum possible communications speed is proportional to the bandwidth of the communications circuit. A full-duplex modem that uses half the bandwidth of a two-wire telephone circuit can carry data at half the speed of a comparable simplex circuit, which can use the full bandwidth. However, modems built to the latest standards use the full bandwidth of a two-wire telephone circuit for both transmitting and receiving. A block diagram of the transmit and receive sections of such a modem is pictured in Figure 9-3.

The **digital signal processor (DSP)** in Figure 9-3 performs the functions of modulation, demodulation, and echo cancellation. Digital data in serial format are input to the DSP, and the DSP generates a digital representation of the modulated carrier. The digital-to-analog converter (D/A) converts the digital output of the DSP to an analog signal, which passes through the hybrid circuit and onto the two-wire telephone line.

**FIGURE 9-2**

Most full-duplex modems divide the telephone circuit into two frequency bands, one for communication in either direction.

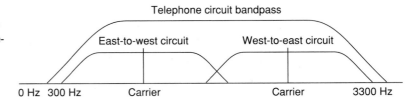

Telephone circuit bandpass

East-to-west circuit    West-to-east circuit

0 Hz  300 Hz        Carrier              Carrier        3300 Hz

**FIGURE 9-3**

Block diagram of the transmit and receive sections of a modem.

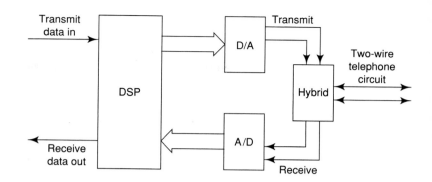

A *hybrid* is a circuit that connects a four-wire line to a two-wire line. In Figure 9-3, the hybrid passes the transmitted signal to the two-wire telephone line and blocks it from entering the modem's receive section and it routes the signal from the telephone line to the modem's receive section.

The received carrier from the two-wire telephone circuit passes through the hybrid to the analog-to-digital converter (A/D), which converts it to a digital format. The DSP demodulates the digitized received signal and outputs the received digital data in serial format.

Part of the transmitted signal leaks through the hybrid into the receive section of the modem. In addition, the telephone circuit reflects part of the transmitted signal back to the modem's receive section. By comparing the transmitted and received signals, the DSP is able to detect and remove any echoes of the transmitted signal that it finds in the received signal.

### 9-1-3 The Importance of Modem Standards

For a communications link to function properly, the modems on either end of the link must be compatible with each other. They must use the same type of modulation and the same protocol, and they must operate at the same speed. All modems built to the same standard ideally should be able to communicate with each other.

There are literally dozens of modem standards, and more are introduced each year. We cannot discuss them all in this book, but we will discuss the more important standards in Chapter 10, including several recent modem standards that use DSP technology to obtain data communications speeds that were thought to be impossible a decade ago.

## 9-2 SHANNON'S LAW

In 1948, Claude Shannon developed a mathematical equation to calculate the maximum rate at which data can be communicated over a given communications channel. The equation is known as **Shannon's Law.** Shannon's Law states that:

$$b/s = BW \log_2(1 \div S/N)$$

where: BW = bandwidth, S = signal power, and N = noise power.

Because logarithms to the base 2 are difficult to work with, the formula can be changed to work with logarithms to the base 10.

$$b/s = 3.32BW \log_{10}(1 + S/N)$$

We can use the formula to calculate the maximum data-carrying capacity of a typical dial-up telephone circuit. If the bandwidth of the line is 3000 Hz and the signal-to-noise ratio is 50 to 1,

$$\begin{aligned} b/s &= 3.32 \times 3000 \times \log_{10}(1 + 50/1) \\ &= 9960 \times 1.71 \\ &\cong 17{,}000 \text{ b/s} \end{aligned}$$

If the bandwidth is reduced to 1500 Hz, as is the case in many full-duplex communications systems, the maximum data-carrying capacity is:

$$\begin{aligned} b/s &= 3.32 \times 1500 \times \log_{10}(1 + 50/1) \\ &= 4980 \times 1.71 \\ &\cong 8500 \text{ b/s} \end{aligned}$$

The formula shows that the information-carrying capacity of a communications link is proportional to its bandwidth. If only half the bandwidth of a telephone circuit is used, as is the case in many full-duplex communications systems, the maximum possible communications speed is also cut in half.

For many years, technology limited data communications speeds to a fraction of the theoretical maximum. Today, a combination of modern DSP-based modems and low-noise telephone circuits allow full-duplex communications speeds over two-wire, dial-up telephone circuits to approach 20,000 b/s.

## 9-3 MODULATION TECHNIQUES

A modem modulates serial digital data onto a sine-wave carrier. Modulation occurs when the data vary some characteristic of the sine wave. The three sine-wave characteristics that can be varied are amplitude, frequency, and phase. Pure amplitude modulation (AM) is seldom used for data communications. Early low-speed modem standards, which are still widely employed, use frequency modulation (FM). In data communications, FM is called **frequency-shift keying (FSK).** Medium-speed modems use phase modulation (PM), which is called **phase-shift keying (PSK)** when it is used for data communications. Modern high-speed modems use a combination of AM and PSK.

### 9-3-1 Bits per Second Versus Baud

The speed of a modem can be measured in two ways, bits per second and baud. Bits per second (b/s) is a baseband measurement that refers to the rate at which a modem can transmit and receive data. As Figure 9-4 illustrates, it is the number of bits the modem can input from the DTE on its transmit data (TD) line for transmission or the number of bits per second it can output to the DTE on its received data (RD) line.

**FIGURE 9-4**
Bits per second refers to the data rate at the baseband side of the modem. Baud refers to the maximum number of changes per second that can take place in the modulated carrier.

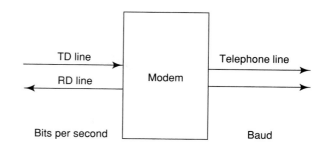

Baud refers to the maximum number of changes per second that can occur in the modulated carrier. It is measured at the analog or telephone line side of the modem. Low-speed FM modems modulate each bit individually onto the carrier. For these modems, the bit rate and the baud rate are the same. Higher-speed PM modems modulate groups of two, three, four, or five bits onto each phase change of the carrier. If a modem modulates groups of two bits onto the carrier, the baud rate is one-half the bit rate. If it modulates groups of three bits onto the carrier, the baud rate is one-third the bit rate.

---

■ **EXAMPLE 9-1**

If a modem transmits and receives at a bit rate of 9600 b/s, and it modulates groups of 4 bits onto the carrier, what is the bit rate of the modem?

**SOLUTION**

Because the modem modulates groups of 4 bits onto the carrier, the baud rate is one-fourth of the bit rate. 9600 ÷ 4 = 2400 baud.

---

In the days when almost all modems used FSK, the bit rate and baud rate of modems were the same. A 300-b/s modem was referred to as a "300-baud modem." Unfortunately, many of us in data communications still use the term *baud* instead of *bits per second* when we talk about the speed of a modem. You will often hear a 2400-b/s modem referred to as a *2400-baud modem,* which is technically incorrect. The 2400-b/s modem may be operating at 600 baud.

### 9-3-2 Amplitude Modulation (AM)

AM, illustrated in Figure 9-5, is the easiest type of modulation to perform. The carrier is transmitted at two different amplitudes. One of the amplitudes represents a mark, and the other represents a space. AM has two disadvantages that make it unsuitable for high-speed data communications: It uses too much bandwidth, and it is very susceptible to noise interference.

Remember that the frequency response of a telephone circuit is from about 300 Hz to 3300 Hz. The circuit's bandwidth is therefore 3300 Hz – 300 Hz, or 3000 Hz. When data are modulated onto a carrier, sidebands are generated. If the modulated

**FIGURE 9-5**
Amplitude modulation uses one amplitude to represent a binary 1 and another amplitude to represent a binary 0.

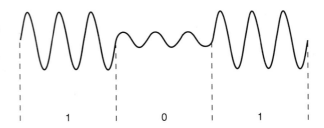

carrier is transmitted over a telephone circuit, the sidebands must fit within the circuit's bandwidth.

Amplitude modulation produces two sidebands. One of the sideband frequencies equals the carrier frequency plus the frequency of the intelligence information, and the other sideband frequency equals the carrier frequency minus the intelligence frequency. Figure 9-6 shows a series of two bits, a 1 and a 0, compared with the frequency of a sine wave. Figure 9-6 illustrates that the fundamental frequency of a serial digital signal is equal to half the bit rate. A serial digital signal of 500 b/s has a fundamental frequency of 250 Hz.

If a digital signal of 500 b/s is modulated onto a 1000-Hz carrier frequency, the bandwidth is the same as if the carrier were modulated by a 250-Hz sine wave. Sidebands are generated at 1000 Hz + 250 Hz, or 1250 Hz, and at 1000 Hz – 250 Hz, or 750 Hz. Total bandwidth is 1250 Hz – 750 Hz, or 500 Hz, equal to the data rate of 500 b/s. As the data speed increases, the required bandwidth increases proportionally. At 1500 b/s, an AM signal would occupy half of the 3000-Hz bandwidth of the telephone circuit. That is the theoretical maximum speed of an AM modem for full-duplex communications without echo canceling.

Mainly because AM is very susceptible to noise, but also because the maximum data speed of an AM modem is limited, the only use of pure AM for data communications over telephone circuits is in the low-speed back channel in some older, half-duplex modems. However, as mentioned earlier, AM and PSK are combined to obtain high communications speeds in many modern modems.

### 9-3-3  Frequency-Shift Keying (FSK)

FSK, which is illustrated in Figure 9-7, uses two different frequencies to represent data. One of the frequencies represents a mark, and the other represents a space.

**FIGURE 9-6**
The fundamental frequency of a serial digital signal is half the bit rate.

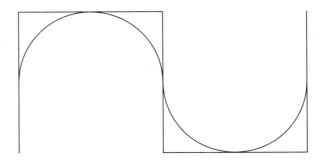

**FIGURE 9-7**
Frequency modulations uses two frequencies. One of the frequencies represents a binary 1, and the other frequency represents a binary 0.

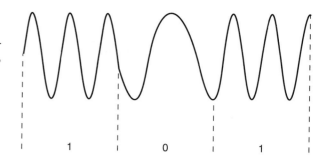

FSK was the first type of modulation that was widely used for data communications, and it is still used in low-speed modems. FSK is much less susceptible to noise interference than is AM. A disadvantage of FSK is that it uses at least as much bandwidth as AM does. The bandwidth of an FSK signal is from two to three times the baud rate. FSK modems modulate each bit separately onto the carrier. Therefore, the bit rate and the baud rate of FSK are the same. For a 3000-Hz-wide telephone circuit, the maximum theoretical speed of a simplex FSK modem is 1500 b/s. Practical FSK modem speeds are much slower. Full-duplex FSK modems typically operate at 300 b/s, and simplex or half-duplex modems operate at speeds up to about 1200 b/s.

### 9-3-4 Phase-Shift Keying (PSK)

Most modern modems use PSK. PSK modulation schemes can be quite complex. The bandwidth of a PSK signal is twice the baud rate. A modem that transmits at 1200 baud has a bandwidth of 2400 Hz. If half the telephone circuit bandwidth is used for full-duplex operation, transmission speeds are limited to about 600 baud for reliable operation over dial-up telephone circuits. However, the bit rate of PSK modems may be several times the baud rate.

#### Binary Phase-Shift Keying (BPSK)

The simplest type of PSK is called **binary phase-shift keying (BPSK)**, which is illustrated in Figure 9-8. BPSK uses two phases, one phase to represent a binary 0 and the other phase to represent a binary 1. Each time the data change from a binary 1 to a binary 0 or from a binary 0 to a binary 1, the transmitting modem shifts the phase of the carrier 180 degrees. Because each data bit is individually modulated onto the carrier, the bit rate and the baud rate of BPSK are equal. The maximum

**FIGURE 9-8**
Binary phase-shift keying uses a phase shift of 180° to indicate when the data change from a binary 1 to a binary 0 or from a binary 0 to a binary 1.

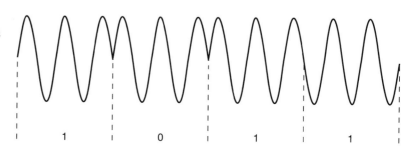

speed of a BPSK modem is limited to approximately 1200 b/s simplex or half-duplex and to about 600 b/s full-duplex without echo canceling for reliable operation over a dial-up telephone line.

Figure 9-9 shows three types of diagrams that are commonly used to represent a BPSK signal. Figure 9-9(a) is a *truth table* that shows the phase of the carrier used to represent a binary 0 and a binary 1. Figure 9-9(b) is a **phasor diagram.** The arrows, or **phasors,** represent both the phase and the amplitude of the carrier for the binary 0 and binary 1 conditions. The length of the phasor represents the amplitude of the carrier, and the position of the phasor indicates its phase angle.

**FIGURE 9-9**
(a) BPSK truth table; (b) BPSK phasor diagram; (c) BPSK constellation diagram.

| Data input | Output phase |
|------------|--------------|
| 0 | 180° |
| 1 | 0° |

(a)

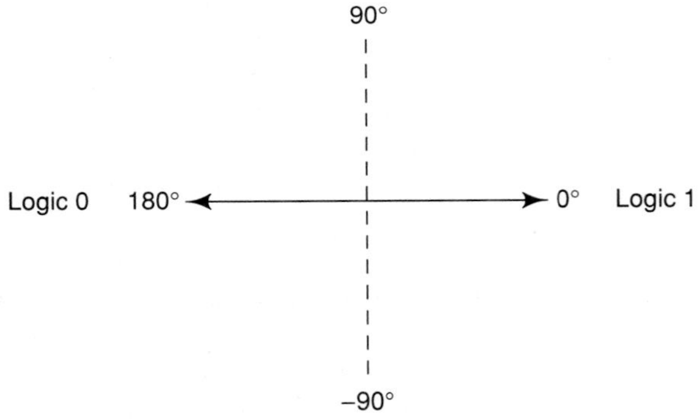

(b)

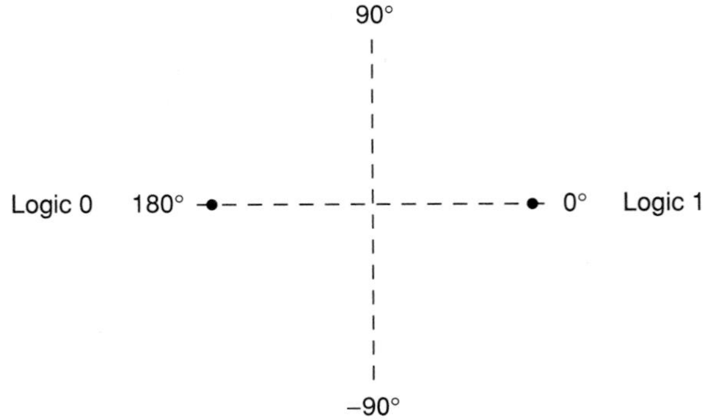

(c)

Figure 9-9(c) is a **constellation diagram.** A constellation diagram is similar to a phasor diagram, but instead of a phasor, it uses a single dot to represent the phase and amplitude of the carrier for each input condition. The dot is placed where the arrowhead of the phasor would be. Some modem standards use many phases and two amplitudes to transmit data. The large number of phasors required to represent the possible output conditions of these modems make a phasor diagram very cluttered and difficult to read. A constellation diagram has the advantage of being easier to interpret.

### Quadrature Phase-Shift Keying (QPSK)

**Quadrature phase-shift keying,** also called *quaternary PSK* or *QPSK,* uses four different phases to represent data. Groups of two bits (called **dibits**) are modulated onto the carrier. As illustrated in Figure 9-10(a), the transmitter section of the modem contains a 2-bit shift register. Serial data from the DTE are shifted into the shift register to form dibits. Each dibit is applied in parallel to the modulator. The modulator uses the dibit to determine the correct phase of the transmitted carrier. Because the carrier is phase shifted every second bit, the baud rate is one-half the bit rate.

Figure 9-10(b) shows how the receive section of the modem functions. The demodulator examines the phase of the received carrier and uses the phase to determine the correct dibit. It outputs the dibit in parallel to a 2-bit shift register, which in turn shifts the data out in serial format to the DTE.

Figure 9-11 shows a truth table and a constellation diagram for the Bell 212A QPSK modem. The phase shifts shown are *differential.* **Differential phase-shift keying** uses the previous dibit as a reference. For example, if the modem sends the dibit 01, there is no phase shift, and the phase of the carrier remains the same as it was

**FIGURE 9-10**
(a) A QPSK modulator modulates 2 bits onto each phase shift of the carrier.
(b) A QPSK demodulator recovers 2 bits from each phase shift of the received carrier.

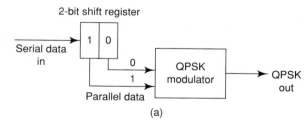

(a)

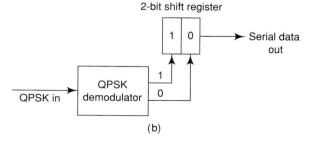

(b)

**FIGURE 9-11**
QPSK uses four phases and modulates a dibits onto the carrier. (a) Truth table for Bell 212A modem. (b) Constellation diagram for Bell 212A modem.

| Dibit | Phase |
|-------|-------|
| 00    | 90°   |
| 01    | 0°    |
| 10    | 180°  |
| 11    | −90°  |

(a)

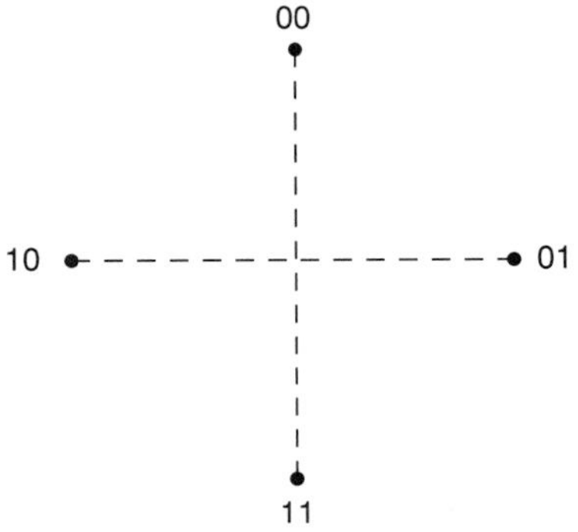

(b)

during the previous dibit. When the dibit 11 is sent, the modem phase shifts the carrier −90° in relation to the carrier phase when the previous dibit was sent.

The advantage of QPSK over two-phase PSK is higher speed. Because groups of 2 bits are modulated onto the carrier, the bit rate is twice the baud rate. Therefore, a QPSK modem operating at 1200 baud has a data rate of 2400 b/s. The disadvantage is that QPSK is more susceptible to errors than is BPSK. Telephone circuits have phase distortion, which causes phase errors in the received carrier. Because BPSK uses a 180°-phase shift, it can tolerate telephone circuit phase distortions approaching 90°. QPSK can tolerate telephone circuit phase distortions approaching 45°.

### Eight-Phase Phase-Shift Keying (8PSK)

**Eight-phase phase-shift keying,** shown in Figure 9-12, uses groups of 3 bits (**tribits**) to determine each phase shift of the carrier. In the transmitting modem, 3 bits are shifted into a shift register and applied in parallel to the modulating circuit. With 3 bits, there are $2^3$, or 8, different phase shifts that can be modulated onto the carrier. The phases are 45° apart, which means that 8PSK modems can tolerate telephone circuit phase distortions approaching 22.5° without error. To make errors easier to detect, 8PSK modems use a special encoding scheme. If you examine the constellation diagram in Figure 9-12(b), you may notice that only one of the bits changes

**FIGURE 9-12**
8PSK uses encodes a tribit onto each phase shift. (a) truth table (b) constellation diagram.

| Tribit | | | Phase Angle |
|:---:|:---:|:---:|:---:|
| 0 | 0 | 0 | −112.5° |
| 0 | 0 | 1 | −157.5° |
| 0 | 1 | 0 | −67.5° |
| 0 | 1 | 1 | −22.5° |
| 1 | 0 | 0 | +112.5° |
| 1 | 0 | 1 | +157.5° |
| 1 | 1 | 0 | +67.5° |
| 1 | 1 | 1 | +22.5° |

(a)

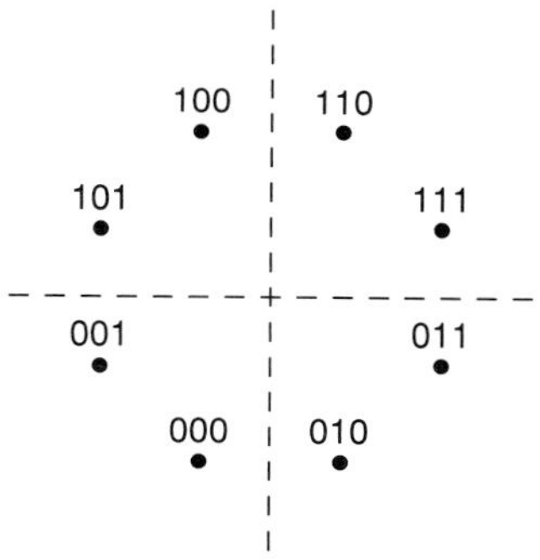

(b)

between adjacent tribits. Because of this encoding scheme, most phase distortion errors cause only 1 bit in a tribit to be received in error.

Because 8PSK uses tribits, the bit rate is three times the baud rate, and bit rates of three times the communications channel bandwidth are possible. For a 3000-Hz-wide telephone circuit, data can theoretically be transmitted at speeds of up to 9000 b/s. In practice, 8PSK is not often used, because a combination of PM and AM modulation, called *quadrature amplitude modulation,* is able to send tribits with fewer errors.

## Quadrature Amplitude Modulation (QAM)

**Quadrature amplitude modulation (QAM)** uses a combination of PSK and AM. Figure 9-13 shows the truth table and constellation diagram for 8QAM. Like 8PSK, 8QAM transmits tribits, and the bit rate is three times the baud rate. The maximum possible bit rate is also three times the bandwidth of the communications circuit. Adjacent points on the 8QAM constellation diagram differ by only 1 bit to make errors easier to detect. Unlike 8PSK, 8QAM needs only 4 phases to represent each of the 8 possible tribits. Each of the 4 phases can have two different amplitudes. The advantage of 8QAM over 8PSK is that 8QAM can tolerate larger phase errors on the communications link, and therefore the bit error rate is lower. A disadvantage

**FIGURE 9-13**
The output of an 8QAM modem.
(a) a truth table (b) constellation
diagram.

| Binary Input | Amplitude | Phase |
|---|---|---|
| 000 | 0.765 V | −135° |
| 001 | 1.848 V | −135° |
| 010 | 0.765 V | −45° |
| 011 | 1.848 V | −45° |
| 100 | 0.765 V | +135° |
| 101 | 1.848 V | +135° |
| 110 | 0.765 V | +45° |
| 111 | 1.848 V | +45° |

(a)

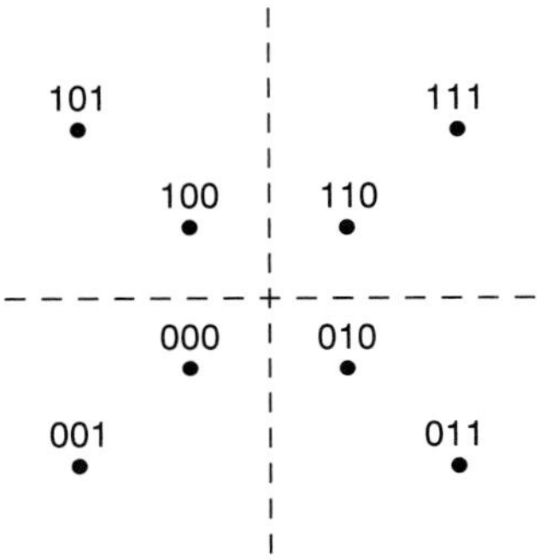

(b)

that 8QAM used to have is that it requires more complicated electronics to combine two types of modulation. However, with modern DSP-based modems, that is no longer a problem.

Figure 9-14 gives the truth table and constellation diagram for 16QAM. **16QAM** uses quadbits to modulate the carrier. The modulated carrier makes use of 12 phase angles and 3 amplitudes to represent the data. The bit rate is 4 times the baud rate, and the maximum bit rate is 4 times the bandwidth of the circuit. As in other QAM modulation schemes, adjacent points on the constellation diagram differ by only 1 bit to reduce errors.

## 9-3-5 Data Compression

Communications engineers are constantly attempting to find new methods of sending more data over a telephone circuit. As the bit rate is increased, the error rate also increases. One method used to increase the apparent speed of a modem is **data compression.** Simply stated, data compression is a method of using fewer bits to represent the same information. We will discuss some specific data compression schemes in Chapter 10. A few simple examples here will serve as an introduction to the topic.

**FIGURE 9-14**
The output of a 16QAM modem.
(a) truth table (b) constellation
diagram.

| Binary Input | Amplitude | Phase |
|---|---|---|
| 0000 | 0.311 V | −135° |
| 0001 | 0.850 V | −165° |
| 0010 | 0.311 V | −45° |
| 0011 | 0.850 V | −15° |
| 0100 | 0.850 V | −105° |
| 0101 | 1.161 V | −135° |
| 0110 | 0.850 V | −75° |
| 0111 | 1.161 V | −45° |
| 1000 | 0.311 V | 135° |
| 1001 | 0.850 V | 175° |
| 1010 | 0.311 V | 45° |
| 1011 | 0.850 V | 15° |
| 1100 | 0.850 V | 105° |
| 1101 | 1.161 V | 135° |
| 1110 | 0.850 V | 75° |
| 1111 | 1.161 V | 45° |

(a)

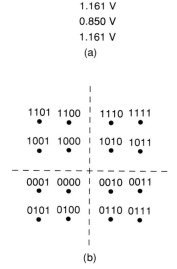

(b)

Much of the information in a text message is repetitive. For example, in an English language message, the word *the* appears quite frequently. If we were developing a data compression scheme based on the English language, we might have our transmitting modems replace the word *the* by the number *1*. This substitution replaces three characters with a single character. Another combination that appears frequently in the English language is the sequence of letters *ion*. This sequence could be replaced by the number *2*. Again, we would replace three characters with a single character. With additional study, many more frequently occurring sequences of letters could be found that could be replaced by shorter characters.

The receive modem would reverse the process. When it received the character *1*, it would replace it with *the*. It would likewise replace the character *2* with *ion*. But what would the modems do if the text contained the actual numbers 1 and 2? The transmitting modem could place a seldom-used character in front of them, such as the backslash (\). The backslash would tell the receiving modem that the following character was not a symbol for a combination of letters but really a number. The number *12,* for example, would be sent as \\*1*\\*2.*

As we will see in Chapter 10, practical data compression schemes look for repeated patterns in the bit stream and replace them with shorter combinations of bits.

### 9-3-6 Synchronous and Asynchronous Modems

You should remember from Chapter 8 that in a synchronous communications system, the clock signals of the transmit and the receive DTEs must be at exactly the same frequency and phase. In an asynchronous communications system, the receive DTE uses the start bit at the beginning of each character to resynchronize itself to the received data. Therefore, the clock frequencies of the transmit and receive DTEs may differ by a few percent in an asynchronous system.

Not only are communications systems divided into synchronous and asynchronous types, but modems are also either synchronous or asynchronous. Synchronous modems require a clock signal of the proper frequency and phase. Asynchronous modems do not require a clock signal, and they must be used in asynchronous communications systems. Synchronous modems can be used in either synchronous or asynchronous communications systems.

FSK modems are asynchronous. They do not require a clock signal to frequency modulate the data onto the carrier. They also do not require a clock signal to demodulate the received data. FSK modems are almost always used in low-speed, asynchronous communications systems.

With their internal shift registers, QPSK and QAM modems are synchronous. The shift registers require a clock signal of the correct frequency and phase, even when they are used in asynchronous communications systems. The receive modem derives its clock signal from the received data stream.

Figure 9-15 shows how the clock signal is supplied to the components of a synchronous communications system. The transmitting DCE usually generates the clock signal and supplies it to the transmitting DTE by means of the RS-232 or other interface. The receive DCE has internal clock recovery circuitry that uses the transitions between 1 and 0 in the incoming bit stream to synchronize an internal clock oscillator so that its signal is the same frequency and phase as the transmit clock sig-

**FIGURE 9-15**
In synchronous transmission, the receive DCE recovers the clock signal from the incoming data.

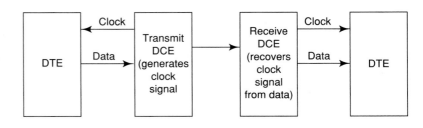

nal. In synchronous communications systems, the receive DCE passes this clock signal on to the receive DTE.

What if QPSK or QAM modems are used in an asynchronous communications system? In fact, a system that uses QPSK or QAM modems is not completely asynchronous. The transmitting DTE and DCE must be synchronized with each other, because the shift register in the DCE must operate in step with the bit stream that the DTE sends to it. The receive DCE must derive a clock signal from the incoming bit stream, because its shift register must be synchronized with that bit stream. The receive DTE is the only part of the system that does not require its clock to be in perfect synchronization with the rest of the system.

When synchronous modems are used in an "asynchronous" communications system, there is really no need to transmit the start and stop bits. The transmitting modem often eliminates the start and stop bits from the data stream in order to speed up communications, and the receive modem adds them back to the data stream. As we will see in Chapter 10, removing the start and stop bits is a simple form of data compression that improves communication speed by 20%.

## ■ SUMMARY

This chapter has presented an overview of the function of the modem (also called a DCE or data set) in a communications system. The modem interfaces between the digital serial signal of the DTE and an analog communications medium such as a telephone line. Most modems today are designed by semiconductor manufacturers, which sell the electronics to modem manufacturers in the form of a chipset consisting of from one to three integrated circuits. A computer manufacturer may build the modem chipset into the motherboard of a computer or terminal. A plug-in modem is built onto a small circuit board that plugs into a slot in the computer's motherboard. Stand-alone modems are built into a separate case located outside of the computer.

Modems may be simplex, half-duplex, or full-duplex. Simplex and half-duplex modems can use the full bandwidth of a two-wire telephone circuit. Older full-duplex modem standards use half the bandwidth of a two-wire circuit for communications in each direction. Shannon's Law states that the maximum possible communications speed is proportional to the bandwidth of the communications channel. Therefore, a full-duplex modem that uses half of the telephone circuit's bandwidth can operate at only half the speed of a simplex or half-duplex modem. Newer DSP-based full-duplex modems with echo canceling use the full bandwidth of a two-wire telephone circuit for both transmitting and receiving.

Bits per second (b/s) and baud are both measurements of modem speed. Bits per second is a baseband measurement and is measured at the DTE side of the modem. Baud is the maximum number of changes per second that can occur in the modulated carrier. FM modems modulate each bit separately onto the carrier. For these modems, b/s and baud are the same. Medium and high-speed modems modulate groups of 2, 3, 4, or 5 bits onto each change in the carrier. These modems can handle more b/s than their baud rate.

The three types of modulation are AM, FSK, and PSK. Low-speed modems use FSK. Medium-speed modems use PSK, and high-speed modems use a combination of PSK and AM known as quadrature amplitude modulation or QAM.

Binary phase-shift keying (BPSK) uses two phases to represent binary data. For BPSK, the bit rate and the baud rate are equal. Quadrature phase-shift keying (QPSK) modulates groups of two bits (called dibits) onto the carrier and uses four different carrier phases to represent the dibits. The bit rate of a QPSK modem is double the baud rate. Eight-phase phase-shift keying (8PSK) uses 8 phases to represent groups of 3 bits (tribits). The bit rate of 8PSK is triple its baud rate. Quadrature amplitude modulation (QAM) uses 4 phases and 2 amplitudes to modulate tribits onto a carrier. QAM can tolerate larger phase errors on the communications link and is therefore preferred over 8PSK for data communications.

Phasor diagrams and constellation diagrams are both used to represent the output of PSK and QAM modems. A phasor diagram uses arrows (called phasors) to represent the phase and amplitude of the carrier. A constellation diagram uses dots instead of arrows. Constellation diagrams are less cluttered and easier to read than phasor diagrams.

Data compression is a method of using fewer bits to represent information. Many modern modems employ data compression to speed communications.

FSK modems, which do not require a clock signal and are therefore asynchronous, are used mainly in slower, asynchronous communications systems. QPSK and QAM modems do require a clock signal, and the sending and receiving modems must be synchronized, even when they are used in communications systems that are otherwise asynchronous. Typically, the sending modem generates the clock signal and also supplies it to the DTE. The receiving modem synchronizes its internal clock to the received bit stream. In a synchronous communications system, the receive modem also passes this clock signal on to the receiving DTE.

## ■ QUESTIONS

1. What are two other names for *modem?*
2. List the five basic functions that a modem performs.
3. What is a modem *chipset?*
4. Who designs the electronic circuitry used in most of the modems produced today?
5. a.  In what three physical forms are modems built?
   b.  Which of the three forms is most popular?
   c.  Why is this the most popular type?
6. Name some applications of simplex modems.
7. a.  Why can half-duplex modems use the full bandwidth of the telephone circuit?
   b.  What are two disadvantages of half-duplex communications?

    c.   What purpose does the low-speed back channel serve in some half-duplex modems?

8. a.   Why can a full-duplex modem that is built to older standards operate at only half the speed of a simplex modem when a two-wire telephone circuit is used?

    b.   What technique makes it possible for full-duplex modems, built to newer standards, to use the full bandwidth of a two-wire telephone circuit for communications in both directions?

9. a.   Which law states the maximum communications speed that is possible over a given communications channel?

    b.   What effect does doubling the bandwidth of a communications channel have on the theoretical maximum communications speed that the channel can handle?

10. What are the three characteristics of a sine wave that can be varied during modulation?

11. a.   What type of modulation is used in low-speed modems?

    b.   What type of modulation is used in medium-speed modems?

    c.   Which two modulation techniques are combined in high-speed modems?

12. a.   Describe the difference between bit rate and baud rate as measurements of communications speed.

    b.   Are the bit rate and the baud rate the same in FSK modems?

    c.   Are the bit rate and the baud rate always the same in PSK modems?

13. a.   What two factors make AM, if used alone, unsuitable for high-speed data communications?

    b.   What application does AM have in some older, half-duplex modems?

14. a.   What is the advantage of FSK compared to AM for data communications?

    b.   What is a disadvantage of FSK?

15. a.   At what speeds do full-duplex FSK modems typically operate?

    b.   At what speeds do simplex and half-duplex FSK modems typically operate?

16. a.   Briefly explain how BPSK modems represent binary data.

    b.   Are the bit rate and the baud rate of a BPSK modem the same, or are they different?

17. a.   What characteristic of a phasor diagram represents the amplitude of the carrier?

    b.   What characteristic of a phasor diagram represents the phase angle of the carrier?

18. a.   What is the difference between a phasor diagram and a constellation diagram?

    b.   Why are constellation diagrams easier to read than phasor diagrams?

19. a. How many phases does QPSK use to represent data?

    b. Why are the bit rate and baud rate of a QPSK modem not equal?

20. What is differential phase-shift keying?

21. a. What is the advantage of QPSK compared to two-phase PSK?

    b. What is the disadvantage of QPSK compared to two-phase PSK.

22. a. In 8PSK modulation, how many bits are modulated onto each phase shift of the carrier?

    b. What technique is used to reduce errors in 8PSK modems?

    c. Why is 8PSK not often used?

23. a. What is the relationship between the bit rate and the baud rate in QAM?

    b. How many phases does 8QAM use to represent data?

    c. What two types of modulation are combined in 8QAM?

    d. Why is QAM superior to 8PSK?

24. a. In 16QAM, what is the relationship between the bit rate and the baud rate?

    b. What is the maximum bit rate of 16QAM in relationship to the bandwidth of the communications circuit?

25. Explain briefly how data compression increases the apparent speed of a modem.

26. a. What is the difference between synchronous modems and asynchronous modems?

    b. Are FSK modems synchronous, or are they asynchronous?

    c. Are QPSK and QAM modems synchronous, or are they asynchronous?

27. a. Which component of a synchronous point-to-point communications system usually generates the clock signal?

    b. From where does the receive DCE get its clock signal?

    c. From where do the transmit and receive DTEs get their clock signals?

# ■ Chapter 10
## MODEM STANDARDS

**OBJECTIVES**

After you have completed this chapter, you should be able to:

- Name the two organizations that have historically set modem standards in North America.
- Discuss the purpose of the AT command set.
- Explain why a computer that uses a modem needs a communications software program.
- Discuss in general terms the features of the Microcom Network Protocol and the V.42 and V.42 bis protocols.
- Explain the difference between Huffman encoding and run-length encoding.
- State the most important characteristics of the following modem modulation standards: Bell 103, Bell 202, Bell 212A, V.22 bis, V.32, and V.32 bis.

**INTRODUCTION**

This chapter discusses the more common modem standards in use today. Modem standards can be divided into three types, (1) standard methods for controlling the operation of a modem, (2) standard methods for compressing data and checking it for transmission errors, and (3) standard methods for modulating data onto a carrier at the sending modem and demodulating it at the receiving end.

Two organizations that have historically set modem standards in North America are the Bell System of telephone companies and the Consultative Committee for International Telegraph and Telephone (CCITT). The Bell System standards were designed for use in North America only, whereas the CCITT standards are designed to be used throughout the world.

The Bell modem standards were developed in the 1960s when the American Telephone and Telegraph Company (AT&T) and the various Bell telephone companies that it controlled dominated the telephone industry in the United States and Canada. Until the late 1960s, North American telephone companies dictated which equipment could be connected to their local loops. Almost the only equipment approved was equipment sold by the telephone companies themselves. Most modems sold in North America were designed and manufactured by Western Electric, the Bell System's manufacturing company. Those modems became North American standards, because they were the only ones that could legally be connected to most telephone company local loops. But in the rest of the world, the CCITT set modem standards. CCITT standards were usually not compatible with those of the Bell System. Modem incompatibility made data communications difficult between North America and the rest of the world.

In 1968 a famous court decision, now known as the **Carterphone decision,** permitted non-Bell equipment to be connected to local loops. That decision drastically altered the telecommunications business in the United States and opened the door to competition in the modem business. Prices dropped drastically. Since the Carterphone decision, any modem, as long as it meets certain safety standards, can be connected to a telephone line. Many new manufacturers entered the modem business, and they wisely abandoned the practice of developing separate modem standards for North America. Instead, they became involved with the CCITT in designing and supporting international modem standards. Most modems manufactured in North American today comply with one or more of the CCITT standards and can be used for international communications.

Today's modems are much more than simple modulators and demodulators. Even a $50 modem has built-in features such as error checking and correction and data compression. A modern modem works together with a computer and its software to place and answer telephone calls without the intervention of a human operator.

## 10-1    CONTROLLING THE MODEM, THE AT COMMAND SET

Early modems were little more than modulators and demodulators. To use one of these modems to send data over a dial-up telephone line, the operator first had to establish the telephone connection using a conventional telephone handset. The operator lifted the handset, listened for a dial tone, and dialed the telephone number of the terminal that was to receive the data. The operator waited for the called modem to answer the call and place a carrier on the telephone line. Upon hearing the carrier, the operator threw a switch to disconnect the handset from the telephone circuit and connect the modem in its place. The operator then pressed a button on the originating terminal to cause it to transmit data. If the operator wished to be sure that the data were successfully communicated to the other end, it was necessary to wait for an acknowledgment from the remote modem. An acknowledgement indicated that the other terminal had received the data without a parity error. If a parity error did occur, the operator had to send the data again. These early modems, which required an operator to perform almost any function, are sometimes called **dumb modems.**

**Intelligent modems** began to appear in the late 1970s. Intelligent modems have built-in microprocessors that can dial telephone numbers, recognize a busy signal, answer incoming calls, correct errors, and perform many other functions. The terminal controls an intelligent modem by sending it special sequences of characters. The modem recognizes the characters as commands. The most common system of commands is the **AT command set,** which is also known as the **Hayes command set.** Hayes Microcomputer Products developed the AT command set for the modems that it manufactures. Other manufacturers also began using the AT command set, and it quickly became a de facto standard. Some of the more common AT commands are shown in Figure 10-1.

### 10-1-1 The AT Command Mode

In the AT command set, all modem commands begin with the ASCII characters *AT,* which stand for ATtention. When the modem is not communicating with another modem, it is in the *command mode,* and it examines any information that the termi-

**FIGURE 10-1**
Some common commands in the AT command set.

| Character(s) | Command |
|---|---|
| AT | Attention |
| A | Answer an incoming call |
| DT | Dial using DTMF tones |
| DP | Dial using pulse dialing |
| E0 | Do not echo transmitted data to terminal screen |
| E1 | Echo transmitted data to terminal screen |
| F0 | Half-duplex communications |
| F1 | Full-duplex communications |
| H | Go on hook (hang up) |
| O | Switch from command to on-line mode |
| Z | Reset modem |
| +++ | Escape code. Switch from on-line to command mode. |

nal sends it by way of the DTE, looking for the ASCII characters AT. When it receives them, it interprets the characters that follow as commands. For example, the ASCII character for $D$ is the command to dial, and $T$ is the command to use DTMF tones instead of pulse dialing. To cause the modem to dial the number 1-(206) 555-1212, the terminal sends the modem the ASCII characters for the string ATDT12065551212.

### 10-1-2 The AT On-Line Mode

When the modem establishes communications with a remote modem, it switches from the command mode to the *on-line mode.* In the on-line mode, the modem treats characters it receives from the terminal, including the AT characters, as data. It modulates them onto the carrier and sends them to the remote modem. The terminal can order the modem to switch from the on-line mode back to the command mode by briefly pausing in the transmission of data, sending a series of three plus signs ($+++$) and pausing again. This sequence is called an **escape code.** The modem responds to the escape code by switching to the command mode, where it again recognizes AT commands. To give an example, $H$ is the command to cause the modem to go on hook, or "hang up," and terminate the telephone call. To end a communications session, the terminal pauses, sends the modem the ASCII characters $+++$, pauses again, and then sends the characters *ATH.* The three plus signs are the escape code that switches the modem into the command mode, the characters *AT* get the modem's attention, and the character $H$ commands the modem to go on hook.

### 10-1-3 Communications Software

Although the user can type AT commands directly into the terminal to control the modem, remembering all of the commands is difficult. It is much more efficient to use a **communications software program.** Remember that most communications terminals are actually computers. A communications software program, also known as a **terminal program,** is computer software that allows the computer to imitate a terminal and aids it in working with the modem. Communications software controls data flow between the terminal and the modem, and it manages the computer's keyboard, display, and disk drives while the modem is in use. Modern communications software allows the computer operator to enter simple commands or click a mouse button to control the modem. For example, to command the modem to dial a telephone number, the user may use the mouse to click on the word *dial* on the computer's screen. The software package will then send the proper AT command to the modem to cause it to dial the number of the remote terminal and establish communications with its modem.

Communications software includes a telephone directory on disk so that the user does not have to type in the telephone number of the remote terminal every time a call is placed. The operator types the names and telephone numbers of frequently called terminals into the directory one time. Along with the telephone number, the operator enters such information as how many data bits and stop bits to use, what type of parity to use, and which data compression and error correction schemes to use with each remote terminal. Once the information is entered into the directory, it is simple to place a call. The computer operator selects a name in the directory, and the communications software takes over from there and directs the computer's modem to dial the telephone number and establish a connection with the remote terminal. For example, someone living in Arizona may have an entry in the directory called "Phoenix Library Catalog." Selecting this entry will cause the communications software to send the modem the necessary commands to cause it to dial the telephone number of the public library in Phoenix, Arizona, and connect itself to one of the modems that serve the library's computerized card catalog.

## 10-2   ERROR CONTROL AND DATA COMPRESSION STANDARDS

Two desirable features in data communications are speed and accuracy, but there is a tradeoff between the two. As communications speed increases, the number of transmission errors in a given block of data also increases. On the other hand, error checking and forward error correction schemes depend on redundant information added to the data stream, and redundant information slows communications. If data must be retransmitted to correct errors, communications are slowed even more. Because they are so closely linked, modern standards to control errors work closely with standards that speed communications.

We saw in Chapter 9 that Shannon's Law limits the speed at which data can be transmitted over an analog telephone line. Chapter 9 also discussed the fact that data compression can significantly increase communications speed by using fewer bits to represent any given amount of information. Figure 10-2 illustrates the principle. The figure shows information being sent from the transmitting DTE to the DCE over the transmit data (TD) line at 4800 b/s. The transmitting modem (DCE) compresses the information so that only half as many bits are needed to represent it and transmits the information over the telephone line at 2400 b/s. The receiving modem decompresses the information to restore it to its original form and sends it to the receive DTE at 4800 b/s. From the point of view of the DTE, the compression is transparent. For all practical purposes, communications takes place at 4800 b/s.

**FIGURE 10-2**
Data compression allows information to be communicated more rapidly without increasing the number of b/s sent over the telephone line.

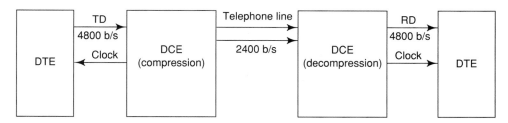

The two most common methods that modems use to compress data and check data for transmission errors are the Micron Network Protocol (MNP) and CCITT standards V.42 and V.42 bis. Both MNP and V.42 divide the transmitted data into blocks, and each block ends with a cyclic redundancy check (CRC) character. The receive modem also calculates a CRC character from the received data and matches it against the CRC character that the transmitting modem sends to it. If the two CRC characters do not match, there is an error in the block of data.

## 10-2-1 MNP Error Control and Compression

The **Microcom Network Protocol (MNP)** is able to both detect and correct errors and to perform data compression. Microcom, Inc., a modem manufacturer, developed MNP for use with its own modems, but it freely licenses the protocol to other manufacturers. MNP has become a de facto standard. This section discusses the five basic levels of the MNP protocol. Simple modems may use only the lower levels of MNP. More complex modems may be capable of using up to level 5.

### Levels 1 and 2 of the MNP Protocol

Levels 1 and 2 perform error detection and correction. Level 1 is used for simplex or half-duplex communications. Level 2 is used with full-duplex communications. Both levels use a CRC character to detect errors. The sending modem divides the transmitted data into blocks, generates a CRC character for each block and transmits the CRC character at the end of the block of data. The receive modem also generates a CRC character for each block of received data and compares it with the CRC character generated by the sending modem. If the two are identical, the receive modem accepts the data and sends an acknowledgment (ACK) back to the sending modem. If they are different, the receive modem assumes that the block contains an error and sends a negative acknowledgment (NAK) to the sending modem to request retransmission. CRC error detection was discussed in greater detail in Chapter 5.

MNP levels 1 and 2 do ensure that data is communicated with fewer errors. However, the information that marks the beginning and end of each block, the CRC character, the ACK or NAK character that the receive modem sends back at the end of each block, and the retransmission of blocks received in error all slow data communications. This slowness is part of the tradeoff between speed and accuracy that was mentioned at the beginning of this section. Given the noisy nature of many telephone circuits, some form of error correction is essential, even if it does slow communications.

### Level 3 of the MNP Protocol

MNP level 3 includes the error checks of level 2, but it also performs a simple type of data compression on asynchronous data by not sending the start and stop bits over the telephone link. As Figure 10-3 illustrates, the transmitting modem eliminates the start and stop bits, and the receive modem adds them back to the data stream. You should remember from Chapter 9 that PSK and QAM modems are synchronous, even when they are used in an asynchronous communications system. Synchronous modems do not need start and stop bits. Eliminating the start and stop bits

**FIGURE 10-3**
By eliminating the start and stop bits, a DCE using MNP level 3 data compression sends asynchronous data 20% faster.

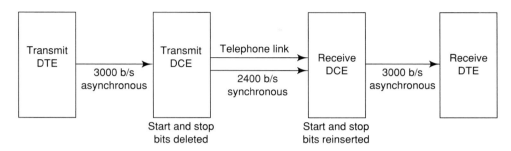

shortens the 10-bit asynchronous data word to an 8-bit synchronous word and improves communications speed between the DTEs by 20%. Even when the overhead of level 2 error checking is added to the data stream, communication using MNP level 3 is slightly faster than communication without MNP. MNP level 3 cannot be used with FSK modems, because FSK modems are asynchronous.

**Level 4 of the MNP Protocol**
MNP level 4 improves error checking and speeds communications by allowing the blocks of data to be of different sizes. When line conditions are good and the modems are encountering few transmission errors, MNP level 4 causes the modems to send long blocks of data, which improves communications speed by reducing the overhead. If line conditions are noisy and errors are occurring more frequently, MNP level 4 causes the modems to shorten the length of the data blocks so that there is a smaller chance for an error to occur in any given block.

**Level 5 of the MNP Protocol**
MNP level 5 adds data compression, which can substantially increase the speed at which data are transferred. MNP level 5 uses two different types of compression, *Huffman encoding* and *run-length encoding.* The two types of encoding are illustrated in Figure 10-4.
    **Huffman encoding** is a data compression scheme that uses fewer bits to represent characters that occur frequently in a transmission and more bits to represent characters that do not occur frequently. Huffman encoding, which is illustrated in Figure 10-4(a), works well with text. It takes advantage of the fact that certain characters occur more frequently than others. For example, the most frequently occurring characters in English-language text are lowercase *a, e, s,* and the space character. Huffman encoding represents the most frequently occurring characters in as few as 4 bits, instead of the 7 or 8 bits that ASCII requires. Letters that rarely occur, for example uppercase *X* in English, are encoded by as many as 11 bits. Figure 10-4(a) illustrates how the sequence ATE might be compressed using Huffman encoding, assuming that *A* and *E* are the most frequently occurring characters in the transmitted text and the character *T* occurs rarely.

**FIGURE 10-4**
MNP level 5 uses two types of data compression: (a) Huffman encoding uses as few as 4 bits to represent frequently used characters. (b) Run-length encoding replaces characters that repeat more than three times with a count.

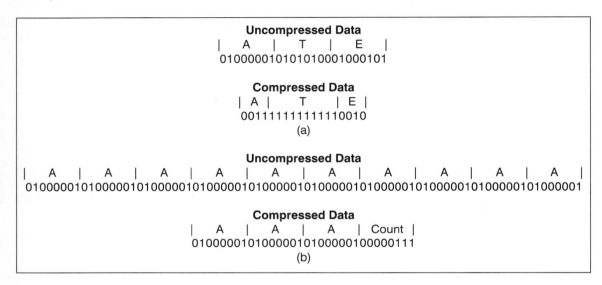

**Run-length encoding,** illustrated in Figure 10-4(b), looks for repeated characters in the data stream, including non-printing characters such as spaces, carriage returns, and line feeds. When it encounters a character that repeats more than three times, it sends the character three times and then sends a count to indicate how many more times the character repeats. Figure 10-4(b) shows how a sequence of 10 consecutive *A* characters could be compressed into 4 bytes of data. Run-length encoding is very effective for sending certain types of computer files such as spreadsheets, data bases, graphics, and some types of computer programs that have many repeated characters. When Huffman encoding and run-length encoding are combined, these files can be sent at several times the speed that they would be sent if no compression were used.

Although only the five basic layers on MNP are discussed here, Microcom continues to add new layers to the protocol to include more sophisticated methods of error correction and data compression. As of this writing, the highest level of MNP is layer 10.

### 10-2-2 V.42 Error Control

The **V.42** standard is an error-correction standard that was developed by Hayes Microcomputer Products, AT&T, and British Telecom to compete with the Microcom protocol. V.42 was published by the CCITT as a recommended international standard for use with asynchronous communications. V.42 actually contains two error-correction schemes. One of the error corrections schemes is called **Link Access Procedure for Modems (LAPM).** The other scheme is the same as MNP level 4. The LAPM scheme is the better of the two, so two modems that both have V.42

capabilities will connect using LAPM. If one of the modems uses V.42 and the other uses only MNP, the V.42 modem will fall back to the highest level MNP that the two modems have in common.

### 10-2-3 V.42 bis Data Compression

*Bis* is a French word that means "twice" or "again." The CCITT uses the word *bis* when it publishes an extension to an existing standard. The V.42 bis standard can therefore be thought of as an extension of the V.42 standard. **V.42 bis** is a data compression standard that is designed to work together with V.42 error correction. The CCITT issued the V.42 bis standard in 1989. It has been claimed that V.42 bis offers 35% more compression than does MNP level 5. Using V.42 bis compression, a 9600 b/s modem can transfer highly redundant data at speeds of up to 38,400 b/s, although a speed of 19,600 b/s is more normal. Most modems that use the V.42 bis standard also have MNP capability, and they will fall back to MNP level 5 if the modem at the other end can use MNP compression but is not capable of using V.42 bis.

## 10-3　MODULATION AND DEMODULATION STANDARDS

As mentioned in the introduction of this chapter, the two organizations responsible for most modem modulation and demodulation standards in North America are the Bell System and the CCITT. The Bell System standards were for all practical purposes the only modem standards used in North America through the 1960s, and modems that use the Bell System standards are still used in some slower communications applications. Many newer modems can fall back to one of the Bell System standards to communicate with those older and slower modems. Today, almost all modems built for computer-to-computer communications over the telephone network adhere to CCITT standards. A list of the more common modem standards for telephone use is shown in Figure 10-5.

**FIGURE 10-5**
Some common modulation standards for modems.

| b/s | Standard | Modulation | Duplex |
|---|---|---|---|
| 300 | Bell 103 | FSK | Full |
| 300 | V.21 | FSK | Full |
| 1200 | Bell 202 | FSK | Half |
| 1200 | Bell 212A | 4PSK | Full |
| 1200 | V.22 | 4PSK | Full |
| 2400 | V.22bis | QAM | Full |
| 9600 | V.32 | QAM | Full |
| 14,400 | V.32 bis | QAM | Full |
| 28,800 | V.34 | QAM | Full |

When one modem calls another over a dial-up telephone circuit, no data can be transferred until the two modems exchange signals with each other, or **handshake,** to decide how they are going to communicate. This handshake procedure is called a **renegotiation protocol.** During the renegotiation protocol, each modem informs the other about its ability to perform error correction and data compression and which modulation standards it can use. As mentioned earlier, most modems can fall back to more primitive modulation standards when necessary. For example, if two modems attempt to communicate with each other, and one of the modems is capable of 2400 b/s while the other has a maximum speed of 1200 b/s, the faster modem will fall back to the speed of the slower. They will decide during the renegotiation protocol to communicate at 1200 b/s. If the telephone circuit is extremely noisy, they may even fall back to a slower rate, say 300 b/s.

If modems have built-in error correction and data compression, they also exchange information about these capabilities during renegotiation. For example, if one modem can use the MNP protocol up to level 3 and the other can use up to level 5, the second modem will fall back to MNP level 3, the highest level that the two have in common.

### 10-3-1 Bell 103/V.21

The **Bell 103** modem standard uses a 200-Hz carrier shift for full-duplex communications at 300 b/s over two-wire dial-up telephone lines. Remember from Chapter 9 that most modems that use two-wire telephone circuits for full-duplex communications divide the telephone circuit's bandwidth in half. The modem that originates the call (the **originate modem**) uses half the bandwidth for sending data, and the modem that receives the call (the **answer modem**) sends data through the other half of the circuit's bandwidth. A Bell 103 standard modem in the originate mode transmits a mark frequency of 1270 Hz and a space frequency of 1070 Hz. In the answer mode it transmits 2025 Hz as a space and 2225 Hz as a mark.

**V.21** is the CCITT version of the Bell 103 standard. Unfortunately V.21 uses different carrier frequencies, which means that Bell 103 modems and V.21 modems cannot communicate with each other. That was not a serious disadvantage decades ago when the standard was published because data communications between North America and other countries over dial-up telephone lines was not as common then. However, in these days of international data communications, it is important that modems standards be used worldwide.

The Bell 103 standard was once widely used for communications between two personal computers. It has also been applied to link a bank's central computer with its automated teller machines and for communication between a credit card company's central computer and credit card verification terminals in retail stores. Today, the Bell 103 standard's 300-b/s communications speed is considered painfully slow for most applications. The fact that Bell 103 modems can be used only in asynchronous communications systems is also a serious disadvantage. Although the Bell 103 standard is out of date, most modems built for use in North America with capabilities up to 2400 b/s have the ability to fall back to the Bell 103 standard to communicate with older modems.

## 10-3-2 Bell 202

**Bell 202** is another early asynchronous FSK modem standard. It was designed for half-duplex communications, and modems built to the Bell 202 standard can therefore use the full bandwidth of the telephone circuit. The greater bandwidth enables Bell 202 modems to operate at higher speed than do Bell 103 modems. Bell 202 modems can operate at 1200 b/s over a dial-up telephone line and at 1800 b/s on a leased, conditioned line. They use a frequency of 1200 Hz to represent a mark and 2200 Hz to represent a space. Bell 202 modems have a low-speed 5-b/s back channel that uses AM with a carrier frequency of 387 Hz that the receiving modem can use to send an ACK or NAK signal at the end of each block of data without the need of turning the circuit around.

## 10-3-3 Bell 212A/V.22

The **Bell 212A** modem standard uses four-phase PSK and is capable of full-duplex communications at 1200 b/s. It operates at 600 baud and modulates dibits onto the carrier. Modems built to the Bell 212A standard are synchronous, and they can therefore be used in either synchronous or asynchronous communications systems. Bell 212A modems frequency divide the bandpass of a telephone circuit into an originate channel and an answer channel. The originate modem uses a carrier frequency of 1200 Hz, and the answer modem uses a carrier frequency of 2400 Hz. When necessary, Bell 212A modems can fall back to the Bell 103 standard to communicate with Bell 103 modems. **V.22** is the CCITT international version of the Bell 212A standard.

## 10-3-4 V.22 bis

**V.22 bis** can be thought of as the second version of the V.22 standard, modified to raise communications speed to 2400 b/s. Because the Bell Telephone monopoly in North America was in the process of being broken up when 2400-b/s modems were developed, the Bell standard for 2400-b/s modems was never accepted. As a result, V.22 bis is used for 2400-b/s communications over dial-up telephone lines throughout the world, including North America. V.22 bis modems operate full-duplex. Like earlier full-duplex standards, V.22 bis divides the telephone circuit bandpass into an originate channel and an answer channel. V.22 bis modems use quadrature amplitude modulation at 600 baud. Although the baud rate is the same as the Bell 212A standard, the higher data rate is achieved by modulating quadbits onto the carrier. V.22 bis modems are synchronous, and they can be used in either synchronous or asynchronous communications systems. To communicate with slower modems, most V.22 bis modems sold in North America can fall back to a number of earlier standards including V.22, Bell 212A, and Bell 103.

To increase effective data communications speed above 2400 b/s, most V.22 bis modems have the ability to use MNP error correction and data compression through level 5 as well as V.42 error correction with V.42 bis data compression. Data compression gives V.22 bis modems the ability to transfer data at speeds of up to about

8000 b/s. As of this writing, an internal V.22 bis modem including MNP levels 2 through 5, V.42, V.42 bis, and a terminal communications software package can be purchased for less than $45.

### 10-3-5 V.32

Modems built to the CCITT **V.32** standard operate full-duplex at up to 9600 b/s over standard two-wire, dial-up telephone circuits. The V.32 standard was made possible by advanced signal processing technology that allows the originate and the answer modem to both transmit at the same time over the full bandwidth of a two-wire dial-up telephone circuit. Because they use the full bandwidth of the telephone circuit and because the digital signal processing circuitry is more immune to errors, V.32 modems operate at modulation rates of up to 2400 baud, much faster than the 600 baud specified in the V.22 and V.22 bis standards. V.32 modems use QAM and modulate quadbits onto the carrier to achieve their 9600-b/s data transfer speed.

When two V.32 modems establish communications with each other, they test the telephone circuit to determine the maximum communications speed that it will support. If the quality of the circuit is good, the modems begin to exchange data at their maximum speed of 9600 b/s. If they experience errors at that speed, they fall back to 7200 b/s. If they still experience errors, they fall back to an even slower 4800 b/s.

Within each modem, a circuit called a **hybrid** isolates the transmitter and receiver from each other. Originally, a hybrid was a type of transformer as illustrated in Figure 10-6, but today it is more likely to be an electronic circuit built into one of the ICs of the modem chipset. The hybrid allows the transmitted signal to pass from the transmitter to the two-wire telephone circuit, but it blocks the transmitted signal from entering the modem's receive section. At the same time, it allows the signal that arrives from the far-end modem over the two-wire line to pass through to the receive section of the modem and blocks it from entering the transmitter section. In practice, no circuit is perfect, and a small portion of the transmitted signal does reflect from the hybrid into the receiver. This reflected signal is called an *echo*.

Additional echoes are reflected back to the receive section of the sending modem by the telephone circuit and the receiving modem. For example, Figure 10-6 shows that modem B's hybrid reflects part of the signal it receives back to modem A. Remember also that an actual dial-up telephone circuit is not as simple as the two parallel conductors shown in the figure. It consists of a two-wire local loop at each end connected by one or several four-wire trunk circuits. Hybrids interface the two-wire local loops to the four-wire trunks, and these hybrids also generate echoes. Any imperfection in the two-wire segment of the telephone connection also generates echoes. As a result, the receive section of a modem receives a number of echoes of the modem's own transmitted signal. These echoes arrive at different times, and they have different amplitudes, but they all occupy the same frequency spectrum as the signal that modem A is receiving from modem B. The receive section of modem A must somehow ignore the echoes of its own signal and demodulate only the signal sent to it by modem B.

When two V.32 modems establish contact, they "learn" the characteristics of the telephone circuit that connects them. As mentioned earlier, part of the learning

**FIGURE 10-6**

If modem A transmits a signal over a two-wire telephone circuit, part of the signal will be echoed back and interfere with the receiver.

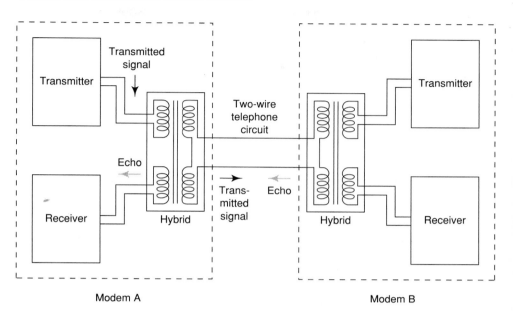

Modem A                                           Modem B

process is to determine the maximum communications speed that the circuit will support without causing excessive errors. As another part of the learning process, each modem transmits a signal and listens for its echoes. Once a V.32 modem learns the time delay and amplitude of a telephone circuit's echoes, it can ignore them during the data exchange.

In order for a modem to filter out echoes, it must be able to rapidly analyze and process the received analog signal. Figure 10-7 shows that at the heart of every V.32 modem is a **digital signal processor (DSP).** As mentioned previously in this book, a DSP is a type of microprocessor that is designed specifically to manipulate analog signals. Because a DSP is a digital device, the analog signals must be converted to digital before the DSP can process them. In the modem, received analog signals pass through an analog-to-digital (A/D) converter before they are passed along to the DSP. In the modem's transmitter section, a digital-to-analog (D/A) converter transforms the DSP's digital output into an analog signal to be sent over the telephone circuit.

The DSP performs many functions within a V.32 modem. It modulates the transmitted carrier, demodulates the received carrier, filters much of the noise from the received signal, and, most importantly, performs echo cancellation. The DSP enables V.32 modems with V.42 error correction and V.42 bis data compression, to transfer certain types of data at speeds up to 38,400 b/s, although speeds of 19,200 b/s are more usual. V.32 modems would not be possible without DSP technology.

**FIGURE 10-7**
A digital signal processor is at the heart of a V.32 modem.

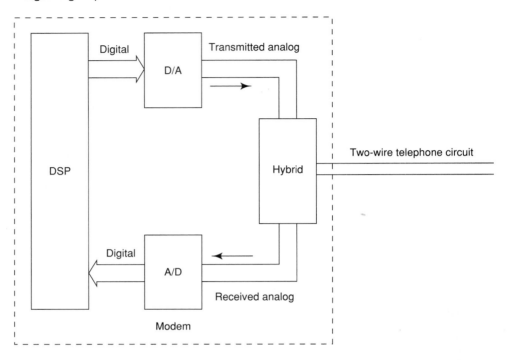

Like other modem circuits, the DSP is not always a separate IC. It can be included with other circuits on one of the larger integrated circuits that make up the modem chipset.

Although it is not shown in Figure 10-7, a V.32 modem also contains a microprocessor that performs routine control functions such as dialing telephone numbers and interpreting AT commands from the terminal. The microprocessor also performs data compression and decompression and error detection and correction. The microprocessor and the DSP together are the heart of a V.32 modem. Both the DSP and the microprocessor execute programs that are stored within the modem in some type of non-volatile memory such as ROM. It may be possible to update a V.32 modem's features by changing the ROM. If the non-volatile memory is flash or EEPROM, updating the modem's features may be even easier. It may be possible to use the modem to dial the manufacturer and have the modem's internal programs updated over the telephone line. If the DSP and other modem circuits are fast enough, a ROM change may be all that is necessary to update a V.32 modem to the newer V.32 bis standard, which is discussed in the following paragraphs.

## 10-3-6 V.32 bis

**V.32 bis** modems include all of the features of V.32 modems with some additional features and higher data speeds. In many cases, the main difference between V.32 and V.32 bis modems is the internal program that the DSP executes. Modems built

This V.32 bis modem operates at 14.4 kb/s over telephone lines or 9.6 kb/s over cellular telephone. Ubiquity 2000 from PCSI. Courtesy of Pacific Communication Sciences, Inc.

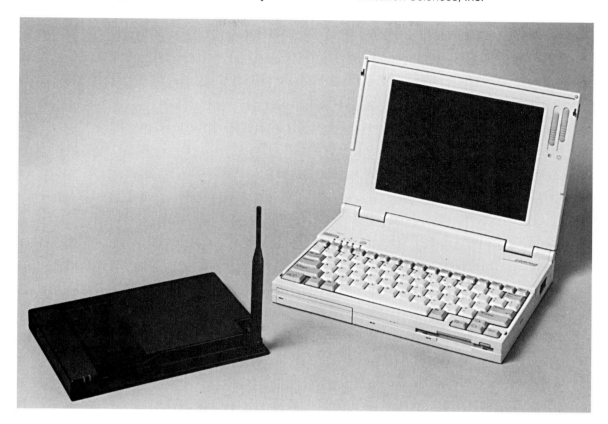

to the V.32 bis standard transfer data at speeds up to 14,400 b/s using full-duplex communications over standard telephone lines. When used with V.42 bis data compression, they can achieve throughputs of up to 57,600 b/s. Like V.32, V.32 bis modems use the full bandwidth of the telephone circuit and depend on DSPs for **echo cancelling.**

V.32 bis modems can communicate at 14,400, 12,000, 9600, 7200, and 4800 b/s. When two V.32 bis modems establish a connection, they analyze the telephone circuit to determine the optimum signaling speed. Like V.32 modems, V.32 bis modems can fall back to a slow speed if line conditions deteriorate. Unlike V.32 modems, they can also *fall forward* to a higher speed if the telephone circuit conditions improve during communications.

### 10-3-7 V.34

**V.34** is the newest modem standard developed by the CCITT. V.34, which was known as V.fast when it was under development, provides signaling speeds from 19,200 b/s to 28,800 b/s over dial-up telephone lines in 2400 b/s increments, depending on the condition of the telephone link. Most V.32 and V.32 bis modems cannot be reprogrammed to the V.34 standard, because the higher data speeds of V.34 require faster and more expensive DSPs.

Many expect that V.34 modems will be the last generation of modems designed for communications over analog telephone circuits. By the time the V.34 standard reaches maturity, the integrated systems digital network (ISDN) should bring digital telephone circuits to the home and office and make modems obsolete. Each ISDN channel will be able to handle 64,000 b/s of digital information. With data compression, speeds will reach several thousand b/s.

## ■ SUMMARY

This chapter has discussed some of the more common modem standards in use. Through the 1960s, the Bell System of telephone companies set the standards in North America for modem modulation and demodulation schemes, and the CCITT set the standards for the rest of the world. Today, CCITT standards are used throughout the world, including North America. Some modem manufacturers have perfected methods of performing certain modem functions. Their methods have been widely accepted by other manufacturers and have become de facto standards.

The AT command set is a de facto standard that was developed by Hayes Microcomputer Products to allow a terminal to control an intelligent modem. The terminal controls the modem by sending it the ASCII characters for the letters *AT* followed by ASCII characters for the commands. The Microcom Network Protocol (MNP) is another de facto standard. MNP performs error correction and data compression. V.42 and V.42 bis are two standards published by the CCITT. V.42 is an error correction standard, and V.42 bis is a data compression standard. Error correction is important for reliable data communications over telephone lines because of the noise encountered in many telephone circuits. Data compression increases communications speed by using fewer bits to represent a given amount of information.

A communications software program or terminal program allows a personal computer to act as a terminal and control a modem. Many modern communications software packages allow the computer operator to use a mouse to "click" on commands that appear on the computer screen. The communications software package converts these screen commands into the proper sequence of AT commands and sends them to the modem.

Bell 103 and Bell 202 are FSK modem standards. Bell 103 operates full-duplex at 300 b/s and Bell 202 operates half-duplex at 1200 b/s. FSK has fallen into disfavor for computer-to-computer communications, because it is slow and because FSK modems are asynchronous. Both MNP and V.42 bis data compression protocols are designed to be used with synchronous modems. Bell 212A is a four-phase PSK modem standard. Like other Bell modem standards, it is not compatible with the CCITT standards that are used internationally. Bell modem standards were used extensively in North America before the breakup of the Bell System telephone monopoly.

The designations of the CCITT standards begin with the letter *V.* V.22 bis modems use QAM at 600 baud to obtain 2400 b/s, full-duplex communications. Like all previous full-duplex modem modulation standards designed for two-wire telephone circuits, V.22 bis modems divide the telephone circuit into an originate and an answer communications channel.

The V.32 standard employs DSPs and sophisticated echo-cancelling techniques to allow the full bandwidth of a two-wire telephone circuit to be used for communications in both directions simultaneously. V.32 modems are capable of full-duplex communications at up to 2400 baud and 9600 b/s. V.32 bis modems use the same echo-cancelling techniques to reach full-duplex communications speeds of up to 14,400 b/s. The latest, and probably the last, CCITT modem standard, designated V.34, can operate at speeds of up to 28,000 b/s. By the time V.34 modems reach maturity, it is expected that ISDN digital telephone lines will make the need for analog modems obsolete.

## ■ QUESTIONS

1. Into what three types can modem standards be divided?

2. What are the two organizations that have historically set modem standards in North America?

3. a. What was the Carterphone decision?

   b. What effect did the Carterphone decision have on the modem business in North America?

4. What is the difference between a *dumb modem* and an *intelligent modem?*

5. What is the most common system of commands used by terminals to control the operation of intelligent modems?

6. What is the difference between the *command mode* and the *on-line mode* of an intelligent modem?

7. What do the letters *AT* stand for in the AT command set?

8. a. What is the AT command set escape code?

   b. What is the purpose of the escape code?

9. a. What is another name for a *communications software program?*

   b. What is the purpose of a communications software program?

10. What is the relationship between speed and accuracy in data communications?

11. a. List the first five levels of the Microcom Network Protocol and state briefly what each level does to improve data communications.

    b. Explain why MNP level 3 data compression will not work with FSK modems.

12. a. Why does Huffman encoding work well to compress text files?

    b. Why is run-length encoding more effective for compressing data that have many repeated characters?

13. Which two error-correction schemes does the V.42 standard use?

14. a.   What is the purpose of the V.42 bis standard?

    b.   What other standard must be used with V.42 bis?

15. a.   What is a *renegotiation protocol?*

    b.   What types of information do modems exchange during renegotiation?

16. a.   At what speed do Bell 103 modems communicate?

    b.   What type of modulation do Bell 103 modems use?

    c.   Why are Bell 103 modems and V.21 modems incompatible with each other?

    d.   What are some disadvantages of the Bell 103 standard for modern data communications?

17. a.   Why can Bell 202 modems communicate faster than Bell 103 modems?

    b.   What feature do Bell 202 modems have that eliminates the need to turn the circuit around at the end of each block of data?

18. a.   What type of modulation do Bell 212A modems use?

    b.   What feature makes it possible for a Bell 212A modem and a Bell 103 modem to communicate with each other?

19. a.   Are V.22 bis modems simplex, half-duplex, or full-duplex?

    b.   How many bits per second can V.22 bis modems send and receive?

    c.   At what baud rate do V.22 bis modems operate?

    d.   What type of modulation do V.22 bis modems use?

20. a.   How many bits per second can V.32 modems send and receive?

    b.   Why can V.32 modems operate at 2400 baud instead of the 600 baud used by some earlier full-duplex modem standards?

21. a.   What is a *hybrid?*

    b.   Why do hybrids in telephones cause problems for data communications?

22. a.   List some of the functions that a DSP performs within a V.32 modem.

    b.   List some of the functions that the microprocessor performs in a V.32 modem.

    c.   How is it possible to update the features of some V.32 modems?

23. a.   What is the main difference between V.32 modems and V.32 bis modems?

    b.   How many bits per second can V.32 bis modems send and receive?

    c.   What is the maximum throughput of a V.32 modem when it uses V.42 bis data compression?

24. a.   What is the maximum communications speed of V.34 modems in bits per second?

    b.   Why do many people expect that V.34 will be the last modem standard designed for communications over analog telephone lines?

# ■ Chapter 11

# NETWORK PROTOCOLS

## OBJECTIVES

After you have completed this chapter, you should be able to:

- ■ Define the word *protocol* as it applies to communications systems.
- ■ State the difference between a character-oriented protocol and a bit-oriented protocol.
- ■ Discuss the general features of the BISYNC protocol.
- ■ Discuss the disadvantages of BISYNC and other character-oriented protocols.
- ■ Discuss the general features of the HDLC protocol.
- ■ Explain the purpose of "bit stuffing" in the HDLC protocol.
- ■ Explain the purpose of I-frames, S-frames, and U-frames in the HDLC protocol.

## INTRODUCTION

For communications to take place, a set of rules must govern the exchange of information. This is true whether the communication is between two human beings or between two data terminals. As part of the rules, there has to be an agreed-upon set of symbols to represent the information. The rules must also specify how the symbols are to be joined together. For communication among human beings, the symbols that represent information are called *words*, and the rules that join them together are called *grammar.*

This book conveys information using the symbols and grammar that make up the English language. If you are fluent in English, communication between the sender (me) and the receiver (you) is likely to be successful. But if I use a different set of symbols and grammar such as German, *was ich sehr einfach machen könnte*, or Spanish, *que no sería difícil tampoco*, you will not receive the information unless you understand the symbols and grammar that make up those languages.

In data communications, the symbols used for communication are called **character sets.** Two character sets discussed earlier in this book are the ASCII and the EBCDIC codes. A **protocol** is a set of rules that governs how characters and other data are communicated. In this chapter we will discuss two of the better known data communications protocols, BISYNC and HDLC. Both of these protocols are used with synchronous communications.

Synchronous data communications protocols must address the following basic problems:

1.  **Framing**—breaking large fields of data into a number of messages, called *blocks* or **frames.** Each block must be short enough to be communicated with a small probability of error.
2.  **Error control**—a method of detecting and correcting transmission errors within a block. The protocols that we will discuss in this chapter most commonly use a cyclic redundancy check (CRC) character at the end of each block to detect errors. They correct errors by retransmitting any block that fails the CRC.
3.  **Sequence control**—a method of numbering blocks so that no block will be lost or duplicated and so that the blocks will be placed in the proper sequence at the receiver.

The following are the two types of synchronous protocols that we will discuss in this chapter:

1.  **Character-oriented protocols**—Character-oriented protocols use special characters, such as the SOH, STX, and ETX to control the flow of information. The character-oriented protocol that we will look at in detail is called *BISYNC.*
2.  **Bit-oriented protocols**—Bit-oriented protocols divide each block into bit fields. Each bit field serves a specific purpose. The bit-oriented protocol that we will look at in detail is called *HDLC* or *SDLC.*

## 11-1  CHARACTER-ORIENTED PROTOCOLS—BISYNC

Character-oriented protocols use special characters, called *control characters,* to facilitate data communication. The best-known character-oriented synchronous protocol is the **Binary Synchronous Communications Protocol (BISYNC),** which IBM introduced in 1968 for communications between its mainframe computers and remote terminals.

Systems that use BISYNC operate half-duplex even if they are otherwise capable of full-duplex operation. BISYNC can be used with either the ASCII or EBCDIC character sets, but it is more commonly used with EBCDIC, which was also developed by IBM. Figure 11-1 lists the more commonly used BISYNC control codes. Many of them can be found in both the ASCII and the EBCDIC tables, which are shown in Figures 11-2 and 11-3. Others, such as ACK0 and ACK1 are 16 bits long and are formed by combinations of two ASCII or two EBCDIC characters. For example, ACK0 is sent as DLE 0 and ACK1 is sent as DLE 1. The SOH, STX, ETB, and ETX characters are called **framing characters** because each of them marks the beginning or end of a specific portion of a BISYNC block, as illustrated in Figure 11-4.

BISYNC has two communications phases that are called the *line control phase* and the *data transmission phase.* During the line control phase, the terminals on the system exchange messages to determine which of them will control the communications circuit during the next data transmission phase. During the data transmission phase, the terminal that has gained control of network sends data messages to another terminal on the network. Once the controlling terminal has finished sending its messages, the system enters another line-control phase to determine which terminal will transmit next.

## 11-1-1 The BISYNC Data Transmission Block

Figure 11-4 shows the format of a BISYNC message block. The transmission begins with at least two SYN characters, which allow the receiver to synchronize itself with the incoming data stream. Following the SYN characters, the block may begin with a header, which is optional. If the header is included, it begins with a **start of header (SOH)** control character. The contents of the header are not specified by the BISYNC protocol and vary from system to system, but they could include such information as the message and block numbers, the data and time that the block was sent, and the message priority.

The text field begins with a **start of text (STX)** character. The text field contains the data. BISYNC does not specify the length of the text field, and this also varies from one communications system to another. The text field should be short enough so that the entire block can be communicated with little chance of error. Block lengths of 256 bytes are typical.

The text field ends with either an **end of text (ETX)** or an **end of transmission block (ETB)** control character. If a message is broken into several blocks, only the text field of the last block terminates with ETX. The text field of each of the earlier blocks ends with ETB.

The **binary check character (BCC)** follows the ETX or ETB character. In systems that use the ASCII character set, the BCC may be a longitudinal parity check character, but in the more common EBCDIC systems, the BCC is a CRC character. The BCC is included to detect errors in the text block.

**FIGURE 11-1**

Some BISYNC control characters.

| | |
|---|---|
| SOH | Start of header. |
| STX | Start of text. |
| ETB | End of transmission block. Marks the end of a block of characters that started with SOH or STX. ETB is followed by BCC, and it requires that the receiving terminal respond with ACK0, ACK1, NAK, WACK, or RVI. |
| ITB | End of intermediate transmission block (called IUS in EBCDIC and US in ASCII). Used in place of ETB when no immediate response is desired from the receiving terminal. Followed by BCC. |
| ETX | End of text. Same as ETB except that it is sent at the end of the last data block. |
| EOT | End of transmission. Also used to respond to a poll when polled terminal has nothing to transmit. |
| NAK | Negative acknowledgment. Previous block was received in error. |
| DLE | Data link escape. Sent as first character of two-character control sequences such as WACK, ACK0, ACK1, and RVI. Also used to mark control characters in transparent data transfer. |
| ENQ | Enquiry. Used to bid for the line in point-to-point systems. Also indicates the end of a poll or selection sequence and is used to request the retransmission of a garbled or missing ACK or NAK. |
| ACK0, ACK1 | Affirmative acknowledgment. Acknowledges receipt of the previous block and indicates that the terminal is ready to receive another block. ACK0 acknowledges even-numbered blocks; ACK1 acknowledges odd-numbered blocks. |
| WACK | Wait before transmit positive acknowledgment. The previous block was received without error, but the receiver is not yet ready for another block. The transmitting station then sends ENQs and the receiver responds to each one with WACK until the receiver is ready. |
| RVI | Reverse interrupt. A positive acknowledgment with a request that the transmitting station terminate transmissions, because the receiving station has an urgent message to send and therefore needs to turn the circuit around. |
| TTD | Temporary text delay. Sent by a transmitting station that is not yet ready to transmit but wishes to retain the line. The receive station responds with NAK, and the transmitting station again sends TTD if it is not ready. |

**FIGURE 11-2**

The ASCII code.

| MS Char → | 000 ($0) | 001 ($1) | 010 ($2) | 011 ($3) | 100 ($4) | 101 ($5) | 110 ($6) | 111 ($7) |
|---|---|---|---|---|---|---|---|---|
| **LS Char** | | | | | | | | |
| 0000 ($0) | NUL | DLE | SP | 0 | @ | P | ` | p |
| 0001 ($1) | SOH | DC1 | ! | 1 | A | Q | a | q |
| 0010 ($2) | STX | DC2 | " | 2 | B | R | b | r |
| 0011 ($3) | ETX | DC3 | # | 3 | C | S | c | s |
| 0100 ($4) | EOT | DCA | $ | 4 | D | T | d | t |
| 0101 ($5) | ENQ | NAK | % | 5 | E | U | e | u |
| 0110 ($6) | ACK | SYN | & | 6 | F | V | f | v |
| 0111 ($7) | BEL | ETB | ' | 7 | G | W | g | w |
| 1000 ($8) | BS | CAN | ( | 8 | H | X | h | x |
| 1001 ($9) | HT | EM | ) | 9 | I | Y | i | y |
| 1010 ($A) | LF | SUB | * | : | J | Z | j | z |
| 1011 ($B) | VT | ESC | + | ; | K | [ | k | { |
| 1100 ($C) | FF | FS | , | < | L | \ | l | \| |
| 1101 ($D) | CR | GS | - | = | M | ] | m | } |
| 1110 ($E) | SO | RS | . | > | N | ^ | n | ~ |
| 1111 ($F) | SI | $\mu$S | / | ? | O | _ | o | DEL |

**FIGURE 11-3**
A partial EBCDIC table.

| Bits 4, 5, 6, & 7 ↓ \ Bits 0, 1, 2, & 3 → | 0000 ($0) | 0001 ($1) | 0010 ($2) | 0011 ($3) | 0100 ($4) | 0101 ($5) | 0110 ($6) | 0111 ($7) | 1000 ($8) | 1001 ($9) | 1010 ($A) | 1011 ($B) | 1100 ($C) | 1101 ($D) | 1110 ($E) | 1111 ($F) |
|---|---|---|---|---|---|---|---|---|---|---|---|---|---|---|---|---|
| 0000 ($0) | NUL | DLE | DS |  | SP | & | - |  |  |  |  |  |  |  |  |  |
| 0001 ($1) | SOH | DC1 | SOS |  |  |  | / |  | a | j |  |  | A | J |  | 1 |
| 0010 ($2) | STX | DC2 | FS | SYN |  |  |  |  | b | k | s |  | B | K | S | 2 |
| 0011 ($3) | ETX | TM |  |  |  |  |  |  | c | l | t |  | C | L | T | 3 |
| 0100 ($4) | PF | RES | BYP | PN |  |  |  |  | d | m | u |  | D | M | U | 4 |
| 0101 ($5) | HT | NL | LF | RS |  |  |  |  | e | n | v |  | E | N | V | 5 |
| 0110 ($6) | LC | BS | ETB | UC |  |  |  |  | f | o | w |  | F | O | W | 6 |
| 0111 ($7) | DL | UIS | ESC | EOT |  |  |  |  | g | p | x |  | G | P | X | 7 |
| 1000 ($8) |  | CAN |  |  |  |  |  |  | h | q | y |  | H | Q | Y | 8 |
| 1001 ($9) |  | EM |  |  |  |  |  |  | i | r | z |  | I | R | Z | 9 |
| 1010 ($A) | SMM | CC | SM |  | ¢ | ! |  | : |  |  |  |  |  |  |  |  |
| 1011 ($B) | VT | CU1 | CU2 | CU3 | . | $ | , | # |  |  |  |  |  |  |  |  |
| 1100 ($C) | FF | IFS |  | DC4 | < | * | % | @ |  |  |  |  |  |  |  |  |
| 1101 ($D) | CR | IGS | ENG | NAK | ( | ) | _ | ' |  |  |  |  |  |  |  |  |
| 1110 ($E) | SO | IRS | ACK |  | + | ; | > | = |  |  |  |  |  |  |  |  |
| 1111 ($F) | SI | IUS | BEL | SUB | \| | ¬ | ? | " |  |  |  |  |  |  |  |  |

**FIGURE 11-4**

BISYNC data transmission block (Header is optional).

| SYN | SYN | SOH | Header | STX | Text | ETX or ETB | BCC |
|-----|-----|-----|--------|-----|------|------------|-----|

## 11-1-2 BISYNC Transparent Data

As mentioned, BISYNC was designed to transmit text using the letters, numbers, symbols, and control codes available in the ASCII and EBCDIC character sets. Today, much of the information sent over data communications networks is binary data such as computer programs, graphics images, digitized sounds, spreadsheets, and data bases that cannot be easily translated into the ASCII or EBCDIC codes. Unfortunately, these data contain bit combinations that are identical to ASCII and EBCDIC control codes. This creates a problem for BISYNC and other character-oriented protocols. If the data in the text field of the block of Figure 11-4 were part of a computer program, it could easily contain the bit pattern 00000011, which is the bit pattern used by both ASCII and EBCDIC to represent the ETX framing character. The receiving terminal would mistake that bit pattern for the ETX character and assume that the end of the text field had been reached.

Figure 11-5 shows a data block format that has been developed for transparent data transmission. **Transparent transmission** means that the control circuitry in the receiving DTE ignores the contents of the text field. The control circuitry passes the text field to the terminal unaltered. In BISYNC transparent transmission, the sending terminal inserts a **DLE** control character in front of all framing characters. If the data block contains a header, for example, the header begins with the characters DLE SOH. The text field begins with the characters DLE STX and ends with either DLE ETX or DLE ETB. The receive terminal obeys the following rules:

1. All characters in the text field whose bit patterns do not match DLE are delivered to the receiver's terminal as data.

2. The receiver deletes any bit pattern from the text field that matches DLE, and it checks the character that follows it to determine if its bit pattern matches ETX or ETB. If it does match, the receiver assumes it has reached the end of the text field, and that the BCC character follows. If the character following DLE has any other bit pattern, it is assumed to be a data character.

3. A bit pattern in the data field that matches the DLE character is sent as DLE DLE. The receiving terminal deletes the first DLE and passes the second one on as data.

**FIGURE 11-5**

BISYNC transparent transmission block for non-text data.

| SYN | SYN | DLE | SOH | Header | DLE | STX | Text (data) | DLE | ETX or ETB | BCC |
|-----|-----|-----|-----|--------|-----|-----|-------------|-----|------------|-----|

### 11-1-3 Acknowledging BISYNC Blocks

BISYNC data blocks are always transmitted by the terminal that was granted control of the communications channel during the line control phase, and they are always transmitted to a single receiving terminal. After each block is transmitted, the circuit is turned around and the receiving terminal sends at least two SYN characters followed by one of the following control characters:

1. **Negative acknowledge (NAK)**—sent when there is a BCC error to request retransmission of the block.
2. **Acknowledge 0 (ACK0,** sent as DLE 0)—indicates that an even-numbered block was received without a BCC error.
3. **Acknowledge 1 (ACK1,** sent as DLE 1)—indicates that an odd-numbered block was received without a BCC error.

You will notice from these characters that the receiving terminal alternates between ACK0 and ACK1 to acknowledge the receipt of data blocks. This is a simple method of sequence control, which you may remember as one of the functions of a communications protocol. If the transmitting terminal receives an ACK0 acknowledgment when it is expecting an ACK1, it indicates that a block has been lost.

### 11-1-4 Point-to-Point BISYNC Systems

As Figure 11-6 illustrates, a point-to-point communications system connects two terminals over a single communications link. Because there are only two terminals, the line control phase of a point-to-point communications system is relatively simple. Either terminal can take control of the data link during a line control phase. When one of the terminals has data to send, it *contends* or *bids* for control of the data link by sending a series of at least two SYN characters followed by a single ENQ characters. If the other terminal has no data to send, it grants control by sending at least two SYN characters followed by ACK0. If both terminals bid for the line, there is a **bid collision** in which case one of the terminals is programmed to relinquish control to the other.

Once a terminal has gained control of the data link, the communications system passes from the line control phase to a data transmission phase. The terminal that has control sends data blocks. The receiving terminal responds to each correctly received block with at least two SYN characters followed alternately by ACK1 and

**FIGURE 11-6**

A point-to-point communications system connects two terminals over a single communications link.

**FIGURE 11-7**

BISYNC communications on a point-to-point system.

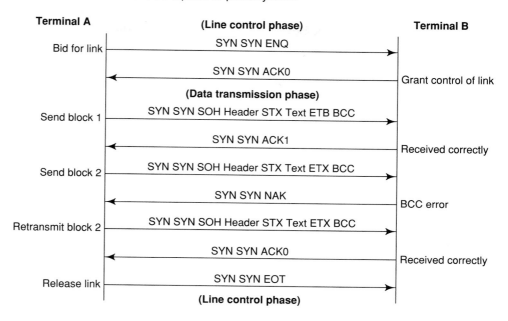

ACK0. It responds to incorrectly received blocks with NAK until the transmitting terminal has sent all of its data. The transmitting terminal then relinquishes control of the data link by sending at least two SYN characters followed by EOT. The system enters another line control phase during which either terminal can bid for control.

Figure 11-7 is a timing diagram showing the exchange of transmission on a point-to-point link using the BISYNC protocol. As shown in the diagram, *all* transmissions are preceded by at least two SYN characters. Assume that terminal A has a message to send to terminal B and that the message is long enough to require two transmission blocks. At the beginning of the diagram, the system is in the line control phase, and terminal A bids for the data link by sending an ENQ character. Terminal B responds with ACK0, which grants control of the link to Terminal A. The system enters the data transmission phase.

Terminal A sends the first block of data. The text field of the data block ends with ETB to indicate that at least one more block is to follow. Terminal B acknowledges that it has received the first block by sending ACK1, and terminal A sends the second block. Because block 2 is the last block of the message, its text field ends with ETX. However, when terminal B receives the block, it fails the BCC. Terminal B transmits NAK to request retransmission of the block. Terminal A retransmits the second block, and this time it is received without error. Terminal B responds with ACK0. Terminal A has no more messages to send, so it transmits an EOT character to release the line. The system enters another line control phase, and either terminal can contend for the data link.

### 11-1-5 Multipoint BISYNC Systems

Figure 11-8 shows a BISYNC multipoint (sometimes called multidrop) system. The system consists of a central computer, called the **supervisor** and a number of remote terminals, called **tributaries.** All of the terminals are connected to the same synchronous data link. The supervisor has overall control of the data link and is always in command during a control phase. A tributary can take temporary control during a data transmission phase, but only when the supervisor grants it permission. All data transmissions take place between the supervisor and one of the tributaries.

The supervisor has two methods of communicating with the tributaries during the BISYNC control phase: it can poll a tributary, or it can select it. As Figure 11-8 shows, each tributary has two addresses, a *poll address* and a *select address.* A *poll* is a command for the addressed tributary to transmit any data messages it may have ready to send to the supervisor. A *selection* commands the addressed tributary to receive a message from the supervisor.

Polling works as follows: When the supervisor has no messages to send, it polls each of the tributaries one at a time by sending the tributary's poll address followed by an ENQ character. If the polled tributary has no messages to send, it responds by sending an EOT character. If a polled tributary does have one or more messages to send, it responds to the poll by entering a data transmission. During the data transmission phase, the tributary controls the data link. The supervisor responds to each block that it receives from the tributary by sending ACK0, ACK1, or NAK as appropriate. When the tributary has finished sending its messages to the supervisor, it transmits an EOT character, and the system reverts to a line control phase with the supervisor again in control of the data link.

**FIGURE 11-8**
In a BISYNC multipoint system, each tributary terminal has both a poll address and select address.

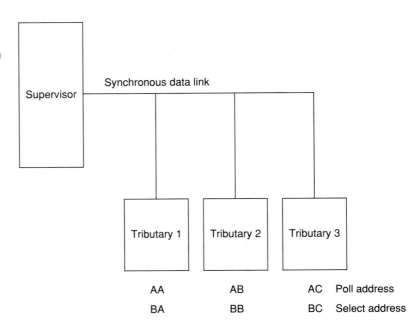

Data transmission from the supervisor to a tributary is handled by selection. The supervisor selects a tributary by sending its select address followed by the ENQ character. If the selected tributary is busy and cannot accept data at that time, it responds by sending the control code WACK. The supervisor responds to WACK by sending EOT and attempts the selection again at a later time. If the tributary is able to accept the data, it responds to the select by sending ACK0. The network then enters a data transmission phase with the host controlling the link. During the data transmission phase, the host transmits blocks of data, and the tributary responds to each block with ACK0, ACK1, or NAK. After the supervisor has sent all the message blocks that it has for the addressed tributary, it sends EOT, and the network again enters a control phase.

Figure 11-9 is a timing diagram that shows some typical transactions that might occur on the BISYNC multipoint communications system pictured in Figure 11-8. At the beginning of the diagram, the system is in a line control phase, and the supervisor is polling the tributaries. As is always the case in BISYNC systems, each transmission begins with at least two SYN characters. The supervisor begins by sending the poll address of tributary 1 followed by an ENQ character. The polled tributary has no messages to send, so it responds to the poll by sending an EOT. Then the supervisor polls tributary 2. Tributary 2 has data to send, so it responds to the poll by sending the first block. This initiates a data transmission phase.

At the end of each block of data, the half-duplex link is turned around so that the supervisor can send an ACK or NAK. The supervisor acknowledges receipt of the first block with ACK1 and the second block with ACK0. The third and final block fails BCC, so the supervisor responds with NAK. The tributary repeats block 3, and this time the supervisor receives it without error and acknowledges the block by sending ACK1. Because the tributary has no more messages to send, it transmits an EOT character to relinquish its temporary control of the link, and the system again enters a line control phase.

The supervisor begins the second line control phase by resuming its poll of the tributaries. It polls tributary 3, which has no traffic and responds with EOT. The supervisor now has a message to send to tributary 1. The supervisor sends tributary 1's select address (BA) followed by an ENQ character. Tributary 1 accepts the selection by transmitting an ACK0 character. The system enters another data transmission phase, and the supervisor sends a one-block message to tributary 1, which tributary 1 acknowledges by sending ACK1. Finally, the supervisor terminates the data transmission phase by transmitting an EOT character.

## 11-1-6 An Assessment of BISYNC

BISYNC has been a very successful protocol. Even though it is outdated for modern data communications, it is still used on systems that are in place in the field. By today's data communications standards, BISYNC and other character-oriented protocols have some disadvantages:

1.  The half-duplex operation of BISYNC makes it slow. After each transmission block, the sending terminal pauses and waits for an acknowledgment from the receiving terminal.

**FIGURE 11-9**
BISYNC communications on a multipoint system.

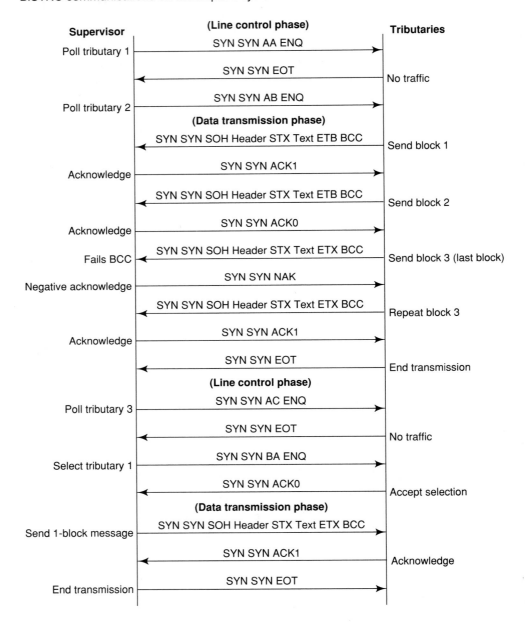

2. BISYNC and other character-oriented protocols are code dependent. They depend on a set of control characters that are defined as part of the character set or sets that they are designed to use.

3. BISYNC and other character-oriented protocols do not deal well with non-text data. Many of the possible bit combinations are reserved for control characters. As was noted in the discussion of BISYNC transparent data transmission, it is possible to modify character-oriented protocols to transmit non-text data, but it is an awkward solution.

## 11-2 BIT-ORIENTED PROTOCOLS—HDLC

Bit-oriented protocols do not use special control characters and do not depend on a specific character set. Unlike character-oriented protocols, they are well suited to communicate non-text data.

The **Synchronous Data Link Control (SDLC)** bit-oriented protocol was published by IBM in 1974. In 1977 the International Standards Organization (ISO) published an updated version of the protocol, which it called **High-Level Data Link Control (HDLC).** This chapter refers to the protocol as HDLC. However, at the introductory level discussed in this book, there is little difference between SDLC and HDLC.

HDLC is a full-duplex protocol although it can be adapted for use on half-duplex systems. A communications system that uses the HDLC protocol has a primary terminal, which controls the link, and one or more secondary terminals.

HDLC has a number of operating modes, which are formally called **classes of procedure.** We will look at the class of procedure used on a multipoint network with one primary terminal and a number of secondaries. The formal name of this class of procedure is the **normal response mode.**

### 11-2-1 The HDLC Frame Structure

Like BISYNC, the HDLC protocol divides longer messages into shorter segments. In BISYNC, we learned that the message segments are called blocks. In HDLC, they are called **frames.** The makeup of an HDLC frame is shown in Figure 11-10. The frame begins with an 8-bit address, which is followed by an 8-bit control field. Next comes a data field, which can consist of any number of bits. Following the data field, the frame ends with a 16-bit CRC character. An 8-bit **flag** is transmitted imme-

**FIGURE 11-10**
The bit fields of an HDLC frame.

| Beginning flag 01111110 | Address 8 bits | Control 8 bits | Data any number of bits | CRC 16 bits | Ending flag 01111110 |
|---|---|---|---|---|---|

diately before and immediately after each frame, and flags also fill any idle time between frames. An HDLC flag serves two purposes: (1) It synchronizes the transmitting and receiving DTEs, much like BISYNC's SYN character, and (2) it notifies the receiver when it has reached the end of a frame.

An HDLC flag consists of a binary 0, six consecutive binary 1s, and another binary 0. When an HDLC terminal is receiving the data field of a frame, it searches for a group of six consecutive 1s in the incoming data stream. When it finds such a group, it assumes it has received the flag that marks the end of the frame, and that the 16 bits prior to the flag are the BCC. The only rule for HDLC transparent data transmission, therefore, is that six consecutive 1s may never occur in the data field. To make sure that they never do, HDLC uses a technique called **zero stuffing.** As Figure 11-11 illustrates, any time a series of five bits occurs during the information field of an HDLC frame, the transmitter inserts or "stuffs" a 0 as the sixth bit. When the receiver detects a series of five 1s in the incoming data stream, it checks the sixth bit. If the sixth bit is a 0, it assumes the 0 was stuffed. It deletes the 0 and treats the received series of bits as data. If the sixth bit is a 1, the receiver assumes it has received the flag that marks the end of a frame and that the preceding 16 bits were the BCC.

Unlike BISYNC, HDLC secondaries have the same address for both poll and selection. SDLC always uses an 8-bit address, which allows up to 256 secondaries. HDLC systems can use 16-bit addresses, but 8-bit addresses are much more common.

The primary has no address in an HDLC system. The primary receives all frames that the secondaries send. The address field in an HDLC frame is always the address of the secondary involved in the communications. When the primary transmits a frame, it sends the address of the secondary that is to receive the message. When a secondary sends a frame, it sends its own address so that the primary will know where the frame came from.

The control field of an SDLC frame is always 8 bits long, whereas HDLC permits control fields of either 8 bits or 16 bits. We will discuss the 8-bit control field format.

The control field divides HDLC frames into three basic types: *information transfer, supervisory,* and *unnumbered* (also referred to as *unsequenced*). If you examine Figure 11-12, you will notice that the two least-significant bits of the control field determine the frame's type. If the least significant bit (b0) of the control field is a 0, the frame is always an information transfer frame. If b0 is a 1 and b1 is a 0, it is a supervisory frame. If b0 and b1 are both 1s, it is an unnumbered frame. Both supervisory and unnumbered frames are further divided into subcategories.

**FIGURE 11-11**
HDLC zero stuffing prevents a series of 1s from being mistaken for a flag.

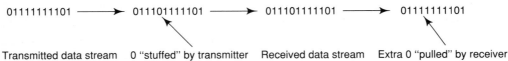

01111111101 ⟶ 011101111101 ⟶ 011101111101 ⟶ 01111111101

Transmitted data stream    0 "stuffed" by transmitter    Received data stream    Extra 0 "pulled" by receiver

**FIGURE 11-12**
The control field of the three basic types of HDLC frames.

| b7 | b6 | b5 | b4 | b3 | b2 | b1 | b0 |
|----|----|----|----|----|----|----|----|
| NR | | | P/F | NS | | | 0 |

**Information Transfer Frame**

| b7 | b6 | b5 | b4 | b3 | b2 | b1 | b0 |
|----|----|----|----|----|----|----|----|
| NR | | | P/F | Type | | 0 | 1 |

**Supervisory Frame**

| b7 | b6 | b5 | b4 | b3 | b2 | b1 | b0 |
|----|----|----|----|----|----|----|----|
| C/R | | | P/F | C/R | | 1 | 1 |

**Unnumbered Frame**

### Information Transfer Frames (I-Frames)

**Information transfer frames** or **I-frames** are the only frames that can be used to transfer data. As Figure 11-12 shows, the control fields of all three types of frames have a **poll/final (P/F) bit.** When the primary transmits a frame with the P/F bit set, the frame is a poll, and the addressed secondary must respond. The secondary sets the P/F bit in the final frame of a message.

The control field of an I-frame has both a *send sequence count (NS)* and a *receive sequence count (NR)* field. The NS count is the frame number. HDLC frames are numbered 0 through 7 (0 through 127 in systems that use a 16-bit control field). When the frame count reaches seven, it rolls over to zero and begins anew.

The NR count is the number of the next frame the terminal expects to receive. For example, suppose a secondary terminal transmits frame number six of a message, and the last frame it received without error from the primary is frame number four. It will set the NS count in the frame to six, and the frame number and the NR count to five, the number of the next frame it expects to receive.

Because a secondary can communicate only with the primary, each secondary terminal maintains a single NS count for the frame it is currently sending to the primary and a single NR count with the number of the next frame it expects to receive from the primary. But the primary communicates with all of the secondaries, so it must maintain a separate NS and NR count for each secondary terminal on the network.

### Supervisory Frames (S-Frames)

In HDLC, **supervisory frames** or **S-frames** serve much the same purpose as the ACK, NAK, and WACK control characters do in BISYNC. Figure 11-13 shows the four types of S-frames: *receive ready (RR), receive not ready (RNR), reject (REJ),* and

**FIGURE 11-13**
The four types of supervisory frames.

| b7 | b6 | b5 | b4 | b3 | b2 | b1 | b0 | Supervisory Type |
|----|----|----|----|----|----|----|----|------------------|
| | NR | | P/F | 0 | 0 | 0 | 1 | Receive ready (RR) |
| | NR | | P/F | 0 | 1 | 0 | 1 | Receive not ready (RNR) |
| | NR | | P/F | 1 | 0 | 0 | 1 | Reject (REJ) |
| | NR | | P/F | 1 | 1 | 0 | 1 | Selective reject (SREJ) |

*selective reject (SREJ)*. Bits 2 and 3 in the control field differentiate among the four types of S-frames.

A **receive ready (RR) frame** is an acknowledgment. The terminal that sends an RR frame acknowledges that it has received all I-frames prior to frame number NR without error and that it now expects to receive I-frame number NR. If a terminal sends an RR frame with an NR sequence count of 3, for example, it has correctly received all I-frames up to and including the I-frame that had an NS count of 2, and it expects the next I-frame to have an NS count of 3. A **receive not ready (RNR) frame** also acknowledges the receipt of all I-frames through NR-1 without error, but it conveys the additional information that the terminal that sent the S-frame has become busy and therefore cannot receive more I-frames at the moment.

REJ and SREJ function much like BISYNC's NAK character. Both indicate that I-frame number NR was received in error. The **reject (REJ) frame** requests the retransmission of *all frames* beginning with NR. For example, suppose a terminal receives a series of I-frames with NS counts of 0 through 5. If the terminal that received those I-frames sends an REJ frame with the NR count set to 3, it is requesting the retransmission of all I-frames beginning with the I-frame that had an NS count of 3.

The **selective reject (SREJ) frame** requests the retransmission of frame number NR *only*. In theory, SREJ is more efficient than REJ, because it requests the retransmission of only one frame. In practice, most systems do not use SREJ on the theory that errors occur infrequently and that the time lost in transmitting a few extra frames is not significant.

### Unnumbered Frames (U-frames)
**Unnumbered frames** or **U-frames** are used to initialize terminals and to place them on- or off-line. Figure 11-14 shows the bit configuration for nine types of U-frames. We will not discuss them in detail, but for reference, a brief description of each type is listed below.

1. *Nonsequenced information (NSI)*—indicates that the information field that follows is unrelated to any sequenced series of frames being sent.

2. *Request for initialization (RQI)*—transmitted by a secondary to request that primary send it a SIM command. If the primary responds with something other than a SIM, the secondary sends another RQI.

**FIGURE 11-14**

Nine types of unnumbered frames.

| b7 | b6 | b5 | b4 | b3 | b2 | b1 | b0 | Unnumbered Type |
|----|----|----|----|----|----|----|----|-----------------|
| 0 | 0 | 0 | P/F | 0 | 0 | 1 | 1 | Nonsequenced information (NSI) |
| 0 | 0 | 0 | F | 0 | 1 | 1 | 1 | Request for initialization (RQI) |
| 0 | 0 | 0 | P | 0 | 1 | 1 | 1 | Set initialization mode (SIM) |
| 1 | 0 | 0 | P | 0 | 0 | 1 | 1 | Set normal response mode (SNRM) |
| 0 | 0 | 0 | F | 1 | 1 | 1 | 1 | Request on line (ROL) |
| 0 | 1 | 0 | P | 0 | 0 | 1 | 1 | Disconnect (DISC) |
| 0 | 1 | 1 | F | 0 | 0 | 1 | 1 | Nonsequenced acknowledgment (NSA) |
| 1 | 0 | 0 | F | 0 | 1 | 1 | 1 | Command reject (CMDR) |
| 0 | 0 | 1 | 1 | 0 | 0 | 1 | 1 | Optional response poll (ORP) |

3. *Set initialization mode (SIM)*—transmitted by the primary to command the secondary to initialize itself. Among other things, the secondary responds to the SIM command by setting both the NR and the NS counts to zero. The expected response to SIM is NSA.

4. *Set normal response mode (SNRM)*—sent by the primary to place the secondary in the normal response mode. In the normal response mode, the secondary may not initiate any transmissions unless primary requests it to do so. SNRM also resets the secondary's NR and NS count to zero. The expected response to SNRM is NSA.

5. *Request on line (ROL)*—sent by a secondary to indicate that it is disconnected.

6. *Disconnect (DISC)*—sent by the primary to place a secondary off-line. An SNRM or SIM is required to reconnect the secondary.

7. *Nonsequenced acknowledgment (NSA)*—the affirmative response to SNRM, DISC, or SIM.

8. *Command reject (CMDR)*—transmitted by a secondary when it receives a non-valid command.

9. *Optional response poll (ORP)*—invites transmission from the addressed secondary station.

## 11-2-2 The Operation of an HDLC System

The timing diagram of Figure 11-15 illustrates an exchange of frames between an HDLC primary and one of its secondaries on a multipoint communications system. The vertical axis of the diagram represents time, and each arrow on the diagram

**FIGURE 11-15**
An exchange of HDLC frames between the primary and one of the secondaries.

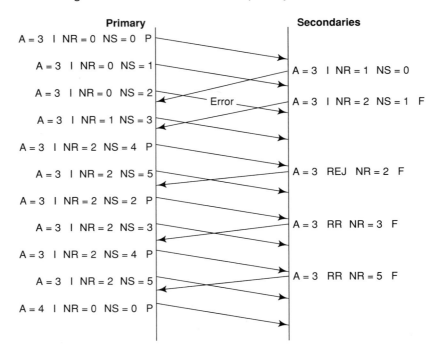

represents the communication of a frame from one terminal to another. The arrows slope down to demonstrate the passage of time during a data transmission. The position of the tail of the arrow represents the time that the sending terminal begins transmitting the frame, and the head of the arrow represents the time when the destination terminal finishes receiving it. The number following the letter A is the address of the secondary involved in the frame transfer. $I$ indicates an I-frame, $REJ$ a reject S-frame, and $RR$ a receive ready S-frame. $NR$ is the receive count, and $NS$ is the frame number or send count. $P$ indicates that the frame is a poll frame, and $F$ indicates that it is a final frame.

   The timing diagram begins with the primary sending the first frame of a six-frame message to secondary number 3. The system has been reset and all counts begin at zero. The first I-frame has the poll bit set, which commands secondary 3 to respond. Once it polls a secondary, the primary may not send another frame until the polled secondary responds with a final frame.

   Because the system is full-duplex, both the primary and the polled secondary transmit at the same time. Secondary 3 also has a message to send, so it responds to the poll by transmitting I-frames, placing its own address in the address field. Secondary 3 also gives the first frame that it transmits an NS count of 0. NR is set to 1 to inform the primary that secondary 3 has received frame NS = 0 without error and is now expecting the primary to send it frame NS = 1. In this way the I-frame serves two purposes: It transmits information and it acknowledges the receipt of frame number 0 without error.

Secondary 3's message is only two frames long, so it sets the final (F) bit when it transmits the second frame. Once it begins to send this final frame, secondary 3 relinquishes its permission to transmit, and it may not transmit any additional frames until it receives another poll from the primary.

Unfortunately, when secondary 3 receives the frame that has an NS count of 2, the frame fails the CRC. Secondary 3 does not have permission to transmit, so it cannot immediately inform the primary of the error. The primary, on the other hand, cannot send another poll until it receives the final frame from secondary 3. The primary continues to send I-frames.

By the time the primary begins to send the frame that has an NS count of 4, it has finished receiving the final frame from secondary 3, so it transmits this frame with the poll bit set. Secondary 3 responds to the poll by sending an REJ frame with the NR count set at 2. This is a request that the primary retransmit all frames beginning with frame 2. The primary does this, polling secondary 3 each time it receives a final frame. Secondary 3 has no more messages to send, so it responds to each poll by sending an RR frame to acknowledge that it has received no frames in error.

At the bottom of the timing diagram, the primary has finished sending frames to secondary 3 and sends an I-frame to secondary 4. Secondary 3 has not acknowledged the reception of the frame that had an NS count of 5. It will acknowledge frame 5 the next time the primary polls it.

## ■ SUMMARY

This chapter has discussed two protocols used for synchronous data communications. A protocol is a set of rules that governs data communications. A protocol must address three basic problems: framing or breaking large fields of data into shorter segments called blocks or frames; error control, the detection and correction of errors; and sequence control, a method of numbering data blocks so that no block will be lost or duplicated and so that the blocks will be placed in the proper order at the receiver.

The protocols discussed in this chapter fall into two categories: character-oriented protocols and bit-oriented protocols. Character-oriented protocols use special control characters to manage the flow of information. Two disadvantages of character-oriented protocols are (1) they are tied to specific character sets and (2) they do not handle non-text data very well.

Bit-oriented protocols use bit fields within each frame to manage the flow of information. Bit-oriented protocols do not depend on the features of a specific character set.

BISYNC is a character-oriented protocol that IBM introduced in 1968. It can be used with either the ASCII or EBCDIC character sets, and it is designed for half-duplex communications. HDLC and SDLC are bit-oriented protocols designed for full-duplex communications. SDLC was published by IBM in 1974. An updated version, renamed HDLC, was published by the International Standards Organization in 1977. SDLC and HDLC are designed for full-duplex communications and are therefore faster than BISYNC. Because they are bit-oriented, SDLC and HDLC can be used with any character set or with pure binary data.

■ **QUESTIONS**

1. Define the word *protocol* as it applies to data communications.
2. Which three basic problems must a synchronous data communications protocol address?
3. What are the two types of synchronous protocols discussed in this chapter?
4. What are the characters called that facilitate the transfer of data in character-oriented protocols?
5. What is the name of the best-known character-oriented synchronous protocol?
6. Which of the following types of communication is BISYNC designed for: simplex, half-duplex, or full-duplex?
7. a. Which two character sets can be used with BISYNC?
   b. Which of these two character sets is *more commonly* used with BISYNC?
8. a. What is the purpose of a *framing character* in BISYNC?
   b. Name four BISYNC framing characters.
9. a. What are the two BISYNC communications phases?
   b. What do the terminals do during the line control phase?
   c. What do the terminals do during the data transmission phase?
10. What is the name of the character that is sent at least two times immediately before each BISYNC message block?
11. a. Which control character is sent immediately before the header of a BISYNC message block?
    b. What type of information could the header contain?
12. Which control character is sent immediately before the text field of a BISYNC message block?
13. When is an ETB character used at the end of the text field in a BISYNC message block, and when is an ETX character used?
14. a. Why is a BCC sent at the end of a BISYNC message block?
    b. What type of BCC is often used in ASCII-based systems?
    c. What type of character is used in EBCDIC systems?
15. Give some examples of types of computer data that cannot be easily represented by the ASCII or EBCDIC codes.

16. Why do binary data create a problem for character-oriented protocols such as BISYNC?

17. a. What is meant by the term *transparent transmission?*

    b. Explain how the BISYNC protocol can be modified to allow transparent transmission.

18. a. Explain the purpose of each of the following BISYNC control characters: NAK, ACK0, ACK1, and WACK.

    b. Why does the receiving terminal alternate between ACK0 and ACK1 to acknowledge the receipt of message blocks?

19. a. In a BISYNC point-to-point communications system, how does a terminal bid for control of the data link?

    b. What procedure does one terminal follow to grant control of the data link to the other terminal?

    c. What procedure does a terminal follow to relinquish control of the data link when it has finished sending data?

20. a. In a BISYNC multipoint communications system, what is the central computer called?

    b. What are the remote terminals called?

21. What is the difference between a *poll* and a *selection?*

22. a. What does the supervisor transmit in order to poll a secondary?

    b. How does the secondary respond to a poll if it has no messages to send?

    c. How does the tributary respond to a poll if it *does* have one or more messages to send?

23. a. What does the supervisor transmit in order to select a tributary?

    b. How does the tributary respond if it is unable to accept data at the time it is selected?

    c. How does the tributary respond to the selection if it *is* able to accept data when it is selected?

24. Name three disadvantages of BISYNC for modern data communications.

25. Why are bit-oriented protocols more suited than character-oriented protocols to communicate non-text data?

26. How are the SDLC and the HDLC protocols related?

27. Name the four bit fields of an HDLC frame.

28. a. Which character is transmitted immediately before and immediately after each HDLC frame?

    b. What two purposes does this character serve?

29. Explain how "bit stuffing" works to ensure that a binary 1 is never sent six consecutive times in the data field of an HDLC frame.

30. a. What are the three basic types of HDLC frames?

     b.    Which of these frame types is used to transfer data?

31.  a.   When does the primary terminal set the P/F bit in an HDLC frame that it transmits?

     b.    When does a secondary set the P/F bit in an HDLC frame that it transmits?

32.  a.   What is the purpose of the NS count in an HDLC frame?

     b.    What is the purpose of the NR count in an HDLC frame?

33.  Describe the purpose of each of the following types of S-frame: a. RR, b. RNR, c. REJ, and d. SREJ.

34.  What purpose do U-frames serve in an HDLC system?

# ■ Chapter 12

# LOCAL AREA NETWORKS

**OBJECTIVES**

After you have completed this chapter, you should be able to:

- ■ Discuss how local area networks make it possible for computer users to enjoy the advantages of distributed computing and still share data and programs.

- ■ Describe layers 1 through 3 of the Open Systems Interconnect Basic Reference Model and discuss why the Model is important to committees that develop data communications standards.

- ■ Discuss the operation of the Ethernet, Token Ring, and FDDI local area networks.

- ■ Discuss the differences among the 10BASE-5, 10BASE-2, and 10BASE-T versions of Ethernet.

- ■ Describe both the CSMA/CD and the token passing methods of controlling transmissions over a LAN.

- ■ Discuss how repeaters, bridges, and routers connect LANs to form an *internetwork.*

## INTRODUCTION

Two decades ago, computers were too expensive for most small businesses to afford. Companies that could justify the purchase of a computer were almost always firms that had to keep track of and manipulate very large amounts of data. The typical business computer installation consisted of a large central computer and a number of remote terminals as illustrated in Figure 12-1. Usually, each terminal was no more than a keyboard and a CRT screen that was connected to the central computer by a serial interface. All computer users had access to the same programs and data, although security codes were used to prevent unauthorized persons from accessing sensitive data such as payroll records. Data stored in a computer in an organized fashion is called a **data base.**

Viewed from the standpoint of today's technology, the centralized computer has a number of disadvantages: It offers poor security, it is vulnerable to failure, it is expensive, and it is difficult to program and customize to the needs of the individual user. There is no guarantee that the shipping clerk will not be able to "crack" the security code for the payroll program and command the computer to issue an extra check. When the central computer "crashes," the whole office may cease to function. In the past, it was not uncommon for programmers to spend a year or more getting a program to work on a central computer, and often the resulting software did not meet the needs of the users. However, the centralized computer has an important advantage. Many users share the same data base, and when one user makes a change in the stored data, that change immediately becomes available to the other users.

As personal computers (PCs) became inexpensive and more powerful, they began to appear on the desks of office workers. They started to replace the central

**FIGURE 12-1**

Early computers were large machines with a number of remote dumb terminals.

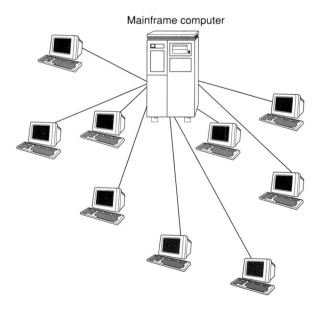

Mainframe computer

computer. The practice of using many smaller computers scattered throughout an office in place of a central machine is called **distributed computing.** Not only can relatively inexpensive PCs perform much of the work that used to be done on the central computer, but they are inexpensive enough to also be put to work at simpler tasks such as word processing. As the PC market grew, a large variety of PC software became available at reasonable prices. Today, most users can buy inexpensive programs off the shelf to meet their needs, and it is seldom necessary to hire programmers to write expensive custom software. The combination of inexpensive PCs and software has made computers affordable for almost all businesses.

Unfortunately, with distributed computing, the advantage of the central computer's shared data base was lost. Office workers exchanged computer files by copying them onto a floppy disk and walking the disk to a coworker's office, a method of data communication jokingly called "Sneakernet." Some better method of sharing data was needed. Computer engineers responded to that need by developing several communications systems to connect PCs together and allow them to share programs and data. These communications systems are called *local area networks* or LANs for short. Some of the LANs became standards and are widely used.

## 12-1 OVERVIEW OF LOCAL AREA NETWORKS

**A local area network** is a communications system that interconnects computers and peripheral devices that are located within a single office, a single building, or adjacent buildings. This chapter discusses Ethernet and Token Ring, the two most popular current LAN standards, and FDDI, a newer and much faster LAN standard that promises to be widely used in the future.

Figure 12-2 shows how the components of a simple LAN might be arranged in an office. Each PC connected to a LAN typically has a limited amount of disk storage, perhaps 40 megabytes. On many LANs, one computer is much more powerful than the others. This more powerful computer is called a **server.** The server is not assigned to an individual user; instead, it serves the needs of all of the PC users on

**FIGURE 12-2**
A network allows several users to share expensive peripherals such as a laser printer or a modem connected to a dedicated telephone line.

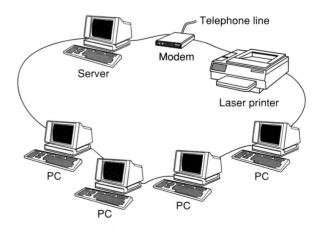

the network. It brings to the LAN users many of the advantages of the old central computer.

The server typically has 500 megabytes or more of disk storage, enough to hold all of the programs used in the office as well as all of the data bases that the individual PC users share. The disk drive of each PC, on the other hand, stores only frequently used programs and the data that are not shared among workers. When a PC accesses one of the programs on the server's disk drive, the server sends the program over the network to the PC where it is temporarily stored in the PC's memory. In most systems, the software that controls the LAN makes the network transparent to the user. The server's disk drives appear on the user's computer screen as if they were attached to the user's PC. With a well-designed LAN, accessing programs and data bases on the server, or even on other PCs on the network, is as easy as accessing programs and data on the user's own computer.

The LAN in Figure 12-2 also allows PC users to share a laser printer and a modem. The average PC user needs these devices only occasionally, so there is no need to purchase a separate printer and modem for each PC. To print a document, the user's PC sends it over the network to the printer. When someone uses the modem, the network establishes a **virtual connection** between the modem and the PC, which means that the transparent network allows the two devices to exchange information as if they were directly connected.

Each of the devices connected to the LAN is called a **terminal,** a **station,** or a **DTE,** terms that are also used to describe devices connected to other communications systems discussed earlier in this book. To differentiate between LANs and earlier communications systems, LAN terminals are often called **nodes.**

To summarize some of the advantages that a LAN brings to distributed computing, it permits each user to enjoy the advantages of having a personal desktop computer while still permitting users to share programs and data bases as they did in the days of centralized computers. A LAN also permits its users to share peripherals such as laser printers and modems. A third advantage, which has not been mentioned so far, is that a LAN enables its users to send messages to each other in the form of *electronic mail.*

## 12-1-1 Electronic Mail

**Electronic mail** is a system of messages that can be sent over a communications network from one computer to another. Electronic mail systems enable any PC on the network to send a message to any other PC, as long as the PCs and the server are running the necessary software. As Figure 12-3 illustrates, most electronic mail systems do not send messages directly from one PC to another. The transmitting computer sends the electronic mail to the server where it is stored on the server's hard disk. If the recipient's computer is operating, the server sends it a shorter message notifying the recipient that there is mail waiting at the server. If the recipient's computer is turned off, the server sends the message the next time it senses, via the network, that the recipient's computer is turned on. The recipient can access the server's hard disk at a convenient time, read the mail, and send it to the printer if a

**FIGURE 12-3**
Electronic mail is stored on the server's hard disk until the recipient deletes it.

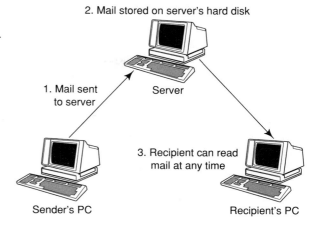

2. Mail stored on server's hard disk

1. Mail sent to server

Server

3. Recipient can read mail at any time

Sender's PC

Recipient's PC

hard copy is needed. The recipient deletes the mail from the server's disk when it is no longer necessary to keep a copy.

Today, not all electronic mail consists of pure text messages. With the proper hardware and software, electronic mail can contain text, graphics, voice, or a combination of the three. When electronic mail, or any other type of data communications, is made up of a combination of text, graphics, and audio, it is called **multimedia communications.**

## 12-1-2 Benefits of LAN Standards

The first LANs were developed by computer manufacturers. At first, many different types of LANs were on the market. However, most LANs were expensive and they would work for only certain types of computers and with certain programs. They also required a great deal of technical expertise to install and maintain.

To resolve these problems, the **Institute of Electrical and Electronic Engineers (IEEE),** formed the 802 Standards Committee. The committee has published several recommended LAN standards, the most popular of which are **Ethernet** (Standard 802.3) and **Token Ring** (Standard 802.5). Ethernet LANs communicate at 10 Mb/s and Token Ring communicates at either 4 or 16 Mb/s, speeds that are adequate for communicating text and most computer programs. For networks that must operate at higher speeds to communicate digitized sounds, still pictures, and even compressed TV pictures, the **American National Standards Institute (ANSI)** has published a LAN standard called the **Fiber Data Distributed Interface (FDDI),** which transfers data at 100 Mb/s.

LAN standards have made it possible for computers and peripheral devices produced by different manufacturers to exchange information. Today it is possible to connect IBM PCs and Apple Macintosh computers to the same Ethernet LAN so that they can share many of the same data bases. LANs have become so common that some computers and printers are sold with Ethernet and Token Ring interfaces built onto the motherboard. As you will see later in this chapter, LAN standards also make it possible to connect two or more LANs through devices called **bridges** and **routers** to form **wide area networks (WANs).** Perhaps most importantly, LAN standards have made it possible for many companies to compete in the LAN market, and the competition has made LAN products affordable.

## 12-2    THE OPEN SYSTEMS INTERCONNECT MODEL

The **International Standards Organization (ISO)** has analyzed the process of data communications among computers and organized that process into seven different groups of functions. It calls each group of functions a *layer.* To show how these layers relate to each other, the ISO has organized them into the **Open Systems Interconnect Basic Reference Model,** which is more commonly referred to as the **OSI Model.** The OSI Model has been officially published by the ISO as Standard 7489 and by the CCITT as Standard X.200. Other standards organizations have agreed to work within the definitions of the OSI Model when they develop new standards for data communications. For example, the 802 Standards Committee published the Ethernet and Token Ring LAN standards to perform the data communications functions described in layers 1 and 2 of the OSI Model.

Figure 12-4 shows the seven layers of the OSI Model. Each layer describes a group of tasks that may need to be performed to communicate data from one computer to another. Simple communications systems may perform only the functions described in the lower layers of the Model. For example, to send a text file from a computer to a printer over a parallel interface cable requires only layers 1 and 2 of the OSI model. However, the OSI model makes it possible for such communications systems to work together with computer software and hardware that operate at the higher levels of the model to produce a sophisticated data communications system. All layers of the OSI Model may be needed if the user of an IBM-compatible PC uses a word processing program to access a graphics file located on the disk of a Macintosh computer.

Although all of the layers of the OSI Model are described in the following paragraphs, the most important layers for you to be familiar with to understand the LANs, bridges, and routers discussed in this chapter are layers 1 and 2, and to some extent, layer 3. Although most of the functions in the OSI Model could theoretically be performed by either hardware or software, in practice layer 1 and layer 2 functions are mainly performed by the types of communications hardware you have been studying in this book. The functions of layers 3 through 7 are mainly performed by software.

Layer 1, the **physical layer** is the physical medium for data flow—in other words, the conductors, fiber-optic cables, or radio waves that link two or more nodes together and the signals that they carry. Layer 1 also defines other aspects of the physical transmission of data such as signal levels and the distance that signals can travel over the physical medium before they must be amplified. Layer 1 should provide a method of informing layer 2 if there is a loss of the physical connection or of electrical power. An example of a communications standard that performs part of the layer 1 function is RS-232C.

**FIGURE 12-4**
The seven layers of the OSI model.

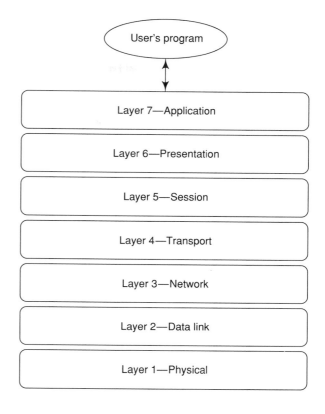

Layer 2, the **datalink layer,** performs error control, framing, synchronization, link initialization and disconnection, addressing, and frame sequence control. Protocols that perform the layer 2 function are responsible for transferring frames to and from the physical medium. An example of a protocol that performs the layer 2 function is HDLC.

Layer 3, the **network layer,** switches and routes information through the network. Standards that operate at this layer establish a virtual connection between the sending and receiving terminals.

Layer 4, the **transport layer,** contains the functions that make the network transparent to the layers above it and to the user. This layer also makes sure that the data move from one end of the network to the other without the user's being concerned with the operation of the network.

Layer 5, the **session layer,** provides a means for data exchange between different user software applications and determines whether the communications should be full-duplex or half-duplex. It also provides a way to recover from major data transfer problems such as a network failure, and it ensures that all data are received before it permits the lower layers to release a connection with the remote terminal.

Layer 6, the **presentation layer,** performs code conversions and data reformatting so that the data are in a format that can be presented to the computer and its application programs. Hardware and software that operate at this layer convert between the ASCII and BISYNC character sets or between data formatted for IBM-compatible PCs and data formatted for Macintosh personal computers. Layer 6 also performs such tasks as screen formatting and data compression and decompression.

Layer 7, the **application layer,** interfaces the communications system to the user's specific application program. It is this layer, for example, that communicates with a word processor program and makes it possible for that word processing program to use the network to access a data file on another computer.

As Figure 12-5 illustrates, each layer in the OSI model adds header information as data move down the model to be sent over the communications system. Each

**FIGURE 12-5**
All OSI layers add overhead to the data to accomplish the layer's function.

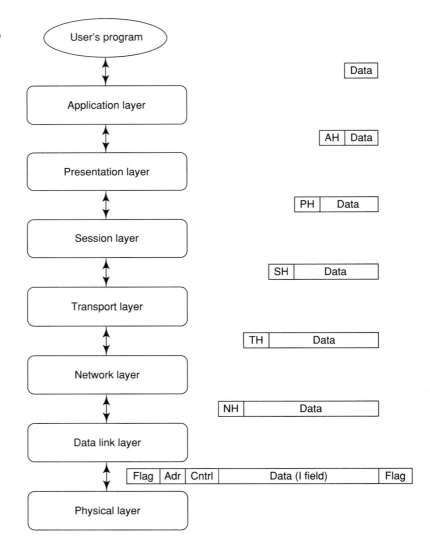

layer also removes header information as data received from the network move up through the layers toward the application program. Assume, for example, that a word processing program on a user's PC stores data to the hard disk of a LAN's server. The user's program hands the data to another program that fulfills the functions of the OSI Model's application layer. This layer manipulates the data and adds a header, which is designated AH for "application header" in Figure 12-5, and passes the data with the attached AH header to the presentation layer. The AH header is a message from the application layer of the sending node to the application layer of the receiving node. The AH header contains information about any data manipulation that the application layer of the transmitting node has performed.

The presentation layer of the transmitting node treats all of the information it receives from the application layer, including the AH header, as data. After the presentation layer performs any necessary code conversions and data reformatting, it adds its own header and passes the data and header to the session layer.

The process continues as the data move down through the layers until the data reach the data link layer. The data link layer adds address and control fields to each frame and marks the beginning and end of each frame with flags. Finally the physical layer transports the data over the network.

As data move up through the OSI Model at the receiving terminal, each layer removes its header and examines it for instructions from the corresponding OSI layer at the sending terminal. For example, the receive node's network layer removes the NH header and examines it to determine how the transmit node's network layer handled the data. The headers enable each OSI layer in the transmitting node to communicate with its corresponding OSI layer in the receiving node.

## 12-3  ETHERNET

Xerox Corporation developed Ethernet in the middle 1970s. By 1980, Xerox had teamed up with Intel Corporation and Digital Equipment Corporation in an attempt to make Ethernet an industry standard. The IEEE's 803.2 Standards Committee adopted Ethernet after adding some safety and signaling features and published a form of the Ethernet standard that is known as **10BASE-5.** The term *10BASE-5* refers to the physical layer specifications. The *10* indicates that this form of Ethernet operates at 10Mb/s, the word *BASE* indicates that the LAN carries baseband data (no carrier is used), and the *5* refers to the fact that the maximum length of a 10BASE-5 network is 500 m unless a repeater is used to amplify the signals.

There are now four physical layer specifications for Ethernet: 10BASE-5 (thick Ethernet), 10BASE-2 (thin Ethernet), **1BASE-5** (StarLAN), and 10BASE-T (twisted-pair Ethernet). Because of its slow data rate, StarLAN has not become popular, so it is not discussed in the following subsections. Ethernet suppliers are experimenting with other methods of transporting Ethernet signals including fiber-optic cable, radio frequency broadcasts, and infrared light, and a fast 100-Mb/s Ethernet standard is under development.

In its early days, Ethernet was considered a LAN better suited to engineering, technical, and graphics computer installations than to business use. Token Ring was considered superior for office installations. Today, that has changed, and Ethernet is preferred for almost all LAN applications. More Ethernet LANs are installed each year than all other LANs combined.

### 12-3-1 10BASE-5 Ethernet

Figure 12-6 shows how computers and other devices are connected to a 10BASE-5 Ethernet network. In the figure, a repeater joins two Ethernet segments. Remember that the maximum cable length of 10BASE-5 Ethernet is 500 m. Additional segments of coaxial cable can be added to the network to extend it beyond the 500-m limit, but a repeater is required to amplify the signals that pass from one segment to the other. Each end of each segment of coaxial cable is terminated in its characteristic impedance of 50 Ω to prevent reflections. The 10BASE-5 Ethernet LAN has a bus or multidrop topology and uses a device called a **media access unit (MAU)** to connect each terminal to the cable. Each connection is called a *tap*. The cable that connects each MAU to its terminal is called a **drop.**

On Ethernet LANs, a terminal is officially called a *station,* but in this book we will use the more general term *node.* Inside each MAU, a *transceiver* transfers the electrical signals between the drop and the coaxial cable.

### 12-3-2 10BASE-2 Ethernet

**10BASE-2** Ethernet is well suited to laboratory and industrial applications where its thick coaxial cable gives it high noise immunity. However, heavy-duty RG-11 coaxial cable is expensive, and cabling rules usually require that it be installed by profession-

**FIGURE 12-6**
The traditional Ethernet topology is a bus network.

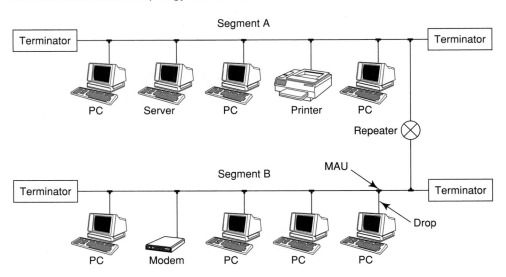

als. The high cost of installing RG-11 coaxial cable inside the walls of an existing office building makes 10BASE-5 Ethernet too expensive for many business applications. To reduce Ethernet's cost, International Computer Ltd., Hewlett-Packard, and 3Com Corporation developed an Ethernet variation that uses thinner, less expensive RG-58 coaxial cable. RG-58 is similar to the cable used to carry TV signals inside many homes. It is cheaper to purchase and cheaper to install than RG-11. The IEEE 803.2 Committee adopted the new Ethernet variation in 1985, and it was given the name *10BASE-2,* although it is more popularly referred to as **Cheapernet** or **Thinwire Ethernet.** 10BASE-2 allows a maximum segment length of almost 200 m (185 m to be exact), which is more than adequate for most offices. 10BASE-2 Ethernet also does away with the MAU, another cost savings. The transceiver is located inside the terminal, and a simple coaxial T-connector connects the terminal to the RG-58 coaxial cable.

### 12-3-3 10BASE-T Ethernet

The lower-cost cable used for 10BASE-2 was an improvement, but for most office installations it was still necessary to pull coaxial cables through the building's walls. Ethernet suppliers began to explore the possibility of using a building's existing telephone wiring to carry Ethernet's 10-Mb/s data stream. The result was **10BASE-T** or **Twisted Pair Ethernet.** 10BASE-T has a maximum segment length of 100 m, and each segment will support a maximum of two nodes connected in a point-to-point communications system. To turn a number of point-to-point connections into a single LAN, 10BASE-T uses a device called an *Ethernet hub* as a central connection point. Figure 12-7 illustrates how an Ethernet hub connects computers to form a 10BASE-T Ethernet LAN. Instead of the bus configuration of earlier Ethernet version, the hub gives 10BASE-T a star topology.

The telephone wiring in an office building usually radiates from a central wiring closet, which makes the wiring closet an ideal location to install the Ethernet hub.

**FIGURE 12-7**
10BASE-T Ethernet uses a star topology and a hub to connect the terminals to the network.

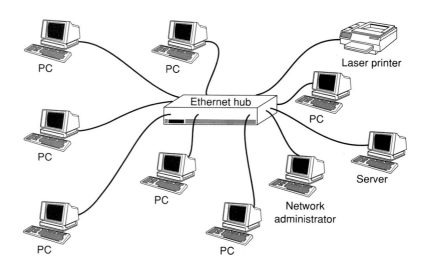

The hub acts as both a central control point and as a repeater for each node on the network. Because it is inexpensive and easy to install, 10BASE-T has become the most popular version of Ethernet.

Each Ethernet connection on the hub is called a **port.** When a node is turned on, its Ethernet transreceiver sends a DC current over the twisted pair to the hub. The hub senses the current and enables the node's port, thereby connecting the node to the network. The port remains enabled as long as the node continues to supply DC current over its twisted-pair connection. If the node is turned off, or if there is an open or short circuit in the twisted pair between the node and the hub, the DC current ceases to flow, and the hub disconnects the port. The rest of the LAN continues to operate normally.

Ethernet hubs may be either intelligent or unintelligent. A network hub is little more than a repeater with a relay at each port to switch the port in or out of the network. An intelligent hub contains sophisticated electronics that make it possible for the network administrator to manage and troubleshoot the network as described in the following section.

### 12-3-4 The Network Administrator

One of the nodes in Figure 12-7 is labeled **network administrator.** The network administrator is an employee whose job it is to make sure that the network functions smoothly. With the aide of an intelligent hub and the proper software, the network administrator monitors and controls the operation of the network. When a problem occurs, the central hub gives the network administrator the ability to isolate the problem to a single port and disconnect that port until the defective equipment can be repaired. If the problem should turn out to be one of the nodes, the network administrator can command the hub to disconnect the defective node from the network until repairs can be made.

The network administrator is also responsible for the operation of the server. The network administrator determines who may access files on the server and establishes passwords for individual users. The network administrator makes sure that each computer on the network has the necessary software and hardware installed to use the network's capabilities and to enable each PC user to perform his or her work.

### 12-3-5 Manchester Encoding

Transmitting baseband 10-Mb/s digital information over long lengths of wire without modulating the information onto an analog carrier requires careful encoding. Ideally, the encoded signal should be high 50% of the time and low 50% of the time to avoid charging up the capacitance of the conductors. It is also helpful if there are frequent transitions between the high and low logic level that can be used to synchronize the clocks of all of the nodes on the network. Ethernet uses the Manchester encoding scheme, illustrated in Figure 12-8, which meets these requirements.

**Manchester encoding** has a transition between the high and the low logic level in the center of each bit. A positive-going transition in the center of the bit indicates

**FIGURE 12-8**
A Manchester-encoded signal.

that the bit is a logic 1. A negative-going transition in the center of the bit indicates that the bit is a logic 0. Another way of looking at it is to say that the first half of the bit is the complement of the data and the second half is the data. There is a logic-level transition at the beginning of a bit only when it follows an identical bit. For example in Figure 12-8, there is a transition at the beginning of the third bit, because the bit before it was also a 0. There is also a transition at the beginning of the fifth bit, because the bit before it was also a 1.

## 12-3-6 Ethernet Data Format

Like HDLC, an Ethernet node breaks transmissions into blocks of data called **frames.** Also like HDLC, an Ethernet frame is made up of bit fields as illustrated in Figure 12-9. The following paragraphs describe each of the bit fields in an Ethernet frame.

1. *Preamble*—The preamble consists of 62 bits of alternating 1s and 0s. The purpose of the preamble is to allow the clock in the receiving node to synchronize with the incoming data stream.
2. *Start frame delimiter*—The start frame delimiter is a series of two logic 1s. Its purpose is to mark the end of the preamble and the beginning of the data frame.
3. *Destination address*—The destination address is the address of the node or nodes that should receive the frame. The address can be the address of a single node, it can be a *group address* assigned to two or more nodes, or it can be a *broadcast address,* which directs the message to all of the nodes on the network.
4. *Source address*—The source address is the address of the node that sends the frame.
5. *Type field*—Ethernet itself does not use the type field. It is placed in the frame for the use of higher layers in the OSI model.
6. *Data field*—The data field contains the information. An Ethernet data field may be from 46 bytes to 1500 bytes long.
7. *CRC*—Ethernet uses a 32-bit CRC for error detection.

**FIGURE 12-9**
An Ethernet frame.

| Preamble | Start frame delimiter | Destination address | Source address | Type field | Data | CRC | End frame delimiter |
|---|---|---|---|---|---|---|---|
| | | | | | | | |

8. *End frame delimiter*—The end frame delimiter is a period of time during which no bits are transmitted. Because Manchester encoding has a transition in the center of each bit, a period with no transitions indicates an end frame delimiter.

### 12-3-7 Carrier Sense Multiple Access with Collision Detection (CSMA/CD)

**Carrier sense multiple access with collision detection** or **CSMA/CD** is a system that Ethernet and some other LANs use to allow nodes to contend for the right to transmit over the network. Under CSMA/CD, the nodes must have full-duplex capability so that while a node is transmitting it can detect a transmission by another node on the LAN (carrier sense). A node may send a frame any time it does not sense another transmission on the line (multiple access). If two or more nodes begin transmitting at the same time, the situation is called a **collision.** When a collision takes place (collision detection), all nodes stop transmission and wait for a short period of time. At the end of the wait, if the LAN is free, any node may begin transmission. If all nodes waited the same period of time before they retransmitted, there would be a second collision. To reduce this possibility, the nodes use a random delay before reattempting transmission.

### 12-3-8 An Ethernet Interface

Figure 12-10 is the block diagram of the Ethernet **network interface controller (NIC)** that is located inside each node on the Ethernet LAN. The NIC may be built into the node's motherboard, but it is more commonly an add-in card that is plugged into a slot on the motherboard. Although the diagram shows six functional blocks, the entire NIC, with the exception of a few components such as capacitors and a crystal, is built into one, two, or at the most, three integrated circuits.

The computer bus interface connects the NIC to the address, data, and control buses of the terminal. The Manchester encoder and decoder converts serial data between the terminal's TTL logic levels and the Manchester-coded signals used on the Ethernet LAN. The deserializer and receive engine block circuit converts

**FIGURE 12-10**
A functional block diagram of an Ethernet network interface controller (NIC).

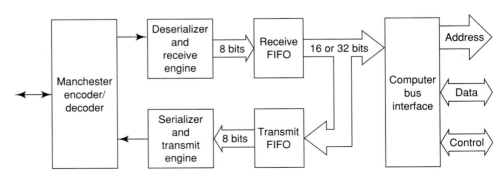

**FIGURE 12-11**
In FIFO memory, each time a byte of parallel data enters the input port, all of the data in the memory shift toward the output port.

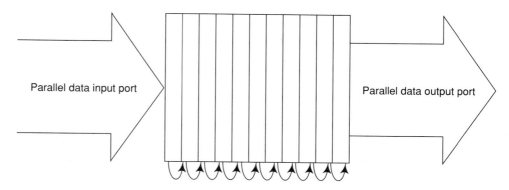

received serial TTL signals to 8-bit parallel bytes of data and passes them on to the receive FIFO memory. The serializer and transmit engine converts parallel data to serial for transmission over the network.

**FIFO** stands for **first in, first out.** Figure 12-11 illustrates the operation of receive FIFO memory. Parallel data enter the memory through the input port. Each time a block of received data enters FIFO memory, the data already in memory move to the right toward the output port to make room for the new data. When the terminal's microprocessor has a few milliseconds of free time, it reads, through the output port, the data that have been accumulated in the FIFO memory. The data are read through the output port. The first data that enter the memory are also the first data to be read from the output port, which gives the memory its name, first in, first out.

FIFO memory acts as a buffer. The receive FIFO acts as a temporary storage location for information received from the LAN until the terminal's processor has the opportunity to read it. In a similar manner, the terminal's processor writes large blocks of data into transmit FIFO memory where they are stored until they can be transmitted over the LAN. Once the processor stores the data to transmit FIFO, it is free to perform other tasks while the Ethernet interface then takes over the task of transmitting the data, one byte at a time.

## 12-4   TOKEN RING NETWORK

Another popular LAN standard is IEEE 802.5, popularly known as **Token Ring.** As its name implies, the first Token Ring LAN used a ring topology as illustrated in Figure 12-12. Today it is more common to use a hub with a Token Ring LAN as illustrated in Figure 12-13. The Token Ring hub is officially called a **multi-station access unit,** abbreviated **MAU.** You may remember that MAU is also the abbreviation used for 10BASE-5 Ethernet's media access unit. To avoid confusion, in this discussion we will use the more popular name *hub.*

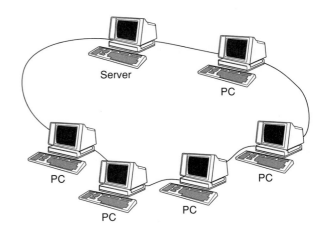

**FIGURE 12-12**
The topology of a Token Ring network.

### 12-4-1 The Star-Ring Topology

Each node in Figure 12-13 is connected to the hub by two pairs of twisted shielded wire. The node transmits over one pair (labeled $T$), and it receives over the other pair (labeled $R$). For simplicity, each pair of wires is represented by a single line in the drawing. Physically, the network has a star configuration because the cables radiate from the central hub to the nodes, but if you trace the electrical path from node to node, you should notice that the nodes are electrically connected in series in the form of a ring. To show its dual nature, this configuration is sometimes called a *star-ring* topology.

One of the disadvantage of the traditional ring topology pictured in Figure 12-12 is that a break in the transmission path anywhere around the ring shuts down the entire network. One loose connection can halt the operation of a 100-node Token Ring LAN. The hub configuration allows defective links or nodes that are not in operation to be bypassed, as node C is bypassed in Figure 12-13. This ability to bypass defective nodes greatly improves the reliability of the Token Ring LAN.

IBM developed the Token Ring LAN, and many Token Ring installations are located in the offices of corporations with large installations of IBM computers. Most Token Ring LANs in place today use a hub with shielded twisted-pair cable and operate at 4 Mb/s. Newer Token Ring computer plug-in cards can operate at either 4 Mb/s or 16 Mb/s. If all of the nodes on the network are capable of 16-Mb/s operation, the network operates at that speed. If one or more of the stations on the network has an older Token Ring card that is capable of only 4-Mb/s operation, the entire ring operates at this slower speed.

### 12-4-2 Token Passing

Unlike Ethernet, the Token Ring nodes do not contend for the right to transmit data. The Token Ring LAN circulates a unique pattern of bits around the ring from station to station. This bit pattern is called a **token.** The token always travels around the ring in the same direction. A node that has a data frame to transmit waits until it

**FIGURE 12-13**
A Token Ring hub bypasses
nodes that are not in service.

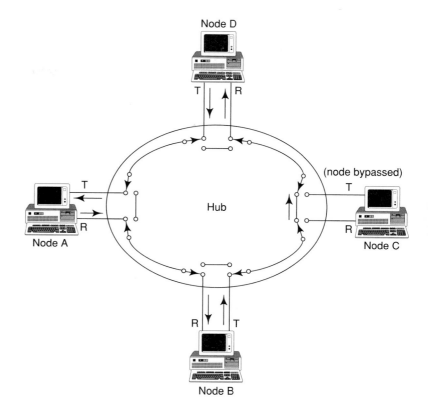

receives the token. The node attaches the frame to the token and transmits the token and its attached frame to the next node on the ring. Like an Ethernet frame, each Token Ring frame has both a source address field and a destination address field. As each node on the ring receives the token, it examines the destination address of the attached frame to determine if the frame is addressed to it. If it is, the node copies the frame into its memory. The node then transmits the token and its attached frame to the next station on the ring.

When a station receives a frame with its own address in the source field, it means that a frame that the node has transmitted has gone all of the way around the ring and that the destination station must have received it. It removes the frame from the token before it transmits the token to the next node on the ring.

To illustrate how the **token-passing protocol** works, assume that node A in Figure 12-14 has an information frame to send to node C. In Figure 12-14(a), node A receives the token from node D, which grants node A permission to transmit. In Figure 12-14(b) node A attaches its information frame to the token and sends the token and attached frame to node B. Node B examines the destination address field of the frame and finds that the frame is not addressed to it. In Figure 12-14(c), node B retransmits the token and attached frame to node C. In Figure 12-14(d), node C also examines the frame's destination address and finds that the frame is addressed

**FIGURE 12-14**
In a Token Ring LAN, the node that has the token has permission to transmit.

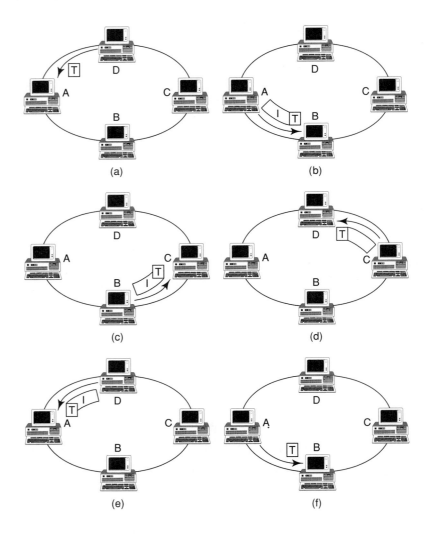

(a)　(b)

(c)　(d)

(e)　(f)

to it, so it makes a copy of the frame in its internal memory. Even though the information frame has reached its destination, node C does not delete the frame from the token. It retransmits the token and frame to node D.

In Figure 12-14(e), node D finds that the frame is not addressed to it, so it retransmits the token and frame to node A. In Figure 12-14(f), node A receives the token and information frame. From the source address field of the frame, it recognizes the frame as one that it has sent and that has circulated around the ring. It deletes the frame and sends the token to node B.

The advantage of token passing compared to the CSMA/CD protocol that Ethernet uses is that token passing avoids the time lost recovering from the collisions that occur on an Ethernet LAN when two nodes try to transmit at the same time. The disadvantage of token passing is that it takes time for the token to pass from node to node, especially if there are many nodes on the LAN. Even though the raw data rate of a fast Token Ring LAN is 16 Mb/s compared to the 10-Mb/s data rate of Ethernet, the actual time it takes to send computer data from one node to another is similar for both types of LANs.

## 12-5 FDDI

The Fiber Distributed Data Interface (FDDI) is a set of standards published by the American National Standards Institute (ANSI) for a high-speed 100-Mb/s LAN, 10 times faster than the Ethernet LAN standard. The topology is a double ring, as pictured in Figure 12-15. One of the rings is designated the **primary ring** and the other is designated the **secondary ring.** Data travels around the two rings in opposite directions. In normal operation, only the primary ring carries data and the secondary ring is reserved as a back-up path in case of problems on the primary. Like Token Ring, the FDDI LAN uses token passing to give a node permission to transmit.

### 12-5-1 Single-Attach and Dual-Attach FDDI Nodes

As Figure 12-15 illustrates, FDDI can use two types of nodes: single-attach and dual-attach. **Dual-attach nodes** are connected to both the primary and the secondary rings. **Single-attach nodes** are connected only to the primary ring by means of a hub-like device called a **concentrator.** Only dual-attach stations can use the secondary ring as a back-up transmission medium if the primary ring is damaged. If the connection between the concentrator and the primary ring is broken, the single-attach stations are disconnected from the network. Dual-attach stations have two fiber-optic transmitters and two fiber-optic receivers, which increases their cost. In many

**FIGURE 12-15**
An FDDI LAN showing dual-attach stations connected to both rings and single-attach stations connected only to the primary ring.

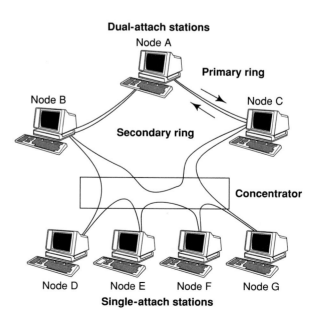

This FDDI evaluation kit contains two computer plug-in cards, the fiber-optic cable, instruction manuals, and software. Courtesy of National Semiconductor.

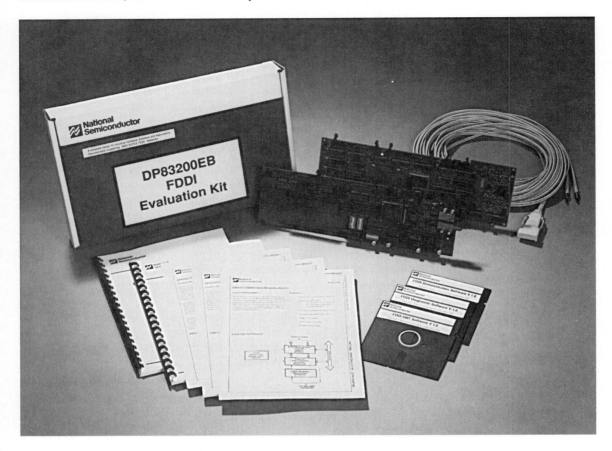

FDDI networks, only critical nodes, such as the network server, are dual-attach. Less important nodes are single-attach to keep the cost of the FDDI LAN within reason.

Like Ethernet and Token Ring hubs, the FDDI concentrator is able to sense when one of the single-attach nodes connected to it is powered down. The concentrator bypasses the node, disconnecting it from the LAN. The concentrator can also bypass defective single-attach nodes to keep them from interfering with the operation of the primary ring.

Figure 12-16 illustrates the **self-healing** feature of the FDDI network. If the fiber-optic cable is broken, the nodes on each side of the break connect the primary and secondary rings to form a single, longer ring. This ability to reconfigure, or perform a **ring-wrap,** makes FDDI a very reliable LAN. In Figure 12-16, all of the nodes, including the single-attach stations, remain connected to the network, despite the cable break.

**FIGURE 12-16**
When a break in the network occurs, dual-attach FDDI stations can loop the network back to keep it running.

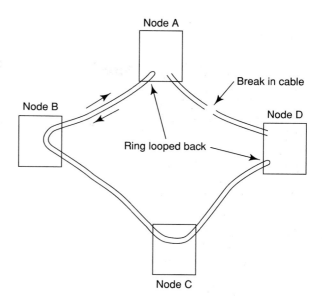

As its name implies, FDDI was originally designed to use fiber-optic cable instead of copper wires as a transmission medium. Fiber-optic cable offered several advantages. It can support very high data transmission rates; it is immune to noise interference; and it does not radiate radio-frequency signals that can cause interference to other equipment. In addition, the cost of fiber-optic cable is also similar to that of copper wire. However, the disadvantage of fiber optics is that the light-emitting diodes and optic detectors that convert between the electric signals of the terminals and the light signals carried by the fiber-optic cable have remained expensive and typically add several hundred dollars to the cost of each FDDI node.

## 12-5-2 Twisted-Pair FDDI

To reduce the cost of installing an FDDI LAN, ANSI has developed a version of the FDDI standard that uses unshielded twisted-pair instead of fiber-optic cable as a physical transmission medium. **Twisted-pair FDDI** also operates at 100 Mb/s, and it uses the same protocol as the fiber-optic version of FDDI. Most standard telephone wiring cannot support the 100-Mb/s data rate, so twisted-pair FDDI requires that data-grade cabling be installed. However, even if new cabling must be installed, the elimination of expensive optical interfaces at each node makes twisted-pair FDDI much more affordable than the fiber-optic version of the network.

Because twisted-pair FDDI has only recently emerged from the ANSI standards committee, there are few installations in place. However, this inexpensive high-speed network is sure to become common as LANs are required to communicate larger amounts of data such as complex graphics, digitized voice, and even digitized and compressed television images.

## 12-6 "INTERNETWORKING"

LANs greatly improve the efficiency of an organization by making it possible for coworkers to exchange computer data and electronic mail. However, LANs are designed for short-distance communications, usually among workers located in the same building. Large international companies often need computer-to-computer communications among workers located in different cities, in different countries, and even on different continents. A number of electronic devices have been developed to connect LANs together to form a *wide-area network (WAN)*. The technique of connecting LANs together has been given the name **internetworking.**

### 12-6-1 Repeaters

**Repeaters** were mentioned in the discussion of the Ethernet LAN. A repeater is the simplest internetworking device. As illustrated in Figure 12-17, repeaters operate at OSI level 1, the physical layer. A repeater is little more than an amplifier that forms a connection between two LAN segments by regenerating or "repeating" digital signals that pass between them so that the segments function as a single larger LAN. Both LAN segments that the repeater connects must use the same protocol and the same data rate.

### 12-6-2 Bridges

As Figure 12-18 illustrates, bridges connect LANs together at layers 1 and 2 of the OSI Model. Layer 2 is the datalink layer. Because they operate at layer 2, bridges can connect LANs that operate at different data rates and that use different protocols. Bridges examine the source and destination addresses of frames they receive and send them to the proper LAN using a process called **selective forwarding.**

**FIGURE 12-17**
A repeater is little more than a bi-directional amplifier that connects two LANs of the same type.

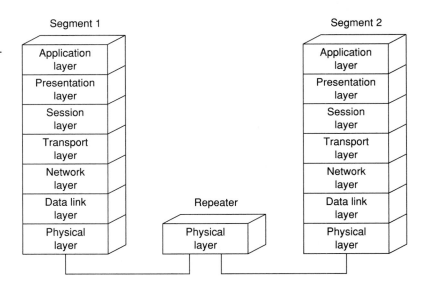

**FIGURE 12-18**
Bridges operate at layers 1 and 2 of the OSI model.

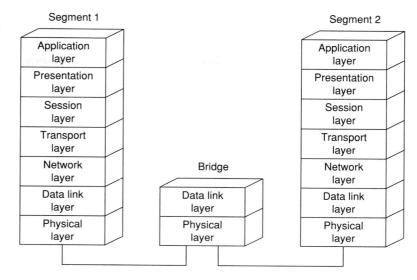

### Selective Forwarding

Figure 12-19 shows a bridge connecting an Ethernet LAN to a Token Ring LAN and illustrates the bridge's selective forwarding feature. In Figure 12-19(a), node A sends a frame to node C. The bridge monitors all frames on the LANs it interconnects, so it also receives the frame. Because the bridge recognizes the destination address of the frame as that of a node on the Ethernet LAN, it does not forward the frame to the Token Ring LAN. In Figure 12-19(b), node A sends a frame to node F, which is located on the Token Ring LAN. When the bridge receives the frame, it recognizes that the frame is addressed to a node on the Token Ring LAN. It converts the frame from Ethernet protocol to Token Ring protocol. When it receives the token from node G, it attaches the frame to the token and sends the token and attached frame to node E to be forwarded to node F. Unlike a repeater, which passes all frames from one network segment to another, a bridge's ability to perform selective forwarding reduces unnecessary network traffic.

### Learning and Routing

A bridge has internal memory in which it maintains a list of all nodes for which it handles traffic along with their addresses and the LAN to which each node is connected. This list is called a **routing table.** Each time a bridge receives a frame, it compares the frame's source address to the addresses in its routing table. If it does not have the node's source address in its routing table, it adds it. Through this process, the bridge "learns" the addresses and locations of the nodes on the networks that it serves. If a new node is added to the network, the bridge learns its address the first time the node transmits a frame. If a node is moved from one LAN to another, the bridge quickly learns the node's new location. The bridge's learning ability makes it possible to add new nodes to the networks the bridge serves without modifying the bridge.

**FIGURE 12-19**
A bridge "knows" which nodes are connected to each network and forwards frames only when necessary to reduce unnecessary traffic. (a) The bridge recognizes the destination address of the frame as node C on the Ethernet LAN and does not forward it. (b) The bridge recognizes the destination address of the frame as that of node F on the Token Ring LAN and forwards it.

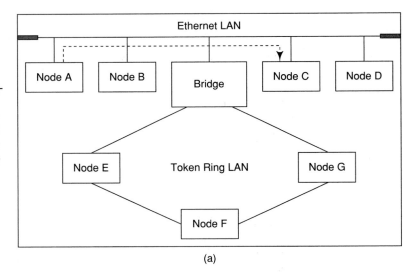

(a)

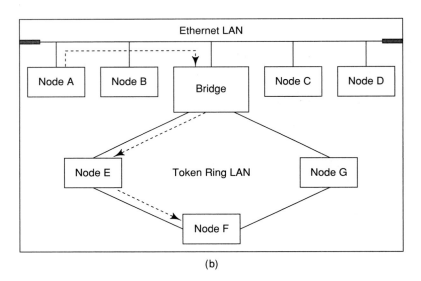

(b)

Bridges often interconnect many LANs. Each LAN that a bridge serves is connected to one of the bridge's ports. When the bridge receives a frame, it examines its routing table to determine to which network the addressed node is connected. If the destination is in the routing table, the bridge forwards the frame to the port where the destination terminal is located. If for some reason the destination address is not in the bridge's routing table, the bridge forwards the frame to all ports except the port from which it was received.

## 12-6-3 Routers

Routers also interconnect LANs, but unlike bridges, they operate at layers 1 through 3 of the OSI model as shown in Figure 12-20. Routers have enough intelligence to support complex network topologies with redundant paths, something that bridges cannot do.

Figure 12-21 shows a group of LANs interconnected by four routers. Such a system of interconnected LANs is sometimes called an *internetwork.* The dashed lines in the figure show two possible routes for the internetwork to communicate frames between LAN A and LAN M. Each router's internal memory contains a sophisticated routing table that not only holds the addresses of the nodes on the internetwork but also lists the various routes between nodes and which of the routes is the best one. If a node on LAN A in Figure 12-21 addresses a frame to a node on LAN M, router 1 determines how to route the frame. Router 1 adds a **routing field** to the frame. The routing field describes the path that router 1 has plotted to transport the frame to its destination. It serves as a set of instructions to the other routers on the internetwork. After it has added the routing field, router 1 then sends the frame to LAN E.

Router 3 examines the frame's routing field and determines that the frame is to be forwarded to Router 4, so it sends the frame to router 4 by means of LAN J. Both router 2 and router 4 received the frame from LAN J, but router 2 determines that the frame has not been routed through it, and ignores it. Router 4 also receives the frame and, following the instructions in the frame's routing field, passes it on to LAN M.

### Static Versus Dynamic Routers

**Static routers** require the network manager to program the routing tables into the individual routers and update the tables whenever changes are made to the internet-

**FIGURE 12-20**
Routers operate at layers 1, 2, and 3 of the OSI model.

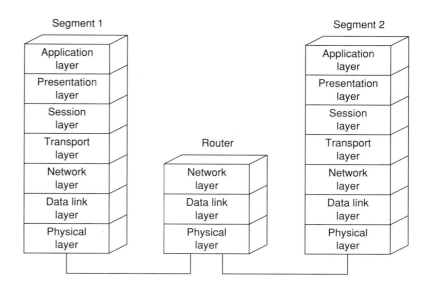

**FIGURE 12-21**
Unlike bridges, routers are able to select among different routes between two nodes.

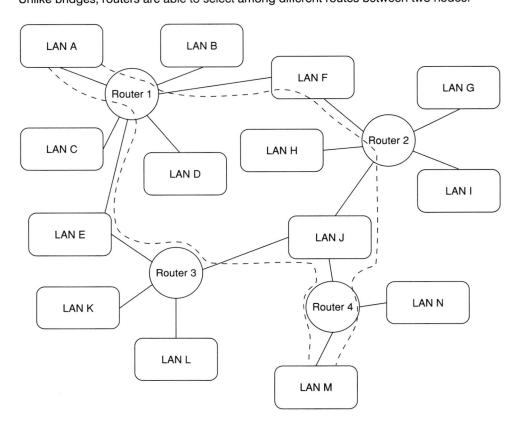

work. A **dynamic router** automatically broadcasts updated routing information throughout the internetwork at regular intervals, perhaps every 30 seconds, and other dynamic routers use this information to update their routing tables. If router 2 should cease operating, the network manager would have to program static routers to route traffic through router 3. An internetwork with dynamic routers would automatically adjust to the situation as the routers broadcast new routing information to each other.

## ■ SUMMARY

This chapter has discussed local area networks (LANs). A local area network is a communications system that interconnects computers and peripheral devices that are located within a single office, a single building, or adjacent buildings. LANs make it possible for PC users to share peripherals, data, and programs and to send each other electronic mail. The three LANs discussed in detail in this chapter are Ethernet, Token Ring, and Fiber Data Distributed Interface (FDDI).

As Figure 12-22 shows, Ethernet is today's most widely used LAN standard, followed by Token Ring. The high cost of fiber-optic transceivers has limited FDDI's popularity, but a less expensive FDDI standard is now available. The new version uses unshielded twisted-pair copper wire instead of optical fiber as its communications medium. FDDI over unshielded twisted-pair copper wire or some other high-speed LAN will be required in the near future to rapidly communicate digitized graphics, voice, and video among computers.

Programs and data are often placed on a server so that they can be shared by many LAN users. A server is a powerful computer with a large hard disk storage capacity that can be accessed by other computers by means of a LAN.

The software that controls a LAN makes the network transparent to its users. The LAN's software and hardware together establish a virtual connection between the user's computer and other devices on the LAN so that the server and other computers connected to the network appear to the extensions of the user's own computer.

With the proper software, LAN users can send each other electronic mail. Electronic mail originally consisted of pure text messages. Today, advanced electronic mail systems can use multi-media, a combination of text, graphics, audio, and even video.

The first LANs were developed by individual manufacturers. They were expensive and difficult to install and maintain. The Institute of Electrical and Electronic Engineers (IEEE) formed the 802 Standards Committee, which published the Ethernet and Token Ring standards, and the American National Standards Institute (ANSI) published the FDDI standard. These and other LAN standards have made it possible for equipment produced by different manufacturers to communicate and have made LANs more affordable by bringing competition to the LAN marketplace.

LANs and other modern communications systems are usually designed to conform to the International Standards Organization's (ISO) Open Systems Interconnect Basic Reference Model (OSI Model). Most LANs implement layers 1 and 2 of the model, and they work closely with communications software that performs the functions of layer 3 and above. OSI layer 1 is the physical layer, which consists of the physical communications medium and electrical signals. Layer 2 is the datalink layer, which performs protocol functions such as error control, framing, synchronization, link initialization and disconnection, addressing, and frame sequence control.

**FIGURE 12-22**
Estimated LAN installations by major type in 1994.

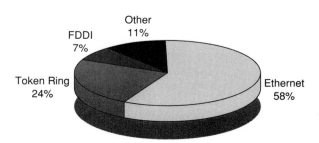

Other 11%

FDDI 7%

Token Ring 24%

Ethernet 58%

**FIGURE 12-23**

A summary of LAN types.

| Type | Access | Media | Topology | Data Rate |
|------|--------|-------|----------|-----------|
| Token Ring | Token passing | Coax<br>Shielded twisted pair | Ring<br>Star or ring | 4 or 16 Mb/s<br>4 or 16 Mb/s |
| Ethernet | CSMA/CD | Thick coax<br>Thin coax<br>Unshielded twisted pair | Bus<br>Bus or star<br>Star | 10 Mb/s<br>10 Mb/s<br>10 Mb/s |
| FDDI | Token passing | Optical fiber<br>Unshielded twisted pair | Double ring<br>Double ring | 100 Mb/s<br>100 Mb/s |

Layer 3 switches and routes information through the network to establish a virtual connection between the sending and receiving terminals.

Figure 12-23 summarizes the differences among the three LANs discussed in this chapter. One of the most important differences is the manner in which a sending node gets permission to transmit. Ethernet, which electrically has a bus topology, requires nodes to contend for permission to transmit using a system called carrier sense multiple access with collision detection (CSMA/CD). Token Ring and FDDI are electrically ring topologies. They circulate a distinctive bit pattern around the ring, which is called a token. The node that has possession of the token has permission to transmit.

There are three main versions of Ethernet: 10BASE-5 (thick coax Ethernet), 10BASE-2 (thin coax Ethernet), and 10BASE-T (twisted-pair Ethernet). All three versions operate at 10 Mb/s and are identical in how they implement OSI layer 2, the datalink layer. The only difference among them is the physical medium over which they send data, OSI layer 1. A fourth version of Ethernet, 1BASE-5 (Star-LAN) exists, but its relatively slow 1-Mb/s speed has kept it from wide acceptance. In addition, wireless versions of Ethernet have been developed. Wireless Ethernet uses either an infrared light beam or radio waves as a communications medium. So far, a combination of high cost and technical problems has kept wireless versions of Ethernet from becoming popular.

10BASE-5 and 10BASE-2 Ethernet use a bus topology. 10BASE-5 Ethernet operates over 50-$\Omega$ RG-11 coaxial cable. A transceiver, called a media access unit (MAU), connects each drop to the Ethernet bus. 10BASE-2 uses less expensive RG-58 coaxial cable, and each node connects to the bus with a simple coaxial T-connector. 10BASE-T Ethernet uses a star topology. Each node connects to the network by means of a centrally located hub. 10BASE-T Ethernet's inexpensive twisted-pair wire medium has made it the most popular version of Ethernet.

The central 10BASE-T Ethernet hub usually has provisions for a network administrator to monitor the LAN's operation. The network administrator is an employee whose job it is to make sure that the network operates smoothly.

Ethernet uses Manchester encoding to place digital information on the LAN. Ethernet transmissions are broken into frames that consist of a preamble, start frame delimiter, destination address, source address, type field, data field, CRC, and end frame delimiter.

The Token Ring network originally used thick coaxial cable as a communications medium, but today it operates over shielded twisted-pair cabling and uses a central hub to connect the individual nodes to the network. Token Ring LANs operate at either 4 Mb/s or 16 Mb/s.

FDDI operates at 100 Mb/s and uses a dual-ring topology. The two rings are called the primary and the secondary and carry data in opposite directions. During normal operation, the primary ring carries all of the data, and the secondary ring serves as a backup.

FDDI has both single-attach and dual-attach nodes. Single-attach nodes connect only to the primary ring through a concentrator. Dual-attach nodes connect directly to both rings. FDDI's ring-wrap feature makes it very reliable. If a break occurs in the LAN's primary ring, the dual-attach nodes on each side of the break connect the primary and secondary rings to form a single, larger ring.

A number of internetworking devices can connect LANs together. Repeaters operate at OSI layer 1 and amplify signals that pass from one LAN segment to another. Bridges operate at OSI layers 1 and 2 and can connect LANs that use different data rates and different protocols. Bridges also use selective forwarding to route frames to the proper LAN. Routers operate at OSI layers 1, 2, and 3. While bridges require that there be only one possible communication path between the sending and receiving nodes, routers can choose the best path to forward a frame through a complex internetwork that contains multiple communication paths.

## ■ QUESTIONS

1. Define the term *data base*.
2. a. Name four disadvantages of using a central computer.
   b. In your opinion, is there any advantage to using a central computer?
3. What does the term *distributed computing* mean?
4. What two factors have made computers more affordable for business use?
5. a. As distributed computing became popular, what advantage of the central computer was lost?
   b. How did computer engineers overcome that disadvantage?
6. Define the term *local area network*.
7. a. What is a server?
   b. What type of information is usually stored on a server's hard disk?
8. In addition to PCs and a server, what other types of devices are often connected to a LAN?

9. Define the term *virtual connection.*

10. State three other names that are sometimes used in place of the word *node* to describe devices connected to a LAN.

11. Name three advantages that a LAN brings to distributed computing.

12. a.  What is *electronic mail?*

    b.  Describe how electronic mail travels over a network from the sending computer to the receiving computer.

13. a.  Why did the IEEE form the 802 Standards Committee?

    b.  What are the two most popular standards that the 802 Standards Committee has published?

14. a.  What does the acronym *ANSI* stand for?

    b.  What important LAN standard has ANSI published?

15. a.  By what name is the Open Systems Interconnect Basic Reference Model more commonly known?

    b.  Into how many layers is the OSI Model divided?

    c.  At which layers of the OSI Model do the Ethernet and Token Ring LAN operate?

16. In your own words, describe layers 1, 2, and 3 of the OSI Model.

17. How do the OSI layers of the transmitting node communicate with the corresponding OSI layers of the receiving node?

18. a.  What do the parts *10, BASE,* and *5* of the name *10BASE-5* stand for?

    b.  What does the letter *T* in the name *10BASE-T* stand for?

19. How can a 10BASE-5 Ethernet LAN be extended to more than 500 m in length?

20. Define the terms *MAU, tap, drop,* and *node* as they apply to 10BASE-5 Ethernet.

21. a.  Why was 10BASE-2 Ethernet developed?

    b.  State two differences between 10BASE-2 and 10BASE-5 Ethernet that make 10BASE-2 cheaper to implement.

    c.  By what other names is 10BASE-2 Ethernet popularly known?

22. a.  What is the maximum segment length of 10BASE-T Ethernet?

    b.  How many nodes will each 10BASE-T Ethernet segment support?

    c.  What device must be used with 10BASE-T Ethernet so that more than two computers can be connected to the LAN?

23. a.  What name is given to the individual connections on an Ethernet hub?

    b.  How does the hub sense whether or not a node is in operation?

24. What is the function of a LAN's *network administrator?*

25. a. What two characteristics does Manchester encoding have that makes it able to transmit 10-Mb/s baseband information over long lengths of wire?

    b. In Manchester encoding, what is the difference between the electrical signal that represents a logical 0 and the electrical signal that represents a logical 1?

26. List the eight fields of an Ethernet frame and briefly describe the purpose of each.

27. a. What do the letters *CSMA/CD* stand for?

    b. Under CSMA/CD, when may a node transmit?

    c. What happens if two nodes begin transmitting at the same time?

28. a. What is a NIC?

    b. List the functions of a NIC.

29. a. What is FIFO memory?

    b. What purpose does FIFO memory serve in a NIC?

30. a. Why is a Token Ring LAN that uses a hub sometimes said to have a *star-ring* topology?

    b. How does a hub improve the reliability of a Token Ring LAN?

31. At what two speeds are newer Token Ring plug-in cards capable of operating?

32. a. How does a node on a Token Ring LAN receive permission to transmit?

    b. How does a node recognize that a Token Ring frame is addressed to it?

    c. What does it mean when a node receives a frame that has the node's own address in the source address field?

33. a. What is the advantage of token passing as compared to CSMA/CD?

    b. What is the disadvantage of token passing as compared to CSMA/CD?

34. What does *FDDI* stand for?

35. a. What purpose does the secondary FDDI ring serve?

    b. What system does FDDI use to give a node permission to transmit?

36. a. What is the difference between single-attach and dual-attach FDDI nodes?

    b. What advantage do dual-attach nodes have compared to single-attach nodes?

    c. Why are dual-attach nodes more expensive than single-attach nodes?

37. What device is used to connect single-attach nodes to an FDDI LAN?

38. Describe the *self-healing* feature of the FDDI LAN.

39. a. What advantages does fiber-optic cable have as a transmission medium compared to copper wire?

    b. What serious disadvantage does fiber-optic cable have compared to copper wire?

    c.    How does the newest version of FDDI overcome fiber-optic's disadvantage?

40.  a.    What is a *WAN?*

    b.    What does the term *internetworking* mean?

41.  a.    What does a LAN repeater do?

    b.    At which layer of the OSI Model does a repeater operate?

42.  a.    At which level of the OSI Model do bridges operate?

    b.    Describe a bridge's *selective forwarding* feature.

    c.    How does a bridge "learn" the addresses and locations of the nodes on the networks that it serves?

43.  a.    At which layers of the OSI model do routers operate?

    b.    What feature do routers have that bridges do not have?

    c.    What is the difference between *static* and *dynamic* routers?

# ■ Appendix A

# THE HAYES AT MODEM COMMAND SET

The terminal can send commands to the modem when the modem is in the command mode. Multiple commands can be sent in a series, but each series must begin with the letters *AT* and end with a carriage return. If the modem is on line, it can be returned to the command mode by sending it the escape sequence (+ + +). After the escape sequence, the terminal should insert one or more commas. Each comma represents a pause, usually of two seconds. Thus the sequence + + +,,ATH would order the modem to enter the command mode, pause for four seconds, and command the modem to go on-hook (disconnect from the telephone line).

All intelligent Hayes-compatible modems that operate at 2400 b/s or faster should support most of the commands on this list, and many of them will support additional commands that are not listed here. When in doubt, consult the modem's documentation.

When a command contains a zero, it is optional. For example, + + +,,ATH0 and + + +,,ATH both command the modem to go on-hook. Commands preceded by a backslash (\) control error correction, and commands preceded by a percent sign (%) control data compression. Spaces can be inserted in a command string to make it easier to read. The modem ignores them. The modem also ignores parentheses and dashes inserted in telephone numbers.

| | |
|---|---|
| **A** | Causes the modem to go off-hook in the answer mode. |
| **A/** | Re-executes the last command that was sent to the modem. |
| **AT** | The command line prefix (attention code), which must be sent at the beginning of all command strings. |
| **B0** | Selects CCITT V.22 operation. |
| **B1** | Selects Bell 212A operation. |
| **DT or DP** | Dials the number that follows the command. DT uses DTMF dialing tones, and DP uses pulse dialing (e.g., ATDT602-555-1212). |
| **E0** | Programs the modem to not echo commands back to the terminal. |
| **E1** | Programs the modem to echo commands back to the terminal. |
| **H0** | Causes the modem to go on-hook. |
| **H1** | Causes the modem to go off-hook. |
| **I0** | Requests the modem to send the product identification code to the terminal. |
| **I1** | Performs a checksum on the modem firmware and sends the checksum to the terminal. |
| **I2** | Performs a checksum on the modem firmware and sends OK or ERROR to the terminal. |
| **L0** | Sets the modem speaker volume to its lowest level. |
| **L1** | Sets the modem speaker volume to its second lowest level. |
| **L2** | Sets the modem speaker volume to medium. |
| **L3** | Sets the modem speaker volume to high. |
| **M0** | Turns the modem speaker off. |
| **M1** | Turns the modem speaker on until the modem detects a carrier from the remote modem. |
| **M3** | Turns the modem speaker on after dialing until the modem detects a carrier from the remote modem. |
| **O0** | Returns the modem from the command mode to the on-line state. |
| **O1** | Returns the modem from the command mode to the on-line state and initiates a retrain sequence. |
| **Q0** | Causes the modem to send result codes (OK, CONNECT, ERROR, etc.) to the terminal. |
| **Q1** | Causes the modem to not send result codes to the terminal. |
| **Q2** | Causes the modem to send result codes to the terminal only when the modem is in the originate mode. |
| **SR=n** | Sets the value of register R to n (e.g., S37=9 loads the value 9 into modem register 37). The modem's internal registers are used to program some of its features. |

| | |
|---|---|
| **SR?** | Causes the modem to return the contents of register R to the terminal (e.g., S37? causes the modem to return the contents of register 37 to the terminal). |
| **V0** | Causes the modem to return short-form numeric result codes to the terminal. |
| **V1** | Causes the modem to return full-word result codes to the terminal. |
| **W0** | Causes the modem to not report the carrier speed and error-correction protocol used to the terminal. |
| **W1** | Causes the modem to report the carrier speed and error-correction protocol used to the terminal. |
| **W2** | Causes the modem to report the carrier speed, but not the error-correction protocol used to the terminal. |
| **X0** | Causes the modem to dial and attempt to connect to the remote modem, even if there is no dial tone or if the modem receives a busy signal. |
| **X1** | The same as X0 except the modem will report to the terminal whether or not it is able to connect to the remote modem. |
| **X2** | The modem checks for a dial tone before dialing, but will attempt to connect to the remote modem, even if it receives a busy signal. |
| **X3** | The modem will not dial until it detects a dial tone, and it will not attempt to connect to the remote modem if it receives a busy signal. |
| **Z** | Resets the modem and initializes it to the user-programmed configuration that was previously stored to the modem's non-volatile memory. |
| **&C0** | Programs the modem to hold the DCD line active. |
| **&C1** | Programs the modem to use the DCD line to report the presence or absence of a received carrier. |
| **&D0** | Programs the modem to ignore the DTR line. |
| **&D1** | Causes the modem to return to the command state if the DTE makes the DTR line inactive. |
| **&D2** | Causes the modem to hang up, enter the command state, and disable auto-answer if the DTE makes the DTR line inactive. |
| **&D3** | Causes the modem to reset the DTE, makes the DTR inactive. |
| **&F** | Restores the modem to the factory-programmed configuration. |
| **&K0** | Programs the modem to not use flow control. |
| **&K3** | Programs the modem and terminal to use the RTS and CTS lines to control the flow of data between them. |
| **&K4** | Programs the modem and terminal to use XON and XOFF characters to control the flow of data between them. |
| **&L0** | Programs the modem to work with a dial-up telephone line. |

| | |
|---|---|
| **&L1** | Programs the modem to work with a leased telephone line. |
| **&M0** | Programs the modem to operate in the asynchronous mode. The terminal and modem must operate at the same speed in this mode. |
| **&M1** | Programs the modem to dial in the asynchronous mode and to switch to synchronous once a connection is established. |
| **&M2** | Programs the modem to dial a stored number in the asynchronous mode when it detects an active DTR and to switch to the synchronous mode once a connection is established. |
| **&M3** | Allows the operator to dial the number on a telset. The modem connects to the telephone line in the synchronous mode when DTR is made active after the last number is dialed. |
| **&P0** | Causes the modem to use pulse dialing with 39% make and 61% break (for the US and Canada). |
| **&P1** | Causes the modem to use pulse dialing with 33% make and 67% break (for use in many countries outside the US and Canada). |
| **&Q0** | The same as &M0. |
| **&Q1** | The same as &M1. |
| **&Q2** | The same as &M2. |
| **&Q3** | The same as &M3. |
| **&R0** | Programs the modem to make CTS track RTS when it is on line and to ignore RTS when it is in the command state. |
| **&R1** | Programs the modem to hold CTS active and to ignore RTS. |
| **&S0** | Causes the modem to hold the RS-232 DSR line active at all times. |
| **&S1** | Causes the modem to operate DSR in accordance with the RS-232 standard. |
| **&T0** | Terminates any modem test program in progress. The escape character must be sent first (+++,,ATT0). |
| **&T1** | Performs an analog loopback, which connects the modem's transmitter output to its receiver input so that any characters that the terminal sends to the modem are echoed back to the terminal. This tests the modem's operation. |
| **&T3** | Performs a remote digital loopback. Characters received from the remote modem are echoed back to it. This tests the communications link and the operation of both modems. |
| **&T4** | Enables the modem to respond to a request from the remote modem to perform a digital loopback test. |
| **&T5** | Prohibits the modem from responding to a request from the remote modem to perform a digital loopback test. |
| **&T6** | Initiates a remote digital loopback. The remote modem echoes back received characters. |

| | |
|---|---|
| **&T7** | The same as &T6 except the modem sends a continuous pattern of alternating marks and spaces and counts the errors in the echoed data. |
| **&T8** | The modem performs a local analog loopback, sends a continuous pattern of alternating marks and spaces, and counts the errors in the echoed data. |
| **&V** | Causes the modem to output the contents of its non-volatile internal memory to the terminal. |
| **&X0** | Causes the modem to generate the transmit clock signal and send it to the DTE over pin 15 of the RS-232 interface. |
| **&X1** | Causes the modem to use the clock signal received from the DTE on pin 24 of the RS-232 interface as the transmit clock. |
| **&X2** | Causes the modem to derive the transmit clock signal from the received data carrier signal and to also send this clock signal to the DTE over pin 15 of the RS-232 interface. |
| **&Z** | Used to store a telephone number in the modem's internal non-volatile memory (e.g., AT&Z=602-555-1212). |
| **\A0** | Sets the maximum MNP block size to 64 characters. |
| **\A1** | Sets the maximum MNP block size to 128 characters. |
| **\A2** | Sets the maximum MNP block size to 192 characters. |
| **\A3** | Sets the maximum MNP block size to 256 characters. |
| **\Bn** | Causes the modem to transmit a break signal for the number of 100 ms internals specified by n (e.g., AT\B3 causes the modem to send a 300 ms break signal). |
| **\N0** | Disables the modem's error correction. The modem buffers information sent to and received from the DTE so that the two can operate at different speeds. |
| **\N1** | Disables the modem's error correction and buffering between the modem and the DTE. The DTE and the modem must operate at the same speed. |
| **\N2** | Sets the modem "reliable mode." The modem attempts to establish an MNP connection. If the remote modem cannot use MNP, the local modem disconnects. |
| **\N3** | Sets the modem "auto-reliable mode." The modem attempts to establish an MNP connection. If the remote modem cannot use MNP, the local modem falls back to a connection without error correction. |
| **\Y** | Causes the modem to attempt to establish an MNP reliable link when it is already connected to a remote modem but not currently using error control. |
| **\Z** | Causes the modem to switch from an MNP connection to a connection with no error control. |
| **%C0** | Disables the modem's data compression. |

| | |
|---|---|
| **%C1** | Enables the modem to use MNP5 data compression. |
| **%C2** | Enables the modem to use V.42 bis data compression. |
| **%C3** | Enables the modem to use both MNP5 and V.42 bis data compression. |
| **%E0** | Disables the modem's auto-retrain capability. |
| **%E1** | Enables the modem to automatically retrain if line conditions change. |
| **%L** | Causes the modem to report the level of the received signal in dBm. |
| **%M0** | Disables V.42 bis data compression. |
| **%M1** | Causes the modem to use V.42 bis data compression for transmit only. |
| **%M2** | Causes the modem to use V.42 bis data compression for receive only. |
| **%M3** | Causes the modem to use V.42 bis data compression for both transmit and receive. |
| **%Q** | Causes the modem to send a number between 0 and 127 to the terminal to report on the quality of the communications line. The higher the number, the poorer the quality of the line. |

## Appendix B

# THE ACIA SPECIFICATION SHEET

# MOTOROLA

# SEMICONDUCTORS

3501 ED BLUESTEIN BLVD., AUSTIN, TEXAS 78721

## MC6850

## ASYNCHRONOUS COMMUNICATIONS INTERFACE ADAPTER (ACIA)

The MC6850 Asynchronous Communications Interface Adapter provides the data formatting and control to interface serial asynchronous data communications information to bus organized systems such as the MC6800 Microprocessing Unit.

The bus interface of the MC6850 includes select, enable, read/write, interrupt and bus interface logic to allow data transfer over an 8-bit bidirectional data bus. The parallel data of the bus system is serially transmitted and received by the asynchronous data interface, with proper formatting and error checking. The functional configuration of the ACIA is programmed via the data bus during system initialization. A programmable Control Register provides variable word lengths, clock division ratios, transmit control, receive control, and interrupt control. For peripheral or modem operation, three control lines are provided. These lines allow the ACIA to interface directly with the MC6860L 0-600 bps digital modem.

- 8- and 9-Bit Transmission
- Optional Even and Odd Parity
- Parity, Overrun and Framing Error Checking
- Programmable Control Register
- Optional ÷1, ÷16, and ÷64 Clock Modes
- Up to 1.0 Mbps Transmission
- False Start Bit Deletion
- Peripheral/Modem Control Functions
- Double Buffered
- One- or Two-Stop Bit Operation

### MOS
(N-CHANNEL, SILICON-GATE)

### ASYNCHRONOUS COMMUNICATIONS INTERFACE ADAPTER

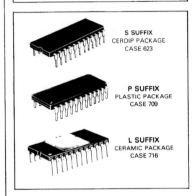

**S SUFFIX**
CERDIP PACKAGE
CASE 623

**P SUFFIX**
PLASTIC PACKAGE
CASE 709

**L SUFFIX**
CERAMIC PACKAGE
CASE 716

### MC6850 ASYNCHRONOUS COMMUNICATIONS INTERFACE ADAPTER BLOCK DIAGRAM

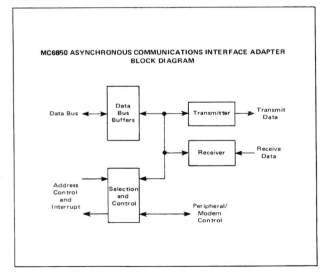

### PIN ASSIGNMENT

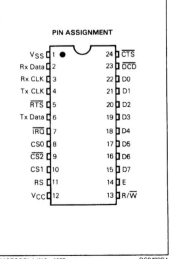

| | | | |
|---|---|---|---|
| V<sub>SS</sub> | 1 | 24 | $\overline{CTS}$ |
| Rx Data | 2 | 23 | $\overline{DCD}$ |
| Rx CLK | 3 | 22 | D0 |
| Tx CLK | 4 | 21 | D1 |
| $\overline{RTS}$ | 5 | 20 | D2 |
| Tx Data | 6 | 19 | D3 |
| $\overline{IRQ}$ | 7 | 18 | D4 |
| CS0 | 8 | 17 | D5 |
| $\overline{CS2}$ | 9 | 16 | D6 |
| CS1 | 10 | 15 | D7 |
| RS | 11 | 14 | E |
| V<sub>CC</sub> | 12 | 13 | R/$\overline{W}$ |

DS9493R4

## MAXIMUM RATINGS

| Characteristics | Symbol | Value | Unit |
|---|---|---|---|
| Supply Voltage | $V_{CC}$ | $-0.3$ to $+7.0$ | V |
| Input Voltage | $V_{in}$ | $-0.3$ to $+7.0$ | V |
| Operating Temperature Range<br>MC6850, MC68A50, MC68B50<br>MC6850C, MC68A50C | $T_A$ | $T_L$ to $T_H$<br>0 to 70<br>$-40$ to $+85$ | °C |
| Storage Temperature Range | $T_{stg}$ | $-55$ to $+150$ | °C |

This device contains circuitry to protect the inputs against damage due to high static voltages or electric fields; however, it is advised that normal precautions be taken to avoid application of any voltage higher than maximum rated voltages to this high-impedance circuit. Reliability of operation is enhanced if unused inputs are tied to an appropriate logic voltage level (e.g., either $V_{SS}$ or $V_{CC}$).

## THERMAL CHARACTERISTICS

| Characteristic | Symbol | Value | Unit |
|---|---|---|---|
| Thermal Resistance<br>Plastic<br>Ceramic<br>Cerdip | $\theta_{JA}$ | 120<br>60<br>65 | °C/W |

## POWER CONSIDERATIONS

The average chip-junction temperature, $T_J$, in °C can be obtained from:

$$T_J = T_A + (P_D \bullet \theta_{JA}) \tag{1}$$

Where:

$T_A \equiv$ Ambient Temperature, °C

$\theta_{JA} \equiv$ Package Thermal Resistance, Junction-to-Ambient, °C/W

$P_D \equiv P_{INT} + P_{PORT}$

$P_{INT} \equiv I_{CC} \times V_{CC}$, Watts — Chip Internal Power

$P_{PORT} \equiv$ Port Power Dissipation, Watts — User Determined

For most applications $P_{PORT} \lessdot P_{INT}$ and can be neglected. $P_{PORT}$ may become significant if the device is configured to drive Darlington bases or sink LED loads.

An approximate relationship between $P_D$ and $T_J$ (if $P_{PORT}$ is neglected) is:

$$P_D = K \div (T_J + 273°C) \tag{2}$$

Solving equations (1) and (2) for K gives:

$$K = P_D \bullet (T_A + 273°C) + \theta_{JA} \bullet P_D2 \tag{3}$$

Where K is a constant pertaining to the particular part. K can be determined from equation (3) by measuring $P_D$ (at equilibrium) for a known $T_A$. Using this value of K, the values of $P_D$ and $T_J$ can be obtained by solving equations (1) and (2) iteratively for any value of $T_A$.

## DC ELECTRICAL CHARACTERISTICS ($V_{CC}$ = 5.0 Vdc ±5%, $V_{SS}$ = 0, $T_A$ = $T_L$ to $T_H$ unless otherwise noted.)

| Characteristic | | Symbol | Min | Typ | Max | Unit |
|---|---|---|---|---|---|---|
| Input High Voltage | | $V_{IH}$ | $V_{SS}+2.0$ | — | $V_{CC}$ | V |
| Input Low Voltage | | $V_{IL}$ | $V_{SS}-0.3$ | — | $V_{SS}+0.8$ | V |
| Input Leakage Current<br>($V_{in}$ = 0 to 5.25 V) | R/$\overline{W}$, CS0, CS1, $\overline{CS2}$, Enable<br>RS, Rx D, Rx C, $\overline{CTS}$, $\overline{DCD}$ | $I_{in}$ | — | 1.0 | 2.5 | µA |
| Hi-Z (Off State) Input Current<br>($V_{in}$ = 0.4 to 2.4 V) | D0-D7 | $I_{TSI}$ | — | 2.0 | 10 | µA |
| Output High Voltage<br>($I_{Load}$ = $-205$ µA, Enable Pulse Width < 25 µs)<br>($I_{Load}$ = $-100$ µA, Enable Pulse Width < 25 µs) | D0-D7<br>Tx Data, $\overline{RTS}$ | $V_{OH}$ | $V_{SS}+2.4$<br>$V_{SS}+2.4$ | —<br>— | —<br>— | V |
| Output Low Voltage ($I_{Load}$ = 1.6 mA, Enable Pulse Width < 25 µs) | | $V_{OL}$ | — | — | $V_{SS}+0.4$ | V |
| Output Leakage Current (Off State) ($V_{OH}$ = 2.4 V) | $\overline{IRQ}$ | $I_{LOH}$ | — | 1.0 | 10 | µA |
| Internal Power Dissipation (Measured at $T_A$ = 0°C) | | $P_{INT}$ | — | 300 | 525* | mW |
| Internal Input Capacitance<br>($V_{in}$ = 0, $T_A$ = 25°C, f = 1.0 MHz) | D0-D7<br>E, Tx CLK, Rx CLK, R/$\overline{W}$, RS, Rx Data, CS0, CS1, $\overline{CS2}$, $\overline{CTS}$, $\overline{DCD}$ | $C_{in}$ | —<br>— | 10<br>7.0 | 12.5<br>7.5 | pF |
| Output Capacitance<br>($V_{in}$ = 0, $T_A$ = 25°C, f = 1.0 MHz) | $\overline{RTS}$, Tx Data<br>$\overline{IRQ}$ | $C_{out}$ | —<br>— | —<br>— | 10<br>5.0 | pF |

*For temperatures less than $T_A$ = 0°C, $P_{INT}$ maximum will increase.

 **MOTOROLA** *Semiconductor Products Inc.*

## SERIAL DATA TIMING CHARACTERISTICS

| Characteristic | | Symbol | MC6850 | | MC68A50 | | MC68B50 | | Unit |
|---|---|---|---|---|---|---|---|---|---|
| | | | Min | Max | Min | Max | Min | Max | |
| Data Clock Pulse Width, Low (See Figure 1) | ÷ 16, ÷ 64 Modes | $PW_{CL}$ | 600 | — | 450 | — | 280 | — | ns |
| | ÷ 1 Mode | | 900 | — | 650 | — | 500 | — | |
| Data Clock Pulse Width, High (See Figure 2) | ÷ 16, ÷ 64 Modes | $PW_{CH}$ | 600 | — | 450 | — | 280 | — | ns |
| | ÷ 1 Mode | | 900 | — | 650 | — | 500 | — | |
| Data Clock Frequency | ÷ 16, ÷ 64 Modes | $f_C$ | — | 0.8 | — | 1.0 | — | 1.5 | MHz |
| | ÷ 1 Mode | | — | 500 | — | 750 | — | 1000 | kHz |
| Data Clock-to-Data Delay for Transmitter (See Figure 3) | | $t_{TDD}$ | — | 600 | — | 540 | — | 460 | ns |
| Receive Data Setup Time (See Figure 4) | ÷ 1 Mode | $t_{RDS}$ | 250 | — | 100 | — | 30 | — | ns |
| Receive Data Hold Time (See Figure 5) | ÷ 1 Mode | $t_{RDH}$ | 250 | — | 100 | — | 30 | — | ns |
| Interrupt Request Release Time (See Figure 6) | | $t_{IR}$ | — | 1.2 | — | 0.9 | — | 0.7 | µs |
| Request-to-Send Delay Time (See Figure 6) | | $t_{RTS}$ | — | 560 | — | 480 | — | 400 | ns |
| Input Rise and Fall Times (or 10% of the pulse width if smaller) | | $t_r$, $t_f$ | — | 1.0 | — | 0.5 | — | 0.25 | µs |

FIGURE 1 — CLOCK PULSE WIDTH, LOW-STATE

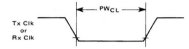

FIGURE 2 — CLOCK PULSE WIDTH, HIGH-STATE

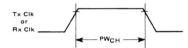

FIGURE 3 — TRANSMIT DATA OUTPUT DELAY

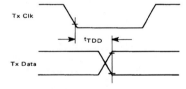

FIGURE 4 — RECEIVE DATA SETUP TIME
( ÷ 1 Mode)

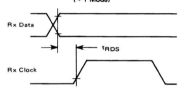

FIGURE 5 — RECEIVE DATA HOLD TIME
( ÷ 1 Mode)

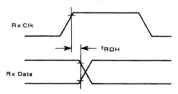

FIGURE 6 — REQUEST-TO-SEND DELAY AND
INTERRUPT-REQUEST RELEASE TIMES

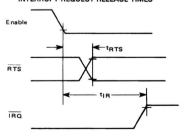

Note: Timing measurements are referenced to and from a low voltage of 0.8 volts and a high voltage of 2.0 volts, unless otherwise noted.

 **MOTOROLA** *Semiconductor Products Inc.*

**BUS TIMING CHARACTERISTICS** (See Notes 1 and 2 and Figure 7)

| Ident. Number | Characteristic | Symbol | MC6850 Min | MC6850 Max | MC68A50 Min | MC68A50 Max | MC68B50 Min | MC68B50 Max | Unit |
|---|---|---|---|---|---|---|---|---|---|
| 1 | Cycle Time | $t_{cyc}$ | 1.0 | 10 | 0.67 | 10 | 0.5 | 10 | µs |
| 2 | Pulse Width, E Low | $PW_{EL}$ | 430 | 9500 | 280 | 9500 | 210 | 9500 | ns |
| 3 | Pulse Width, E High | $PW_{EH}$ | 450 | 9500 | 280 | 9500 | 220 | 9500 | ns |
| 4 | Clock Rise and Fall Time | $t_r, t_f$ | — | 25 | — | 25 | — | 20 | ns |
| 9 | Address Hold Time | $t_{AH}$ | 10 | — | 10 | — | 10 | — | ns |
| 13 | Address Setup Time Before E | $t_{AS}$ | 80 | — | 60 | — | 40 | — | ns |
| 14 | Chip Select Setup Time Before E | $t_{CS}$ | 80 | — | 60 | — | 40 | — | ns |
| 15 | Chip Select Hold Time | $t_{CH}$ | 10 | — | 10 | — | 10 | — | ns |
| 18 | Read Data Hold Time | $t_{DHR}$ | 20 | 50* | 20 | 50* | 20 | 50* | ns |
| 21 | Write Data Hold Time | $t_{DHW}$ | 10 | — | 10 | — | 10 | — | ns |
| 30 | Output Data Delay Time | $t_{DDR}$ | — | 290 | — | 180 | — | 150 | ns |
| 31 | Input Data Setup Time | $t_{DSW}$ | 165 | — | 80 | — | 60 | — | ns |

*The data bus output buffers are no longer sourcing or sinking current by $t_{DHR}$max (High Impedance).

**FIGURE 7 — BUS TIMING CHARACTERISTICS**

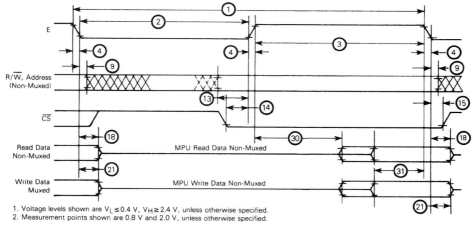

1. Voltage levels shown are $V_L \leq 0.4$ V, $V_H \geq 2.4$ V, unless otherwise specified.
2. Measurement points shown are 0.8 V and 2.0 V, unless otherwise specified.

**FIGURE 8 — BUS TIMING TEST LOADS**

Load A
(D0-D7, RTS, Tx Data)
5.0 V
$R_L = 2.5$ kΩ
MMD6150 or Equiv.
Test Point
C     R
MMD7000 or Equiv.

Load B
(IRQ Only)
5.0 V
3 kΩ
Test Point
100 pF

C = 130 pF for D0-D7
  = 30 pF for RTS and Tx Data

R = 11.7 kΩ for D0-D7
  = 24 kΩ for RTS and Tx Data

**MOTOROLA** *Semiconductor Products Inc.*

FIGURE 9 — EXPANDED BLOCK DIAGRAM

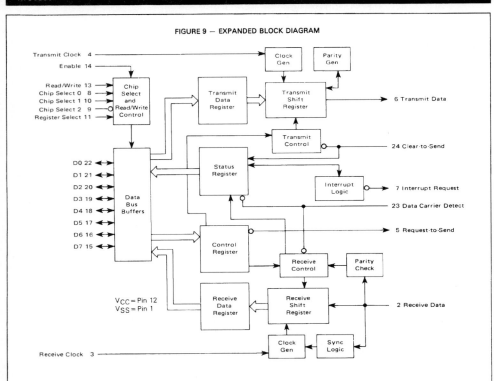

## DEVICE OPERATION

At the bus interface, the ACIA appears as two addressable memory locations. Internally, there are four registers: two read-only and two write-only registers. The read-only registers are Status and Receive Data; the write-only registers are Control and Transmit Data. The serial interface consists of serial input and output lines with independent clocks, and three peripheral/modem control lines.

## MASTER RESET

The master reset (CR0, CR1) must be set immediately after power-up to insure the reset condition and prepare for programming the ACIA functional configuration when the communications channel is required. During the first master reset, $\overline{IRQ}$ and $\overline{RTS}$ outputs are held at level 1. On all other master resets, the $\overline{RTS}$ output can be programmed high or low with the $\overline{IRQ}$ output held high. Control bits CR5 and CR6 should also be programmed to define the state of $\overline{RTS}$ whenever master reset is utilized. After master resetting the ACIA, the programmable Control Register can be set for

a number of options such as variable clock divider ratios, variable word length, one or two stop bits, and parity (even, odd, or none).

## TRANSMIT

A typical transmitting sequence consists of reading the ACIA Status Register either as a result of an interrupt or in the ACIA's turn in a polling sequence. A character may be written into the Transmit Data Register if the status read operation has indicated that the Transmit Data Register is empty. This character is transferred to a Shift Register where it is serialized and transmitted from the Transmit Data output preceded by a start bit and followed by one or two stop bits. Internal parity (odd or even) can be optionally added to the character and will occur between the last data bit and the first stop bit. After the first character is written in the Data Register, the Status Register can be read again to check for a Transmit Data Register Empty condition and current peripheral status. If the register is empty, another character can be loaded for transmission even through the first character is in the process of being transmitted (because of double buffering). The second character will be automatically transferred into the Shift Register when the first character transmission is completed. This sequence continues until all the characters have been transmitted.

## RECEIVE

Data is received from a peripheral by means of the Receive Data input. A divide-by-one clock ratio is provided for an externally synchronized clock (to its data) while the divide-by-16 and 64 ratios are provided for internal synchronization. Bit synchronization in the divide-by-16 and 64 modes is initiated by the detection of 8 or 32 low samples on the receive line in the divide-by-16 and 64 modes respectively. False start bit deletion capability insures that a full half bit of a start bit has been received before the internal clock is synchronized to the bit time. As a character is being received, parity (odd or even) will be checked and the error indication will be available in the Status Register along with framing error, overrun error, and Receive Data Register full. In a typical receiving sequence, the Status Register is read to determine if a character has been received from a peripheral. If the Receiver Data Register is full, the character is placed on the 8-bit ACIA bus when a Read Data command is received from the MPU. When parity has been selected for a 7-bit word (7 bits plus parity), the receiver strips the parity bit (D7 = 0) so that data alone is transferred to the MPU. This feature reduces MPU programming. The Status Register can continue to be read to determine when another character is available in the Receive Data Register. The receiver is also double buffered so that a character can be read from the data register as another character is being received in the shift register. The above sequence continues until all characters have been received.

## INPUT/OUTPUT FUNCTIONS

### ACIA INTERFACE SIGNALS FOR MPU

The ACIA interfaces to the M6800 MPU with an 8-bit bidirectional data bus, three chip select lines, a register select line, an interrupt request line, read/write line, and enable line. These signals permit the MPU to have complete control over the ACIA.

**ACIA Bidirectional Data (D0-D7)** — The bidirectional data lines (D0-D7) allow for data transfer between the ACIA and the MPU. The data bus output drivers are three-state devices that remain in the high-impedance (off) state except when the MPU performs an ACIA read operation.

**ACIA Enable (E)** — The Enable signal, E, is a high-impedance TTL-compatible input that enables the bus input/output data buffers and clocks data to and from the ACIA. This signal will normally be a derivative of the MC6800 $\phi$2 Clock or MC6809 E clock.

**Read/Write (R/$\overline{\text{W}}$)** — The Read/Write line is a high-impedance input that is TTL compatible and is used to control the direction of data flow through the ACIA's input/output data bus interface. When Read/Write is high (MPU Read cycle), ACIA output drivers are turned on and a selected register is read. When it is low, the ACIA output drivers are

turned off and the MPU writes into a selected register. Therefore, the Read/Write signal is used to select read-only or write-only registers within the ACIA.

**Chip Select (CS0, CS1, $\overline{\text{CS2}}$)** — These three high-impedance TTL-compatible input lines are used to address the ACIA. The ACIA is selected when CS0 and CS1 are high and $\overline{\text{CS2}}$ is low. Transfers of data to and from the ACIA are then performed under the control of the Enable Signal, Read/Write, and Register Select.

**Register Select (RS)** — The Register Select line is a high-impedance input that is TTL compatible. A high level is used to select the Transmit/Receive Data Registers and a low level the Control/Status Registers. The Read/Write signal line is used in conjunction with Register Select to select the read-only or write-only register in each register pair.

**Interrupt Request ($\overline{\text{IRQ}}$)** — Interrupt Request is a TTL-compatible, open-drain (no internal pullup), active low output that is used to interrupt the MPU. The $\overline{\text{IRQ}}$ output remains low as long as the cause of the interrupt is present and the appropriate interrupt enable within the ACIA is set. The $\overline{\text{IRQ}}$ status bit, when high, indicates the $\overline{\text{IRQ}}$ output is in the active state.

Interrupts result from conditions in both the transmitter and receiver sections of the ACIA. The transmitter section causes an interrupt when the Transmitter Interrupt Enabled condition is selected (CR5•$\overline{\text{CR6}}$), and the Transmit Data Register Empty (TDRE) status bit is high. The TDRE status bit indicates the current status of the Transmitter Data Register except when inhibited by Clear-to-Send ($\overline{\text{CTS}}$) being high or the ACIA being maintained in the Reset condition. The interrupt is cleared by writing data into the Transmit Data Register. The interrupt is masked by disabling the Transmitter Interrupt via CR5 or CR6 or by the loss of $\overline{\text{CTS}}$ which inhibits the TDRE status bit. The Receiver section causes an interrupt when the Receiver Interrupt Enable is set and the Receive Data Register Full (RDRF) status bit is high, an Overrun has occurred, or Data Carrier Detect ($\overline{\text{DCD}}$) has gone high. An interrupt resulting from the RDRF status bit can be cleared by reading data or resetting the ACIA. Interrupts caused by Overrun or loss of $\overline{\text{DCD}}$ are cleared by reading the status register after the error condition has occurred and then reading the Receive Data Register or resetting the ACIA. The receiver interrupt is masked by resetting the Receiver Interrupt Enable.

## CLOCK INPUTS

Separate high-impedance TTL-compatible inputs are provided for clocking of transmitted and received data. Clock frequencies of 1, 16, or 64 times the data rate may be selected.

**Transmit Clock (Tx CLK)** — The Transmit Clock input is used for the clocking of transmitted data. The transmitter initiates data on the negative transition of the clock.

**Receive Clock (Rx CLK)** — The Receive Clock input is used for synchronization of received data. (In the ÷1 mode, the clock and data must be synchronized externally.) The receiver samples the data on the positive transition of the clock.

 **MOTOROLA** *Semiconductor Products Inc.*

## SERIAL INPUT/OUTPUT LINES

**Receive Data (Rx Data)** — The Receive Data line is a high-impedance TTL-compatible input through which data is received in a serial format. Synchronization with a clock for detection of data is accomplished internally when clock rates of 16 or 64 times the bit rate are used.

**Transmit Data (Tx Data)** — The Transmit Data output line transfers serial data to a modem or other peripheral.

## PERIPHERAL/MODEM CONTROL

The ACIA includes several functions that permit limited control of a peripheral or modem. The functions included are Clear-to-Send, Request-to-Send and Data Carrier Detect.

**Clear-to-Send (CTS)** — This high-impedance TTL-compatible input provides automatic control of the transmitting end of a communications link via the modem Clear-to-Send active low output by inhibiting the Transmit Data Register Empty (TDRE) status bit.

**Request-to-Send (RTS)** — The Request-to-Send output enables the MPU to control a peripheral or modem via the data bus. The RTS output corresponds to the state of the Control Register bits CR5 and CR6. When CR6 = 0 or both CR5 and CR6 = 1, the RTS output is low (the active state). This output can also be used for Data Terminal Ready (DTR).

**Data Carrier Detect (DCD)** — This high-impedance TTL-compatible input provides automatic control, such as in the receiving end of a communications link by means of a modem Data Carrier Detect output. The DCD input inhibits and initializes the receiver section of the ACIA when high. A low-to-high transition of the Data Carrier Detect initiates an interrupt to the MPU to indicate the occurrence of a loss of carrier when the Receive Interrupt Enable bit is set. The Rx CLK must be running for proper DCD operation.

## ACIA REGISTERS

The expanded block diagram for the ACIA indicates the internal registers on the chip that are used for the status, control, receiving, and transmitting of data. The content of each of the registers is summarized in Table 1.

## TRANSMIT DATA REGISTER (TDR)

Data is written in the Transmit Data Register during the negative transition of the enable (E) when the ACIA has been addressed with RS high and R/W low. Writing data into the register causes the Transmit Data Register Empty bit in the Status Register to go low. Data can then be transmitted. If the transmitter is idling and no character is being transmitted, then the transfer will take place within 1-bit time of the trailing edge of the Write command. If a character is being transmitted, the new data character will commence as soon as the previous character is complete. The transfer of data causes the Transmit Data Register Empty (TDRE) bit to indicate empty.

## RECEIVE DATA REGISTER (RDR)

Data is automatically transferred to the empty Receive Data Register (RDR) from the receiver deserializer (a shift register) upon receiving a complete character. This event causes the Receive Data Register Full bit (RDRF) in the status buffer to go high (full). Data may then be read through the bus by addressing the ACIA and selecting the Receive Data Register with RS and R/W high when the ACIA is enabled. The non-destructive read cycle causes the RDRF bit to be cleared to empty although the data is retained in the RDR. The status is maintained by RDRF as to whether or not the data is current. When the Receive Data Register is full, the automatic transfer of data from the Receiver Shift Register to the Data Register is inhibited and the RDR contents remain valid with its current status stored in the Status Register.

TABLE 1 — DEFINITION OF ACIA REGISTER CONTENTS

| Data Bus Line Number | Buffer Address | | | |
|---|---|---|---|---|
| | RS • R/W<br>Transmit Data Register<br>(Write Only) | RS • R/W<br>Receive Data Register<br>(Read Only) | RS • R/W<br>Control Register<br>(Write Only) | RS • R/W<br>Status Register<br>(Read Only) |
| 0 | Data Bit 0* | Data Bit 0 | Counter Divide Select 1 (CR0) | Receive Data Register Full (RDRF) |
| 1 | Data Bit 1 | Data Bit 1 | Counter Divide Select 2 (CR1) | Transmit Data Register Empty (TDRE) |
| 2 | Data Bit 2 | Data Bit 2 | Word Select 1 (CR2) | Data Carrier Detect (DCD) |
| 3 | Data Bit 3 | Data Bit 3 | Word Select 2 (CR3) | Clear to Send (CTS) |
| 4 | Data Bit 4 | Data Bit 4 | Word Select 3 (CR4) | Framing Error (FE) |
| 5 | Data Bit 5 | Data Bit 5 | Transmit Control 1 (CR5) | Receiver Overrun (OVRN) |
| 6 | Data Bit 6 | Data Bit 6 | Transmit Control 2 (CR6) | Parity Error (PE) |
| 7 | Data Bit 7*** | Data Bit 7** | Receive Interrupt Enable (CR7) | Interrupt Request (IRQ) |

\* Leading bit = LSB = Bit 0
\*\* Data bit will be zero in 7 bit plus parity modes.
\*\*\* Data bit is "don't care" in 7 bit plus parity modes.

 **MOTOROLA** *Semiconductor Products Inc.*

## CONTROL REGISTER

The ACIA Control Register consists of eight bits of write-only buffer that are selected when RS and R/W̄ are low. This register controls the function of the receiver, transmitter, interrupt enables, and the Request-to-Send peripheral/modem control output.

**Counter Divide Select Bits (CR0 and CR1)** — The Counter Divide Select Bits (CR0 and CR1) determine the divide ratios utilized in both the transmitter and receiver sections of the ACIA. Additionally, these bits are used to provide a master reset for the ACIA which clears the Status Register (except for external conditions on C̄T̄S̄ and D̄C̄D̄) and initializes both the receiver and transmitter. Master reset does not affect other Control Register bits. Note that after power-on or a power fail/restart, these bits must be set high to reset the ACIA. After resetting, the clock divide ratio may be selected. These counter select bits provide for the following clock divide ratios:

| CR1 | CR0 | Function |
|-----|-----|----------|
| 0 | 0 | ÷ 1 |
| 0 | 1 | ÷ 16 |
| 1 | 0 | ÷ 64 |
| 1 | 1 | Master Reset |

**Word Select Bits (CR2, CR3, and CR4)** — The Word Select bits are used to select word length, parity, and the number of stop bits. The encoding format is as follows:

| CR4 | CR3 | CR2 | Function |
|-----|-----|-----|----------|
| 0 | 0 | 0 | 7 Bits + Even Parity + 2 Stop Bits |
| 0 | 0 | 1 | 7 Bits + Odd Parity + 2 Stop Bits |
| 0 | 1 | 0 | 7 Bits + Even Parity + 1 Stop Bit |
| 0 | 1 | 1 | 7 Bits + Odd Parity + 1 Stop Bit |
| 1 | 0 | 0 | 8 Bits + 2 Stop Bits |
| 1 | 0 | 1 | 8 Bits + 1 Stop Bit |
| 1 | 1 | 0 | 8 Bits + Even parity + 1 Stop Bit |
| 1 | 1 | 1 | 8 Bits + Odd Parity + 1 Stop Bit |

Word length, Parity Select, and Stop Bit changes are not buffered and therefore become effective immediately.

**Transmitter Control Bits (CR5 and CR6)** — Two Transmitter Control bits provide for the control of the interrupt from the Transmit Data Register Empty condition, the Request-to-Send (R̄T̄S̄) output, and the transmission of a Break level (space). The following encoding format is used:

| CR6 | CR5 | Function |
|-----|-----|----------|
| 0 | 0 | R̄T̄S̄ = low, Transmitting Interrupt Disabled. |
| 0 | 1 | R̄T̄S̄ = low, Transmitting Interrupt Enabled. |
| 1 | 0 | R̄T̄S̄ = high, Transmitting Interrupt Disabled. |
| 1 | 1 | R̄T̄S̄ = low, Transmits a Break level on the Transmit Data Output. Transmitting Interrupt Disabled. |

**Receive Interrupt Enable Bit (CR7)** — The following interrupts will be enabled by a high level in bit position 7 of the Control Register (CR7): Receive Data Register Full, Overrun, or a low-to-high transition on the Data Carrier Detect (D̄C̄D̄) signal line.

## STATUS REGISTER

Information on the status of the ACIA is available to the MPU by reading the ACIA Status Register. This read-only register is selected when RS is low and R/W̄ is high. Information stored in this register indicates the status of the Transmit Data Register, the Receive Data Register and error logic, and the peripheral/modem status inputs of the ACIA.

**Receive Data Register Full (RDRF), Bit 0** — Receive Data Register Full indicates that received data has been transferred to the Receive Data Register. RDRF is cleared after an MPU read of the Receive Data Register or by a master reset. The cleared or empty state indicates that the contents of the Receive Data Register are not current. Data Carrier Detect being high also causes RDRF to indicate empty.

**Transmit Data Register Empty (TDRE), Bit 1** — The Transmit Data Register Empty bit being set high indicates that the Transmit Data Register contents have been transferred and that new data may be entered. The low state indicates that the register is full and that transmission of a new character has not begun since the last write data command.

**Data Carrier Detect (D̄C̄D̄), Bit 2** — The Data Carrier Detect bit will be high when the D̄C̄D̄ input from a modem has gone high to indicate that a carrier is not present. This bit going high causes an Interrupt Request to be generated when the Receive Interrupt Enable is set. It remains high after the D̄C̄D̄ input is returned low until cleared by first reading the Status Register and then the Data Register or until a master reset occurs. If the D̄C̄D̄ input remains high after read status and read data or master reset has occurred, the interrupt is cleared, the D̄C̄D̄ status bit remains high and will follow the D̄C̄D̄ input.

**Clear-to-Send (C̄T̄S̄), Bit 3** — The Clear-to-Send bit indicates the state of the Clear-to-Send input from a modem. A low C̄T̄S̄ indicates that there is a Clear-to-Send from the modem. In the high state, the Transmit Data Register Empty bit is inhibited and the Clear-to-Send status bit will be high. Master reset does not affect the Clear-to-Send status bit.

**Framing Error (FE), Bit 4** — Framing error indicates that the received character is improperly framed by a start and a stop bit and is detected by the absence of the first stop bit. This error indicates a synchronization error, faulty transmission, or a break condition. The framing error flag is set or reset during the receive data transfer time. Therefore, this error indicator is present throughout the time that the associated character is available.

**Receiver Overrun (OVRN), Bit 5** — Overrun is an error flag that indicates that one or more characters in the data stream were lost. That is, a character or a number of characters were received but not read from the Receive Data Register (RDR) prior to subsequent characters being received. The overrun condition begins at the midpoint of the last bit of the second character received in succession without a read of the RDR having occurred. The Overrun does not occur in the Status Register until the valid character prior to Overrun has

 **MOTOROLA** *Semiconductor Products Inc.*

been read. The RDRF bit remains set until the Overrun is reset. Character synchronization is maintained during the Overrun condition. The Overrun indication is reset after the reading of data from the Receive Data Register or by a Master Reset.

**Parity Error (PE), Bit 6** — The parity error flag indicates that the number of highs (ones) in the character does not agree with the preselected odd or even parity. Odd parity is defined to be when the total number of ones is odd. The parity error indication will be present as long as the data

character is in the RDR. If no parity is selected, then both the transmitter parity generator output and the receiver partiy check results are inhibited.

**Interrupt Request (IRQ), Bit 7** — The IRQ bit indicates the state of the IRQ output. Any interrupt condition with its applicable enable will be indicated in this status bit. Anytime the IRQ output is low the IRQ bit will be high to indicate the interrupt or service request status. IRQ is cleared by a read operation to the Receive Data Register or a write operation to the Transmit Data Register.

ORDERING INFORMATION

| Package Type | Frequency (MHz) | Temperature | Order Number |
|---|---|---|---|
| Ceramic<br>L Suffix | 1.0 | 0°C to 70°C | MC6850L |
| | 1.0 | −40°C to 85°C | MC6850CL |
| | 1.5 | 0°C to 70°C | MC68A50L |
| | 1.5 | −40°C to 85°C | MC68A50CL |
| | 2.0 | 0°C to 70°C | MC68B50C |
| Cerdip<br>S Suffix | 1.0 | 0°C to 70°C | MC6850S |
| | 1.0 | −40°C to 85°C | MC6850CS |
| | 1.5 | 0°C to 70°C | MC68A50S |
| | 1.5 | −40°C to 85°C | MC68A50CS |
| | 2.0 | 0°C to 70°C | MC68B50S |
| Plastic<br>P Suffix | 1.0 | 0°C to 70°C | MC6850P |
| | 1.0 | −40°C to 85°C | MC6850CP |
| | 1.5 | 0°C to 70°C | MC68A50P |
| | 1.5 | −40°C to 85°C | MC68A50CP |
| | 2.0 | 0°C to 70°C | MC68B50P |

 **_MOTOROLA_** *Semiconductor Products Inc.*

## PACKAGE DIMENSIONS

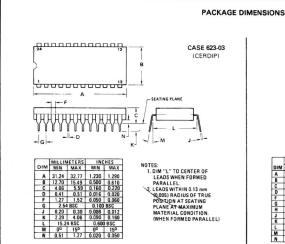

CASE 623-03
(CERDIP)

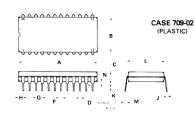

CASE 709-02
(PLASTIC)

| DIM | MILLIMETERS | | INCHES | |
|-----|-----|-----|-----|-----|
| | MIN | MAX | MIN | MAX |
| A | 31.24 | 32.77 | 1.230 | 1.290 |
| B | 12.70 | 15.49 | 0.500 | 0.610 |
| C | 4.06 | 5.59 | 0.160 | 0.220 |
| D | 0.41 | 0.51 | 0.016 | 0.020 |
| F | 1.27 | 1.52 | 0.050 | 0.060 |
| G | 2.54 BSC | | 0.100 BSC | |
| J | 0.20 | 0.30 | 0.008 | 0.012 |
| K | 2.29 | 4.06 | 0.090 | 0.160 |
| L | 15.24 BSC | | 0.600 BSC | |
| M | 0° | 15° | 0° | 15° |
| N | 0.51 | 1.27 | 0.020 | 0.050 |

NOTES:
1. DIM "L" TO CENTER OF LEADS WHEN FORMED PARALLEL.
2. LEADS WITHIN 0.13 mm (0.005) RADIUS OF TRUE POSITION AT SEATING PLANE AT MAXIMUM MATERIAL CONDITION. (WHEN FORMED PARALLEL)

| DIM | MILLIMETERS | | INCHES | |
|-----|-----|-----|-----|-----|
| | MIN | MAX | MIN | MAX |
| A | 31.37 | 32.13 | 1.235 | 1.265 |
| B | 13.72 | 14.22 | 0.540 | 0.560 |
| C | 3.94 | 5.08 | 0.155 | 0.200 |
| D | 0.36 | 0.56 | 0.014 | 0.022 |
| F | 1.02 | 1.52 | 0.040 | 0.060 |
| G | 2.54 BSC | | 0.100 BSC | |
| H | 1.65 | 2.03 | 0.065 | 0.080 |
| J | 0.20 | 0.38 | 0.008 | 0.015 |
| K | 2.92 | 3.43 | 0.115 | 0.135 |
| L | 15.24 BSC | | 0.600 BSC | |
| M | 0° | 15° | 0° | 15° |
| N | 0.51 | 1.02 | 0.020 | 0.040 |

NOTES:
1. POSITIONAL TOLERANCE OF LEADS (D), SHALL BE WITHIN 0.25 mm (0.010) AT MAXIMUM MATERIAL CONDITION, IN RELATION TO SEATING PLANE AND EACH OTHER.
2. DIMENSION L TO CENTER OF LEADS WHEN FORMED PARALLEL.
3. DIMENSION B DOES NOT INCLUDE MOLD FLASH.

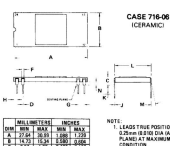

CASE 716-06
(CERAMIC)

| DIM | MILLIMETERS | | INCHES | |
|-----|-----|-----|-----|-----|
| | MIN | MAX | MIN | MAX |
| A | 27.64 | 30.99 | 1.088 | 1.220 |
| B | 14.73 | 15.34 | 0.580 | 0.604 |
| C | 2.67 | 4.32 | 0.105 | 0.170 |
| D | 0.38 | 0.53 | 0.015 | 0.021 |
| F | 0.76 | 1.40 | 0.030 | 0.055 |
| G | 2.54 BSC | | 0.100 BSC | |
| H | 0.76 | 1.78 | 0.030 | 0.070 |
| J | 0.20 | 0.30 | 0.008 | 0.012 |
| K | 2.54 | 4.57 | 0.100 | 0.180 |
| L | 14.99 | 15.49 | 0.590 | 0.610 |
| M | — | 10° | — | 10° |
| N | 1.02 | 1.52 | 0.040 | 0.060 |

NOTE:
1. LEADS TRUE POSITIONED WITHIN 0.25mm (0.010) DIA (AT SEATING PLANE) AT MAXIMUM MATERIAL CONDITION.
2. DIM "L" TO CENTER OF LEADS WHEN FORMED PARALLEL.

 **MOTOROLA** *Semiconductor Products Inc.*

3501 ED BLUESTEIN BLVD., AUSTIN, TEXAS 78721 • A SUBSIDIARY OF MOTOROLA INC.

# Glossary

### 1BASE-5 Ethernet
An Ethernet version that uses twisted-pair wire as a medium and operates at a speed of 1 Mb/s. Also known as *StarLAN*. 1BASE-5 Ethernet is not popular because of its slow speed compared to 10BASE-T.

### 2B+D
See *Basic ISDN*.

### 8PSK
See *Eight-phase phase-shift keying*.

### 10BASE-2 Ethernet
An Ethernet version that uses thin coaxial cable as a medium, operates at 10 Mb/s, and has a maximum network length of 185 m. Also called *Cheapernet, Thin Ethernet,* and *Thinwire Ethernet*.

### 10BASE-5 Ethernet
An Ethernet version that uses thick coaxial cable as a medium, operates at 10 Mb/s, and has a maximum network length of 500 m.

### 10BASE-T Ethernet
An Ethernet version that uses twisted-pair wire as a medium, operates at a speed of 10 Mb/s, and uses a hub and a star topology. Also known as *Twisted-Pair Ethernet*.

**16QAM**
A modem modulation scheme that uses 12 phase angles and 3 amplitudes to represent data and that modulates quadbits onto the carrier.

**ACIA**
An abbreviation for *asynchronous communications interface adapter.* A type of UART.

**ACK (acknowledge)**
A character that the receiver sends in some character-oriented protocols to acknowledge that it has correctly received a block of DATA.

**ACK0**
Sent by the receiver in a BISYNC system to acknowledge that an even-numbered block of data was received without error.

**ACK1**
Sent by the receiver in a BISYNC system to acknowledge that an odd-numbered block of data was received without error.

**Acknowledge 0**
See *ACK0.*

**Acknowledge 1**
See *ACK1.*

**A/D**
See *Analog-to-digital converter.*

**Aliasing**
The production of extraneous frequency components in a sampled signal caused by undersampling. Aliasing is a type of distortion.

**American National Standards Institute (ANSI)**
A membership organization that is devoted to the development of standards for American industry and is a member of the International Standards Organziation (ISO), which sets worldwide standards.

**American Standard Code for Information Interchange (ASCII)**
A 7-bit code that is widely used in data communications, especially for the communication of text.

**Analog-to-digital converter (A/D)**
A circuit that converts an analog signal to a digital value.

**ANSI**
See *American National Standards Institute.*

**Answer modem**
The modem that does not originate communication in a full-duplex communications system.

**Application layer**
The top layer (layer 7) of the OSI model. The application layer interfaces the communications system to the user's specific application programs.

**ARQ**
See *Automatic request for repetition.*

**ASCII**
See *American Standard Code for Information Interchange.*

**Asynchronous communications**
A form of communications that uses a start bit to frame the beginning and a stop bit to frame the end of each data word and allows independent transmit and receive clock signals.

**Asynchronous communications interface adapter (ACIA)**
See *ACIA.*

**AT command set**
A de facto set of standard commands that control the operation of intelligent modems. Also known as the *Hayes command set.*

**Automatic request for repetition (ARQ)**
A 7-bit code based on Baudot with the addition of redundant bits for error checking. Each ARQ character has 3 binary 1s and 4 binary 0s.

**Back channel**
See *Reverse channel.*

**Backbone network**
A high-speed network that links several slower networks. An FDDI network may serve as a backbone to several Ethernet or Token Ring LANs.

**Baseband signal**
Any information signal that is *not* modulated onto a carrier.

### Basic ISDN

A form of the integrated services digital network designed for residential subscribers. Basic ISDN operates over the local loop and provides two 64-kb/s B channels for information transfer and one 16-kb/s D channel for supervisory signals. Also called *Basic Rate Interface (BRI)* or *2B+D*.

### Basic Rate Interface

See *Basic ISDN.*

### Baudot

A 5-bit digital code once widely used in data communications but now largely replaced by ASCII and other more modern codes.

### BCC

See *Binary check character* or *Block check character.*

### B channel

See *Bearer channel.*

### Bearer channel (B channel)

A 64-kb/s Integrated Services Digital Network (ISDN) channel that carries any type of digitized information including voice, facsimile, and computer data.

### Bell 103

A 300 b/s full-duplex FSK modem standard. The CCITT version is V.21.

### Bell 202

A half-duplex FSK modem standard that operates at 1200 b/s over dial-up telephone lines and 1800 b/s over leased, conditioned lines.

### Bell 212A

A full-duplex 4PSK modem standard that operates at 1200 b/s and 600 baud. The CCITT version is V.22.

### Bid collision

A contention situation in the BISYNC protocol caused when two terminals bid (contend) for the communications link at the same time. To resolve a bid collision, one of the terminals must back down and allow the other to transmit.

### Binary check character (BCC)

A redundant character sent at the end of a block of data and used to detect transmission errors. Checksums and cyclic redundancy check characters are examples of BCCs. Also called a *block check character.*

### Binary phase-shift keying

A modulation scheme that uses two phases to represent data, one to represent a mark and the other to represent a space.

### Binary Synchronous Communications Protocol (BISYNC)
A character-oriented synchronous protocol developed by IBM.

### BISYNC
See *Binary Synchronous Communications Protocol.*

### Bit-oriented protocol
A set of rules for communicating data that uses individual bits in a block of data as control codes. HDLC and SDLC are examples of bit-oriented protocols.

### Block check character (BCC)
An extra data word added to the end of a data transmission to aid in error detection. Also called *binary check character.*

### BPSK
See *binary phase-shift keying.*

### Break
A constant space that is transmitted in some communications systems to signal the remote terminal to stop sending data.

### BRI
Basic Rate Interface. See *Basic ISDN.*

### Bridge
A device that operates at OSI Model levels 1 and 2 to connect two or more LANs so that data can pass from one LAN to the other.

### Broadcast address
An address assigned to all terminals on a network.

### Built-in modem
A modem whose electronics are integrated into the motherboard of a terminal or computer.

### Bus network
A network topology that uses a single communications link to connect three or more terminals. Also called a *multidrop network.*

### Carrier Sense Multiple Access with Collision Detection (CSMA/CD)
A protocol that Ethernet and some other LANs use to control the manner in which nodes contend for the right to transmit over the network.

### Carterphone decision
A 1968 decision that permitted users to connect their own station equipment to local telephone loops in the United States.

## CCITT
See *Consultative Committee for International Telegraph and Telephone.*

## Centronics interface
A de facto parallel interface standard for connecting printers and other peripherals to a computer.

## Champ connector
Another name for the Amphenol 57-30360 connector used at the printer end of a Centronics interface cable.

## Character-oriented protocol
A set of rules for communicating data that relies upon special characters, such as SOH, STX and ETX, to control the flow of information. BISYNC is an example of a character-oriented protocol.

## Character set
A collection of symbols and codes that are used for communication and to store text in computers. The ASCII and EBCDIC codes are examples of commonly used character sets.

## Cheapernet
See *10BASE-2.*

## Checksum
A block check character that is formed by taking the arithmetical sum of the binary numbers that form a block of data. The checksum is transmitted as the last character in the block, and it is used for error detection.

## Chipset
A set of integrated circuits that supply all or most of the circuitry needed to build an item of electronic equipment. Most modems and computers are built from chipsets.

## Cladding
The outer layer of glass or plastic of a fiber-optic cable that surrounds the core.

## Class of Procedure
The formal name for *operating mode* in the HDLC protocol.

## Code
A system of symbols used to represent information. ASCII and EBCDIC are two binary codes used in data communications.

## Codec
Coder/decoder. A single integrated circuit that contains both an A/D and a D/A and which performs both pulse code modulation and demodulation.

**Collision**

The term for contention in the CSMA/CD protocol. A collision occurs when two nodes attempt to transmit at the same time.

**Combinational network**

A communications network that uses two or more topologies. A combinational network often results from linking several previously independent networks to form a single, larger network.

**Comité Consulatif International Télégraphique et Téléphonique (CCITT)**

Committee that publishes international communications standards. Known in English as the *Consultative Committee for International Telegraph and Telephone.* The CCITT is a permanent organ of the International Telecommunications Union (ITU) headquartered in Geneva, Switzerland.

**Common-mode noise**

A noise signal that appears on both conductors of a balanced circuit. Common-mode noise signals are of equal amplitude and cancel each other out when they appear on the input of a balanced amplifier.

**Communication**

The transfer of information from one location to another.

**Communications channel**

A single link from the transmitter to the receiver in a communications network.

**Communications port**

A connector on a terminal through which data are input and/or output.

**Communications software program**

See *Terminal program.*

**Compression**

See *Data compression.*

**Concentrator**

A hub-like device used on FDDI networks to connect several single-attach nodes to the network's primary.

**Conditioned line**

A telephone circuit that has had its frequency response and/or delay characteristics adjusted for optimum performance.

**Constellation diagram**

A diagram that uses dots to represent all possible phases and amplitudes of a modulated carrier.

### Consultative Committee for International Telegraph and Telephone (CCITT)

The English name for a committee that publishes international communications standards. The committee's original French name is *Comité Consulatif International Télégraphique et Téléphonique.* The CCITT is one of four permanent organs of the International Telecommunications Union (ITU), headquartered in Geneva, Switzerland.

### Contention

The situation that occurs when two or more terminals try to transmit over the same communications link at the same time.

### Control code

A special character that causes some special action at the receiving terminal. For example, a *line feed* character moves the cursor to the next line on the receiving terminal's screen.

### Core

The inner layer of glass or plastic of a fiber-optic cable. The core is surrounded by another layer called the *cladding.*

### CR

The abbreviation for the control register of a programmable integrated circuit such as the Asynchronous Communications Interface Adapter.

### CSMA/CD

See *Carrier Sense Multiple Access with Collision Detection.*

### Cyclic redundancy check (CRC)

A type of block check character that is very effective in detecting communications errors. CRC characters are commonly 12, 16, 24, or 32 bits long.

### D/A

See *Digital-to-analog converter.*

### Data

In this book, the word *data* means information that is stored in digital form before it enters a communications system. In common usage, the word *data* is used to refer to any type of information. Data is the plural form; the singular form is *datum.*

### Data base

Information stored in a computer in an organized fashion.

### Data channel

A 16-kb/s Integrated Services Digital Network (ISDN) channel that carries control information and can also be used for low-speed data.

### Data communications
The transfer of information that is in digital form before it enters the communications system.

### Data communications equipment (DCE)
A device that serves as the interface between the DTE and the communications medium. A DCE is often a modem that modulates digital signals onto an analog carrier and sends them over an analog communications link. The DCE also demodulates received analog signals to recover the digital information.

### Data compression
A method of recording information to reduce the number of bits that are needed to represent it. Data compression allows higher communications speeds and allows more information to be stored on a disk.

### Datalink layer
Layer 2 of the OSI model. The datalink layer defines error control, framing, synchronization, link initialization and disconnection, addressing, and frame sequence control.

### Data set
Telephone company jargon for *modem.*

### Data terminal equipment (DTE)
A device that converts data from the parallel format used within a terminal to the serial format used on a communications link.

### Datum
The singular form of the word *data.* See *Data.*

### DCE
See *Data communications equipment.*

### D channel
See *Data channel.*

### DDD
See *Direct distance dial network.*

### Demultiplexing (DEMUX)
The process of separating a transmission that contains two or more intermixed signals into its original and separate intelligence signals.

### DEMUX
See *Demultiplexing.*

### Dial tone
A tone that a telephone switch sends to a telset to notify the subscriber that the switch is ready to receive dialing signals.

### Dibit
A group of two data bits that are modulated onto a carrier as a single unit.

### Differential phase-shift keying
A modulation scheme used in some modems in which each carrier phase shift becomes the new zero degree reference for the following phase shift.

### Digital pulse modulation
Another name for *pulse code modulation.*

### Digital signal processor (DSP)
A device similar to a microprocessor but which is specially designed to process analog signals. The analog signal is first digitized by an A/D converter. After the DSP processes the digitized signal, the signal may pass through an A/D converter to change it back to analog form. In a modem, a DSP may perform modulation, demodulation, and echo cancellation.

### Digital-to-analog converter (D/A)
A circuit that converts a digital value to an analog voltage.

### Direct distance dial (DDD) network
A telephone network over which the subscriber may directly dial long-distance telephone calls.

### Distributed computing
The practice of using many smaller computers in place of a distributed machine.

### DLE
A character that is sent immediately before a control character in BISYNC transparent transmission.

### Drop
A cable that connects a terminal to a multidrop (bus) network.

### DSP
See *Digital signal processor.*

**DTE**
See *Data terminal equipment.*

**DTMF**
See *Dual-tone multifrequency signaling.*

**Dual-attach node**
An FDDI terminal that connects to both the primary and secondary rings. A dual-attach node has two input ports and two output ports.

**Dual-tone multifrequency signaling (DTMF)**
A system of tones used as dialing signals in the telephone network. A combination of two tones represents each digit. Also called *Touch Tone.*

**Dumb modem**
A modem that has no built-in microprocessor and must be directly controlled by an operator.

**Dynamic router**
A router that automatically broadcasts routing information throughout the internetwork at regular intervals. Other dynamic routers on the internetwork use this information to update their internal routing tables.

**EBCDIC**
See *Extended Binary Coded Decimal Interchange Code.*

**Echoplex**
A simple form of error detection. The receiving terminal echoes typed characters back to the sending terminal, where they are displayed on the terminal's screen. Echoplex relies on the operator to detect errors.

**Echo suppresser**
A circuit once commonly used on analog long-distance telephone circuits to prevent echoes by opening one side of a four-wire circuit while the other side carries audio. A modem must transmit a tone to disable the echo suppressers for full-duplex communication. In today's digital telephone network, echo suppressers have been largely replaced by digital echo cancellation techniques.

**Eight-phase phase-shift keying**
A seldom-used modem modulation scheme that modulates tribits onto the carrier and uses eight carrier phase shifts.

### Eighty-milliampere (mA) loop
A de facto serial interface standard that uses an 80-mA current to represent a mark and a 0-mA current to represent a space.

### Electronic communications
The transfer of information from one location to another with the use of electronic circuits.

### Electronic mail (E-mail)
Electronic messages that are sent over a communications network from one computer to another.

### E-mail
See *Electronic mail.*

### Encoding
The process of putting information into digital format such as converting text to ASCII or audio to PCM.

### End of text
See *ETX.*

### End of transmission block
See *ETB.*

### Equalizer
A device used to compensate for certain types of distortion on a circuit.

### Error control
The detection and correction of errors in data communications.

### Escape code
A series of three plus signs (+ + +) that is sent to a modem to switch it from the on-line mode to the command mode.

### ETB (end of block)
A control character sent at the end of the text field in all but the final block of data in a character-oriented protocol.

### Ethernet
A LAN standard, also known as IEEE 802.3, that connects personal computers by means of coaxial cable or twisted-pair conductors and uses a bus or star topology. Most Ethernet LANs operate at 10 Mb/s.

### ETX (end of text)
A control character sent at the end of the text field in the last block of a transmission in character-oriented protocols.

### Extended Binary Coded Decimal Interchange Code (EBCDIC)
An 8-bit code developed by IBM Corporation and widely used to communicate text.

### Facsimile (fax)
A communications terminal for the transmission of graphics and documents.

### Fax
See *Facsimile.*

### FDDI
See *Fiber Data Distributed Interface.*

### FDX
See *Full-duplex.*

### FEC
See *Forward error correction.*

### Fiber Data Distributed Interface (FDDI)
An ANSI LAN standard that uses fiber-optic cable or twisted-pair wire and operates at 100 Mb/s using a dual-ring topology.

### FIFO
See *First-in, first-out memory.*

### First-in, first-out (FIFO) memory
A type of memory with separate input and output ports. The first data to enter the input port are the first to exit the output port. FIFO memory within a network interface controller (NIC) serves as a buffer between the terminal's data bus and the LAN.

### Flag
An 8-bit sequence of bits (01111110) that is transmitted in the HDLC protocol immediately before and after each frame and to fill any idle time between frames.

### Forward error correction (FEC)
Any system that allows a terminal to both detect and correct errors in the data it receives.

### Fractional T1
A portion of the bandwidth of a T1 carrier system that a user can lease from a telecommunications provider in 64-kb/s increments.

### Frame
Another name for a block of data.

### Framing
The process of breaking large fields of data into a number of smaller units such as blocks or characters.

### Framing character
A control character that marks the beginning or end of a field in character-oriented protocols such as BISYNC. Examples are SOH (start of header), STX (start of text), ETB (end of block), and ETX (end of text).

### Framing error
A communications error that occurs because the receiving terminal is unable to determine where one data word ends and the next data word begins.

### Frequency-shift keying (FSK)
A simple form of frequency modulation that low-speed modems use for data transmission over analog communications links such as telephone lines. An FSK signal shifts between two carrier frequencies. One carrier frequency represents a mark, and the other represents a space.

### FSK
See *Frequency-shift keying.*

### Full-duplex (FDX) communications
Communications that takes place in both directions at the same time. FDX communication traditionally required two communications channels, one for communication in each direction, but modern digital echo-canceling techniques now make FSK possible over a single channel.

### General Purpose Interface Bus (GPIB)
See *IEEE 488 interface.*

### Group address
An address assigned to more than one terminal on a network.

### Half-duplex (HDX) communications
Communications that can take place in either direction, but in only one direction at a time.

### Handshaking
A set of signals that coordinate the transfer of data from one device to another.

### Hayes Command Set
See *AT Command Set.*

## HDLC
See *High-Level Data Link Control.*

## HDX
See *Half-duplex.*

## Hewlett-Packard Interface Bus (HP-IB)
See *IEEE 488 interface.*

## Hierarchical network
A network topology organized in the form of a pyramid with one terminal at the top and increasing numbers of terminals at each lower level. Also called a *tree network.*

## High-Level Data Link Control (HDLC)
A bit-oriented protocol published by the International Standards Organization in 1977. HDLC is based on IBM's Synchronous Data Link Control (SDLC) protocol.

## Hook switch
A switch within a telset that closes when the handset is lifted from the telset and closes when the handset is replaced or "hung up."

## Horizontal and vertical parity check
An error detection scheme that relies on normal parity plus a block check character at the end of each transmission and which can correct 1-bit errors at the receiver without a need for retransmission.

## HP-IB
Hewlett-Packard Interface Bus. See *IEEE 488 interface.*

## Hub
A central point in a star network. Each of the terminals in a hub network connects to the hub by means of an individual point-to-point link.

## Huffman encoding
A data compression scheme that uses fewer bits to represent characters that occur frequently in a transmission and more bits to represent characters that do not occur frequently. Huffman encoding works well with text-based information. Also see *Run-length encoding.*

## Hybrid
A telephone circuit that joins a two-wire line to a four-wire line. Originally, hybrids were transformers, but today they are electronic circuits.

### IEEE
See *Institute for Electrical and Electronic Engineers.*

### IEEE 488 interface
A parallel interface designed to connect test and measurement equipment to a computer. Also called the *General Purpose Interface Bus (GPIB)* and the *Hewlett-Packard Interface Bus (HP-IB).*

### I-frame
See *Information frame.*

### Index of refraction
The ratio of the speed of light in a vacuum to the speed of light through another medium, such as glass. When light passes from one medium to another, it bends. The amount of bending is determined by the difference between the indices of refraction of the two media.

### Information frame (I-frame)
The only type of HDLC frame that can be used to send data.

### Institute for Electrical and Electronic Engineers (IEEE)
A membership organization founded in 1963 with over 290,000 members. Among other activities, the IEEE publishes computer and communications standards.

### Integrated Services Digital Network (ISDN)
A telephone service that brings a digital local loop to the telephone subscriber's premises. ISDN can use the same channel to communicate digitized voice, graphics, and data.

### Intelligent modem
A modem with an internal microprocessor that performs such functions as automatic dialing, answering an incoming call, automatic error correction, and data compression.

### International Standards Organization (ISO)
An organization that is involved in setting worldwide standards and that is made up of the national standards organizations of more than 75 countries. The ISO developed the Open Systems Interconnect (OSI) communications model. The US member organization is the American National Standards Institute (ANSI).

### Internetworking
The technique of connecting individual LANs to form a larger network.

### Interoffice trunk
A telephone circuit that connects two telephone company offices.

### Interrupt
A signal sent to a terminal's microprocessor to cause it to temporarily suspend the execution of one program in order to execute another short program, called an interrupt service routine, that inputs or outputs information.

### Interrupt line
Line over which an interrupt signal is sent.

### Interrupt request (IRQ)
An MPU control line that a peripheral can use to temporarily interrupt the program that the MPU is executing so that the MPU can input data from or output data to the peripheral.

### IRQ
See *Interrupt request.*

### ISDN
See *Integrated services digital network.*

### ISO
See *International Standards Organization.*

### LAN
See *Local area network.*

### LAPM
See *Link Access Procedure for Modems.*

### Leased line
A telephone circuit that continuously connects two or more points and is continuously available to the subscriber.

### Linefinder switch
A device located in a telco central office that connects the local loop to the central office switch when the subscriber's telset is taken off-hook and returns a dial tone to the telset.

### Line (loop) start operation
A process that connects a telset to the telco switching equipment when the telset is taken off hook.

### Line termination (LT)
An ISDN interface between the local loop and the telco central office switch.

### Link Access Procedure for Modems (LAPM)
A communications error-detection and correction protocol.

**Listener**
A device that is programmed to receive data over an IEEE 488 interface.

**Local area network (LAN)**
A communications system that connects computers and peripheral devices that are located within a single office, a single building, or in adjacent buildings and allows its users to share programs, information, and peripheral devices such as printers and modems.

**Local loop**
A telephone circuit that connects a subscriber's station equipment to the switching equipment in the telco local office.

**Local office switch**
A telephone switch that serves all subscribers connected to a single telephone exchange.

**Loop start operation**
See *Line start operation.*

**Manchester encoding**
A coding scheme that several LANs use to send data over their communications links. Manchester encoding has a logic transition in the center of each bit. If the transition is positive, the bit is a logic 1, and if the transition is negative, the bit is a logic 0.

**Mark**
Another name for a binary 1 in a data communication.

**Master**
The controlling terminal in a communications network. Also called the *primary.*

**Master-slave system**
A communications system with one controlling terminal (master) and one or more subordinate terminals (slaves).

**MAU**
See *Media access unit* and *Multi-station access unit.*

**Media**
See *Medium.*

**Media access unit (MAU)**
A device used to connect a terminal to a 10BASE-5 Ethernet LAN.

## Medium (pl. media)
The path information travels from the transmitter to the receiver in a communications system.

## Mesh network
A network topology that features numerous possible communications links among the terminals.

## Micron Network Protocol (MNP)
A system of error-checking and data compression protocols that has become a de facto standard for modem communications.

## Mnemonic
An abbreviation that is designed to be easy to remember, such as RTS for request to send.

## MNP
See *Micron Network Protocol.*

## Modem
Short for modulator/demodulator. See *Data Communications Equipment.*

## Modem turnaround time
A short time delay to allow for the direction of data transmission to reverse in a half-duplex communications circuit.

## Morse code
A system of using long and short sounds to communicate the letters of the alphabet, numbers, and certain other symbols.

## Multidrop network
See *Bus network.*

## Multi-media communications
A communication that is made up of a combination of text, graphics, audio, and video.

## Multiplexing (MUX)
A process of combining several signals so that they can be sent simultaneously over a single communications link. A demultiplexer (DEMUX) at the receiving end of the link separates the signals.

## Multipoint network
A communications network that connects three or more terminals.

### Multi-station access unit (MAU)
A Token Ring hub. The MAU gives the Token Ring LAN the physical appearance of a star network, although electrically it is a ring.

### MUX
See *Multiplexing.*

### NAK (negative acknowledge)
A character that a receiver sends in character-oriented protocols to indicate that it received a block of data that contains an error.

### Negative acknowledge
See *NAK.*

### Network administrator
A person who is responsible for the efficient operation of one or more communication networks.

### Network interface controller (NIC)
A circuit that is usually located within a terminal and that interfaces a LAN to the terminal's address, data, and control buses.

### Network layer
Layer 3 of the OSI model. The network layer defines how data are switched and routed through the network.

### Network terminator (NT)
A Basic ISDN interface installed at a subscriber's premises to multiplex two 64-kb/s B channels and a 16-kb/s D channel onto the telco local loop.

### NIC
See *Network interface controller.*

### Node
A terminal on a LAN or other data communications network.

### Non-linear quantizing
A form of pulse code modulation in which the quantizing levels are spaced closer together at low signal levels and further apart at high signal levels.

### Normal response mode
The HDLC operating mode that is used in a multipoint network with one primary and a number of secondaries.

### NT
See *Network terminator.*

### Null modem cable
A cable used to connect the RS-232 ports of two DTEs to each other. A null modem cable is wired internally to make it appear to each DTE that it is communicating with a DCE.

### Nyquist rate
A sampling rate equal to twice the maximum frequency of the signal that is sampled.

### Open Systems Interconnect (OSI) Model
A communications reference model developed by the International Standards Organization that divides the data communications process into seven layers.

### Originate modem
The modem that initiates communication in a full-duplex communications system. Some full-duplex modem standards assign a specific carrier frequency to the originate modem and a different carrier frequency to the answer modem.

### OSI model
See *Open Systems Interconnect Model.*

### Overrun error
The error that occurs when the terminal does not read a data word from the DTE's receive register before another word is received and overwrites it.

### Oversampling
Sampling at a rate greater than twice the maximum frequency of the sampled signal. Practical pulse modulation systems oversample.

### PAM
See *Pulse amplitude modulation.*

### Parity bit
A redundant bit that is added to each data word in a message to aid in error detection. All words in the message have the same parity. If odd parity is used, all data words have an odd number of 1s, and if even parity is used, all data words have an even number of 1s.

### Parity error
The error that occurs in a DTE when a received data word has the wrong parity.

### PBX (also PABX)
See *Private branch exchange.*

**PDM**
Abbreviation for *pulse duration modulation.* See *Pulse width modulation.*

**P/F bit**
See *Poll/final bit.*

**PFM**
See *Pulse frequency modulation.*

**Phase-locked loop (PLL)**
An electronic circuit that consists of a phase detector, low-pass filter and voltage-controlled oscillator. A PLL can be used as an FSK demodulator.

**Phase-shift keying (PSK)**
A type of phase modulation used by many modems.

**Phasor**
An arrow used to represent the instantaneous phase and amplitude of a phase-modulated carrier.

**Phasor diagram**
A diagram that uses arrows (phasors) to represent all possible phases and amplitudes of a modulated carrier.

**Physical layer**
The lowest layer (layer 1) of the OSI Model that defines the physical medium for data communications.

**Plug-in modem**
A modem built onto a circuit board which plugs into a slot on the motherboard of a terminal or computer.

**Point-to-point network**
A communications network that connects two terminals.

**Poll/final (P/F) bit**
A bit used in all HDLC frames. The primary sets the P/F bit to indicate that the frame is a poll, and a secondary sets the P/F bit to indicate that the frame is the final frame in a message.

**Polling**
The process of asking each terminal on a network, one at a time, if it has data to send.

**Port**
See *Communications port.*

**PPM**
See *Pulse position modulation.*

### Prefix
In the United States and Canada, the first three digits of a seven-digit local telephone number.

### Presentation layer
Layer 6 of the OSI model. The presentation layer performs code conversions and data reformatting, formats information for display on the terminal's screen, and performs data compression and decompression.

### PRI
Primary rate interface. See *Primary ISDN.*

### Primary
The controlling terminal in a communications network. Also called the *master.*

### Primary ISDN
A form of the Integrated Services Digital Network designed for business subscribers. Primary ISDN uses the bandwidth of a T1 carrier system.

### Primary ring
The data path that carries communications on an FDDI network during normal operation. There is also a secondary ring, which serves as a backup if the primary ring is damaged.

### Private branch exchange (PBX or PABX)
Telephone company jargon for a switchboard located on the subscriber's premises.

### Protocol
A system of rules that controls the operation of a communications system.

### PSK
See *Phase-shift keying.*

### PTM
See *Pulse time modulation.*

### Pulse amplitude modulation (PAM)
A type of pulse modulation in which the amplitude of the pulses represents the amplitude of the sampled signal.

### Pulse code modulation (PCM)
A form of pulse modulation that converts each sample of the intelligence signal into a binary number.

### Pulse duration modulation (PDM)
See *Pulse width modulation.*

**Pulse frequency modulation (PFM)**
A form of pulse time modulation in which the frequency of the sample pulses is proportional to the amplitude of the sampled signal.

**Pulse position modulation (PPM)**
A form of pulse time modulation in which the position of the pulse in time represents the amplitude of the sampled signal.

**Pulse time modulation (PTM)**
Any form of pulse modulation in which some characteristic of the pulse timing is varied. PTM includes pulse width modulation (PWM), pulse frequency modulation (PFM), and pulse position modulation (PPM).

**Pulse width modulation (PWM)**
A form of pulse time modulation in which the width of the sample pulse is proportional to the instantaneous amplitude of the sampled signal. Also called *pulse duration modulation*.

**PWM**
See *Pulse width modulation*.

**QAM**
See *Quadrature amplitude modulation*.

**QPSK**
See *Quadrature phase-shift keying*.

**Quadrature amplitude modulation (QAM)**
A combination of phase-shift keying and amplitude modulation used in high-speed modems.

**Quadrature phase-shift keying (QPSK)**
A modem PSK modulation scheme that uses four phases to represent data. Each phase represents 2 bits (a dibit) in the data stream. Also called *Quaternary PSK*.

**Quantizing**
The process of assigning a binary number to a sample during pulse code modulation.

**Quantizing error**
The difference between the actual amplitude of a sample of an intelligence signal and the level assigned to it during pulse code modulation.

**Quantizing level**
The binary number assigned to a sample of the intelligence signal during pulse code modulation.

### Quaternary coding
A coding scheme that uses four different voltage levels to represent information. Basic ISDN uses quaternary coding for transmission over the local loop.

### Quaternary PSK
See *Quadrature phase-shift keying.*

### RDR
Abbreviation for the receive data register of the Asynchronous Communications Interface Adapter.

### Receive not ready (RNR) frame.
An HDLC S-frame that the receiving terminal sends to the transmitting terminal to acknowledge the receipt of I-frames and to indicate that the receiving terminal is not ready to receive more information.

### Receiver
The destination of information in a communication system.

### Receive ready (RR) frame
An HDLC S-frame that acknowledges the correct receipt of I-frames.

### Redundant data
Data that are not necessary to the information content of a transmission. Redundant data are often added to a communication to aid in the detection of errors.

### Refraction
The bending of a light ray when it passes from one medium (such as air) into another medium (such as glass), or when it passes from one type of glass to another in an optical fiber.

### Reject (REJ) frame
An HDLC S-frame that a receiving terminal sends to the transmitting terminal to request the retransmission of all I-frames beginning with a specified frame number.

### REJ frame
See *Reject frame.*

### Renegotiation protocol
A protocol that two modems use when they first establish contact with each other to negotiate such factors as the communications speed, data compression speed, and error correction scheme that they will use to communicate.

### Repeater
A device that operates at OSI Model level 1 and connects two smaller LAN segments to form a larger network.

### Reverse channel

A low-speed channel used with some half-duplex modems so that the receiving terminal can send control codes back to the transmitting terminal. The reverse channel is also called the *back channel* or *supervisory channel.*

### Ring

The conductor of a telephone local loop circuit that is at ground potential. The other conductor is called the tip and has a potential of –48 V when the telset is on hook.

### Ringer

A device in a telset that sounds to alert the subscriber when there is an incoming call.

### Ring network

Any network topology that connects its terminals in a loop or ring. Two widely used ring networks are Token Ring and FDDI.

### Ring-wrap

See *Self-healing.*

### RNR frame

See *Receive not ready frame.*

### Router

A device that connects two or more LANs to each other and that operates at OSI Model layers 1 through 3. A router is able to select among multiple paths to route a frame between the source and destination nodes.

### Routing field

Information that a router adds to a frame to specify the path that the frame should travel from the LAN where it originated to the LAN where the destination node is located.

### Routing table

A table of the addresses of the various nodes on the LANs served by a bridge or other internetworking device. The routing table allows frames to be forwarded to the LAN where their destination node is located.

### RR frame

See *Receive ready frame.*

### RS-232

A recommended serial standard published by the EIA that is frequently used to interface a DTE and a DCE.

## RS-422

A recommended standard published by the EIA to specify electrical signal levels of a serial interface. RS-422 uses balanced circuits and is designed to be used with the RS-449 mechanical specification.

## RS-423

A recommended standard published by the EIA to specify electrical signal levels of a serial interface. RS-423 uses unbalanced circuits and is designed to be used with the RS-449 mechanical specification.

## RS-449

A recommended standard published by the EIA to specify the functional and mechanical interface between a DTE and a DCE. RS-449 is designed to replace RS-232, but it does not specify the electrical signals. RS-449 is often used with the RS-422 and RS-423 electrical standards.

## Run-length encoding

A data compression scheme that replaces repeated characters in a data stream with a shorter code. Run-length encoding works well with many types of computer files. Also see *Huffman encoding*.

## Sample and hold circuit

A circuit that periodically takes a sample of an intelligence signal and holds that sample on its output long enough for an A/D converter to quantize it.

## Sampling theorem

A theorem that states that any analog signal can be reconstructed from its samples if the sampling frequency is at least twice the frequency of the sampled signal. Also see *Nyquist rate*.

## SDLC

See *Synchronous Data Link Control*.

## Secondary

A subordinate terminal in a communications network. Also called a *slave, remote,* or *tributary* terminal.

## Secondary ring

A data path that serves as a backup communications link on an FDDI network in case the primary ring is damaged.

## Selection

The process of choosing a terminal on a network to receive data.

**Selective forwarding**
The ability of a bridge or other internetworking device to forward from one LAN to another only those frames that are addressed to a node on the output side of the bridge. Selective forwarding reduces unnecessary traffic on the internetwork.

**Selective reject (SREJ) frame**
An HDLC S-frame that the receiving terminal sends to the transmitting terminal to request the retransmission of a specified I-frame.

**Self-healing**
A feature of an FDDI LAN that permits the nodes on either side of a break in the primary and secondary rings to connect the two rings together to bypass the break. The resulting configuration is sometimes called a ring-wrap.

**Sequence control**
A method of numbering blocks of data so that no block will be lost or duplicated and so that the blocks can be placed in the proper sequence at the receiver, even if they are not received in the order in which they were sent.

**Server**
A computer that stores programs and data that are accessible to users by means of a network.

**Session layer**
Layer 5 of the OSI model. The session layer provides a method for data exchange among different software applications and provides a way to recover from major data transfer problems.

**S-frame**
See *Supervisory frame.*

**Shannon's Law**
A prediction of the maximum speed that data can be sent over a communications link. This maximum speed depends on the link's bandwidth and signal-to-noise ratio.

**Simplex communications**
Communications in one direction only.

**Single-attach node**
An FDDI terminal that is not connected to the secondary ring of the network. It is connected to the primary ring by means of a concentrator.

**Slave**
A subordinate terminal in a communications network. Also called a *secondary.*

**SOH**
(Start of header) a character sent before the header information in a block of data in some character-oriented protocols.

### Space
A binary 0 in a data communications. A binary 1 is called a *mark*.

### SR
The abbreviation for the status register of a programmable integrated circuit such as the Asynchronous Communications Interface Adapter.

### SREJ frame
See *Selective reject.*

### Stand-alone modem
A modem that is physically located outside the terminal it serves and connects to the terminal by means of an RS-232 or other serial interface. A stand-alone modem usually has its own power supply, although some stand-alone modems that are designed for portable use take their power from the RS-232 interface lines.

### StarLAN
See *1BASE-5 Ethernet.*

### Star network
A network topology with a central hub and a number of remote terminals that are connected to the hub by individual point-to-point links.

### Start bit
A space placed at the beginning of each data word in asynchronous communications.

### Start of header
See *SOH.*

### Start of text
See *STX.*

### Static router
A router whose routing table must be reprogrammed by the network manager every time a change is made to the internetwork. Dynamic routers, on the other hand, update their own routing tables from information that they periodically broadcast to each other through the internetwork.

### Station
A terminal on an Ethernet LAN.

### Station equipment
All parts of the telephone network that are located on the subscriber's premises including telsets, modems, switchboards, and wiring.

### Stop bit
A mark placed at the end of each data word in asynchronous communications.

### STX
(Start of text) a character sent to mark the beginning of the text field in a block of data in some character-oriented protocols such as BISYNC.

### Subscriber
A customer of a telephone company.

### Supervisor
Name of the master terminal in a BISYNC multipoint communications system.

### Supervisory channel
See *Reverse channel.*

### Supervisory frame (S-frame)
An HDLC frame that a receiving terminal uses to respond to communications from a transmitting terminal. The four types of S-frames are receive ready (RR), receive not ready (RNR), reject (REJ), and selective reject (SREJ).

### Switching equipment
Equipment located in the telco offices that makes the connection between the station equipment of two or more subscribers.

### SYN
(Synchronization) a character transmitted in some synchronous communications systems to synchronize the receiving terminal to the incoming data stream.

### Synchronous communications
A form of communications in which the sending and receiving terminals operate from the same clock signal and which does not use start and stop bits to frame each data word.

### Synchronous Data Link Control (SDLC)
A bit-oriented synchronous protocol published by IBM in 1974.

### T1 digital carrier system
A digital communications link that operates at 1.544 Mb/s in North America and Japan.

### T2 carrier system
A digital communications link that is formed by multiplexing three T1 systems. North American T2 systems operate at 6.312 Mb/s.

### T3 carrier system
A digital communications link that is formed by multiplexing seven T2 systems. In North America, T3 systems operate at 47.736 Mb/s.

### Talker
A device that is programmed to send data over the IEEE 488 interface.

### Tandem switch
A telephone company switch that establishes connections among other switches.

### Tandem trunk
A telephone circuit that connects a tandem switch to a local office switch.

### TDR
The transmit data register of the Asynchronous Communications Interface Adapter.

### Telco
A short form of the words *telephone company.*

### Telset
Telephone jargon for a standard telephone set.

### Terminal
The device on a digital network that sends or receives data. A terminal is often a computer.

### Terminal program
A communications software package that controls an intelligent modem and performs other communications functions.

### Thinwire Ethernet
See *10BASE-2.*

### Tip
The conductor of a telephone local loop circuit that is at –48 V potential. The other conductor, called the ring, is at ground potential.

### Token
A unique bit pattern that controls which terminal has permission to transmit on a Token Ring network. See *Token passing.*

### Token passing
A protocol that gives a terminal permission to transmit on a Token Ring LAN. The token is a unique bit pattern that circulates around the ring from terminal to terminal. The terminal that possesses the token has permission to transmit.

### Token Ring
A LAN standard, also known as IEEE 802.5, that uses a ring topology to connect personal computers. Token Ring LANs operate at either 4 Mb/s or 16 Mb/s.

### Toll center
A telephone company office that processes long-distance telephone calls.

### Topology
The physical layout of a communications network. Some popular topologies are bus, ring, star, and point-to-point.

### Touch Tone
See *Dual-tone multifrequency signaling (DTMF)*.

### Transmission equipment
Telephone circuits that carry information from one subscriber to another.

### Transmitter
A device that sends information in a communications system.

### Transmitter start code (TSC)
A code, similar to an address, that commands a specific terminal on a network to transmit.

### Transparent
A term that means that during normal operation the telephone user is unaware of the equipment's operation.

### Transparent transmission
A type of transmission used in BISYNC in which the receiving DTE ignores the contents of the text field. Transparent transmission is used to communicate non-text data where a data word in the text field could be confused with a control character.

### Transport layer
Layer 4 of the OSI model. The transport layer defines standards that make the network transparent to the user.

### Tree network
See *Hierarchical network.*

### Tribit
A group of three data bits that is modulated onto a carrier as a single unit.

### Tributary
Name given to a secondary terminal in a BISYNC multipoint communications system.

**Trunk**
A telephone circuit that connects two telephone switches or two telco local offices.

**TSC**
See *Transmitter start code.*

**Twenty-milliampere loop**
A de facto serial interface standard that uses 20 mA to represent a mark and 0 mA to represent a space.

**Twisted-pair Ethernet**
See *10BASE-T Ethernet.*

**Twisted-pair FDDI**
A new FDDI LAN standard that uses twisted-pair wire instead of fiber-optic cable as a communications medium. Twisted-pair FDDI is more economical, because it eliminates the expensive interface between each node and the fiber-optic cable.

**UART**
See *Universal asynchronous receiver/transmitter.*

**U-frame**
See *Unnumbered frame.*

**Undersampling**
Sampling at a rate less than twice the maximum frequency of the signal that is sampled. Undersampling is undesirable, because it produces *aliasing,* a type of distortion.

**Universal asynchronous receiver/transmitter (UART)**
A DTE that is used in asynchronous communications systems.

**Universal synchronous/asynchronous receiver/transmitter (USART)**
A DTE that can be used in either synchronous or asynchronous communications systems.

**Universal synchronous receiver/transmitter (USRT)**
A DTE that is used in synchronous communications systems.

**Unnumbered frame (U-frame)**
A data block in the HDLC and SDLC protocols that is used to initialize terminals and to place them on or off line.

**USART**
See *Universal synchronous/asynchronous receiver/transmitter.*

**USRT**
See *Universal synchronous receiver/transmitter.*

**V.21**
A CCITT 300-b/s full-duplex FSK modem standard. The North American version is Bell 103.

**V.22**
A CCITT full-duplex 4PSK modem standard that operates at 1200 b/s and 600 baud. The North American version is Bell 212A.

**V.22 bis**
A CCITT full-duplex QAM modem standard that operates at 2400 b/s and 600 baud.

**V.24**
The CCITT version of the RS-232 serial interface standard.

**V.32**
A CCITT full-duplex QAM modem standard that operates at 9600 b/s and 2400 baud.

**V.32 bis**
A CCITT full-duplex modem standard that operates at 14,400 b/s.

**V.34**
A CCITT full-duplex modem standard that operates at a speed of up to 28,800 b/s. While it was under development, the standard was known as V.fast.

**V.42**
A CCITT error-checking standard that is used for modem communications.

**V.42 bis**
A CCITT data compression standard that is used for modem communications.

**V.fast**
See *V.34.*

**VCO**
See *Voltage-controlled oscillator.*

**Virtual connection**
A data path between two terminals that appears to the user as if the two terminals were connected directly to each other, although in reality no direct connection exists.

### Voltage-controlled oscillator (VCO)

An oscillator whose output frequency is controlled by an input voltage signal. A VCO can be used as an FSK modulator.

### WAN

See *Wide area network.*

### Wide area network (WAN)

A network that uses a system of bridges and routers to connect two or more local area networks and allow communication between them.

### Zero stuffing

A procedure used in the HDLC protocol to make sure that a series of six binary 1s never occurs in the data field. A series of six 1s would be interpreted by the receiver as a flag. The transmitting DTE "stuffs" an extra 0 before the sixth 1, and the receiver DTE removes it.

# ■ Index